Governance of Welfare State Reform

GLOBALIZATION AND WELFARE

Series Editors: Denis Bouget, *MSH Ange Guépin, France,* Jane Lewis, *Professor of Social Policy, London School of Economics, UK and* Giuliano Bonoli, *Professor of Social Policy, Swiss Graduate School of Public Administration (IDHEAP), Switzerland*

This important series is designed to make a significant contribution to the principles and practice of comparative social policy. It includes both theoretical and empirical work. International in scope, it addresses issues of current and future concern in both East and West, and in developed and developing countries.

The main purpose of this series is to create a forum for the publication of high quality work to help understand the impact of globalization on the provision of social welfare. It offers state-of-the-art thinking and research on important areas such as privatization, employment, work, finance, gender and poverty. It includes some of the best theoretical and empirical work from both well established researchers and the new generation of scholars.

Titles in the series include:

Governing Home Care
A Cross-National Comparison
Viola Burau, Hildegard Theobald and Robert H. Blank

Party Politics and Social Welfare
Comparing Christian and Social Democracy in Austria, Germany and the Netherlands
Martin Seeleib-Kaiser, Silke van Dyk and Martin Roggenkamp

Families, Ageing and Social Policy
Intergenerational Solidarity in European Welfare States
Edited by Chiara Saraceno

The Labour Market Triangle
Employment Protection, Unemployment Compensation and Activation in Europe
Edited by Paul de Beer and Trudie Schils

Governance of Welfare State Reform
A Cross National and Cross Sectoral Comparison of Policy and Politics
Edited by Irene Dingeldey and Heinz Rothgang

Governance of Welfare State Reform

A Cross National and Cross Sectoral Comparison of Policy and Politics

Edited by

Irene Dingeldey

Institute Labour and Economy, University of Bremen, Germany

Heinz Rothgang

Centre for Social Policy Research, University of Bremen, Germany

GLOBALIZATION AND WELFARE

Edward Elgar
Cheltenham, UK • Northampton, MA, USA

Published by
Edward Elgar Publishing Limited
The Lypiatts
15 Lansdown Road
Cheltenham
Glos GL50 2JA
UK

Edward Elgar Publishing, Inc.
William Pratt House
9 Dewey Court
Northampton
Massachusetts 01060
USA

A catalogue record for this book
is available from the British Library

Library of Congress Control Number: 2009933363

ISBN 978 1 84720 143 0

Printed and bound by MPG Books Group, UK

Contents

Contributors

Giuliano Bonoli, Institut de Hautes Etudes en Administration Publique (IDHEAP), Switzerland

Robert Henry Cox, School of International and Area Studies, University of Oklahoma, USA

Irene Dingeldey, Institute Labour and Economy, University of Bremen, Germany

Thomas Gerlinger, Johann Wolfgang Goethe University of Frankfurt on Main; Institute for Medical Sociology at the Center for Health Sciences of the University's Clinical Centre, Germany

Thorsten Hippe, Faculty of Sociology, University of Bielefeld, Germany

Anja P. Jakobi, The Collaborative Research Centre 597 'Transformations of the State', University of Bremen, Germany

Michael Baggesen Klitgaard, Faculty of Social Sciences, Department of Political Science and Public Management, Centre for Welfare State Studies, University of Southern Denmark, Denmark

Kerstin Martens, The Collaborative Research Centre 597 'Transformations of the State', University of Bremen, Germany

Herbert Obinger, Centre for Social Policy Research; The Collaborative Research Centre 597 'Transformations of the State', University of Bremen, Germany

Heinz Rothgang, Centre for Social Policy Research; The Collaborative Research Centre 597 'Transformations of the State', University of Bremen, Germany

Peter Starke, The Collaborative Research Centre 597 'Transformations of the State', University of Bremen, Germany

1. Introduction: Governance and Comparative Welfare State Research

Irene Dingeldey and Heinz Rothgang

INTRODUCTION

Governance has been one of the major research topics in sociology and political science in recent years. To date, however, analysts of governance have paid scant attention to social policy or welfare state reform. Equally, little consideration has been given to changing forms of governance in the extensive literature on welfare state change and its consequences for convergence or divergence. In many cases, the analyses in question are limited to changes in the public – private mix of finance and service provision and ignore other aspects of the changes in governance. The reform process that is driving these changes is generally not incorporated systematically into the analysis. And analysts have so far paid equally little attention to the question of how far changes in governance are influencing the variance in the evolution of welfare states. Consequently, there is a gap in the literature with regard to the governance of welfare state reform. It is this gap that the present volume is intended to fill. Our interest in this topic is directed primarily towards three questions, the answers to which may help to further understanding of the developments taking place.

1. *How are policies and regulatory structures changing?* Is regulatory responsibility shifting from the state towards private actors, such as market-based organisations, third-sector organisations or networks? Are modes of interaction changing, i.e. from hierarchy to competition or self-responsibility?
2. *How are the reform processes in different policy areas or countries being shaped?* How is the change in governance being influenced by institutional settings and by different actors and/or discourses? What are the factors assisting and hindering the change in governance?

3. *Are there signs of convergence or divergence across different welfare state types?* How are the 'old' regulatory structures influencing the specific reconfigurations of the policy areas analysed in the different welfare states? How is the dissemination of new ideas and related discourses influencing policy change?

In order to be able to address these questions, we need first to outline the notion of governance and critically survey the current state of research on governance and social policy. It will become clear that, even within this one field of research, there are many different approaches to the changes in governance. Thus in order to construct a common framework to be used in the various comparative analyses for describing and evaluating the governance of welfare state reform, we will firstly offer some clarifications on the typing of the various forms of governance with regard to social policy and on the convergence and divergence of welfare state development. The perspective adopted in this book will then be outlined and explained and the various chapters briefly summarised.

GOVERNANCE AND THE WELFARE STATE: CONCEPT AND STATE OF RESEARCH

The notion of governance, which was developed originally by institutional economists (Williamson 1979), has been used and further developed in many different contexts (for a general overview see Benz 2004: 21ff.; Kooiman 1999: 68; Pierre 2000; Schuppert 2003: 395ff.). Following Renate Mayntz, two basic uses of the term can be identified. The first is the use of governance as a generic term for various modes of coordinating social action (through hierarchies, markets, communities, organisations, etc.); in this usage, the term primarily denotes the structures rather than the process of governance or steering. The second, which developed primarily in the context of international relations, is the use of governance as an explicit counter concept to hierarchical forms of government in which state authorities exert control over the people in a given society;[1] in this usage, the term refers primarily to the processes of governance or control.

Renate Mayntz now proposes that these two uses of the term should be combined and that governance should be used as a generic term denoting 'all co-existing forms of collective regulation of societal matters, from those based solely on the state to those based solely on civil society' (Mayntz 2004). Thus governance denotes the structures as well as the processes of regulation and control (Mayntz 2005: 15; Pierre and Peters 2000: 14). According to this definition, the notion of governance can refer to the reform process (politics) and to the factors influencing that process as well as to the results of the process as reflected in changes in policies and politics.

Depending on the academic approach adopted, most of the empirical research that has been conducted to date on governance in social policy has focused exclusively either on politics or on policies.[2] In both approaches, however, the notion of governance is widely associated with change.

Post-marxist regulation theory describes the developments triggered by globalisation as a change in the regulatory regime characterised essentially by changes in the function of social policy and/or welfare state arrangements. Accordingly, the transition from the Keynesian welfare state to the Schumpeterian workfare post-national regime is attributed to the increased use of social policy to safeguard labour market flexibility and competitiveness in international markets (Jessop 1991, 1994). To date it has been mainly the recent reforms in labour market policy that have been adduced as evidence for these hypotheses, and in particular the reductions in transfer payments and their increased conditionality, as well as the increased compulsion to work (Jessop 2004; Torfing 1999). The strength of the regulationist approach is that it considers institutional and regulatory changes in a broad context, i.e. with reference to both the regime and policies. However, besides its strongly normative evaluation of the changes observed, the principal weakness of the regulationist approach is that political processes are not included in the analysis and that no tools for detailed comparative analysis of change have been developed.

Post-structuralist analyses use the term governance in order to reveal changes in power and control in the modern state, the discursive construction of modern societies and the paradoxes associated with institutional change in the public sector (Clarke and Newman 1997, Hillyard and Watson 1996; Newman, et al. 2004). Most of them adopt a Foucauldian perspective and examine the recent reform processes from the point of view of 'the kinds of knowledge and power through which social activity is regulated and through which actors – citizens, workers, organisations – are constituted as self-disciplining subjects' (Newman 2001: 20). Using cultural and discursive analyses, the construction of social arrangements is interpreted as the outcome of the production of specific meaning and the associated repression of alternative meaning.

In this strand of governance research, which is particularly prominent in the UK, the emphasis is on analysis of neo-liberal ideologies and 'third way' rhetoric in the context of the implementation of activating or investment-oriented social policy. A particular focus of attention is the redefinition of relations between the state and social actors (including professions and local bureaucracies or families (Barnes, et al. 2004: 8)) or between the state and citizens (Clarke 2004; Clarke and Newman 1997). The emphasis in these analyses is on the reinterpretations of values and rights in social policy (Hay 1999) and the consequent redefinition of citizenship in the welfare state (Lister 1998, 2002, 2003). Thus the post-structuralist school places the new social policy objectives and their discursive incorporation into policy-making processes at the heart of their analyses, while the changed mode of institutional regulation is largely ignored.

In the institutionalist approaches, governance is analysed with regard to both policies and politics, albeit in different strands.

In one strand, the *EU is regarded as having a virtually independent governance structure* (Benz 2003; Börzel 2005; Kohler-Koch 1999). Although in fact relatively few regulatory or implemental functions have so far been shifted to the EU level, an extensive body of research is developing whose primary aim is to investigate the EU's influence on national policies. One object of research in this strand is the implementation of the social policy directives adopted to date by the EU (Falkner 2005; Hartlapp 2005). Considerable attention is also being paid in research on social policy to the open coordination method as a new form of governance (de la Porte and Pochert 2001; Ferrera, et al. 2002; Schmid and Kull 2004; Schulte 2002). Recent studies of the influence of other international organisations, such as the OECD, on national social policies can be regarded as an extension of this research strand (Armingeon and Beyeler 2004; Weymann and Martens 2005). It should be noted in this regard, however, that the internationalisation of regulatory competences and the influence exerted by international organisations on national policies ultimately reflect just one aspect of the change in governance.

Political economists engaged in research on political steering and/or governance[3] have adopted a considerably broader approach, in which the changes in or erosion of the capacity of national economies to control their own affairs are investigated against the background of economic internationalisation or globalisation. In an approach characterised as actor-centred institutionalism (Mayntz and Scharpf 1995; Scharpf 2000), in which rational choice or game theory is sometimes applied, one focus of research has been the interaction between 'institutional rules defining actor constellations and their modes of interaction, and the orientations – perceptions and preferences – of the policy actors involved' (Scharpf and Schmidt 2000a: 17,18) in the resolution of specific economic and social problems, such as unemployment, for example. The analyses in question investigate decision-making processes, with an emphasis on the influence of actors in different institutional settings (Scharpf 1987, 1988; Scharpf and Schmidt 2000b). Although more recent studies have increasingly emphasised the importance of ideas and discourses in explaining welfare state reforms (Hemerijck and van Kersbergen 1999; Schmidt 2002a; Schmidt 2002b), the much-publicised paradigm shift in social policy to the social investment state (Giddens 1998), the enabling state (Gilbert 2002) or the activating state (Dingeldey 2006) and associated shift in policies has hitherto been largely ignored in this strand of governance research. One exception is Cox (2001).

Finally, the strand of governance research (and the closely associated policy research strand) that derives its analytical framework more from *political and administrative science* has concentrated on structures and processes in policy implementation. As far as the analysis of changes in governance is concerned, particular attention has been paid to shifts in responsibilities away from the central state towards the transational or international level and to the devolvement of responsibilities to sub-national (public) organisations as a result of the implementation of new public management theories. Other research objects have included privatisation and marketisation processes and the transfer of previously public duties and responsibilities to network structures (for a survey see Jann and Wegerich 2004; Mayntz 1997; Rhodes 1997, 2000).

Interpretations of the changes that have taken place diverge considerably. Some authors have spoken of the 'hollowing out of the state' (Rhodes 1994, Rhodes 2000), that is of the erosion of the nation state and of its responsibilities and decision-making capacities. Other authors, in contrast, point to a change in the function of the state, a change to which they attach largely positive connotations. In the German debate, this change has been characterised more precisely as the shift to the cooperative (Benz 1997; Ritter 1979) or ensuring state (Hoffmann-Riem 2000; Schuppert 1997, 1999, 2005).

In the analyses of various areas of social policy that fall within the scope of this strand, some of which are comparative, the main focus is also on the change in the division of responsibilities between the state and social actors. They include studies of the governance of education systems (Windzio, et al. 2005), the regulation of privatised old-age insurance schemes (Leisering 2006), the re-regulation of healthcare systems (Rothgang 2006; Wendt, et al. 2005) and the change of regulatory structures in labour market policy (Schmid 2004). In addition, there are countless studies that examine changes in individual instruments, such as the introduction of contracts (Finn 2005; Sol and Westerfeld 2005) and of voucher systems (Kühnlein and Klein 2003; Steuerle, et al. 2000). These studies, many of which are comparative, usually give a very detailed picture of the changes in institutions and regulatory structures but say virtually nothing about the political processes underlying the reforms.

This brief survey of the current state of research confirms that, to date, virtually no analyses of the governance of welfare state reform extending beyond individual policy areas have been carried out. At the same time, however, it has become clear that social policy itself is undergoing a change of governance of which, to date, insufficient account has been taken in studies on the convergence and divergence of different types of welfare state. However, in order to be able to put the notion of governance to profitable use in a comparative analysis of welfare states and social policy, further clarification of the typologising of the various forms of governance and of our understanding of them is required.

FORMS OF GOVERNANCE: AN INTERACTIVE APPROACH

In governance research, the standard set of regulatory forms (hierarchy, market and community) is extended to include networks as a new basic form of governance[4] (Marin and Mayntz 1991; Pierre and Peters 2000: 14). In all the various typologies, however, the individual regulatory structures and their basic characteristics, such as the modes of steering or governance, are usually described as 'pure' forms. This has led critics to observe that the typologies cannot adequately characterise combinations of governance forms and the problems of institutional politics that arise in such hybrid forms of governance (Benz 2004: 25). This criticism of the typologies is further strengthened by the fact that the frequently observed network-based cooperation between state and social actors (Bevir and Rhodes 2003; Rhodes 2000b) is also based on a mixture of different institutionalised regulatory systems and/or a blurring of the boundaries between the state and civil society (Benz 2004: 25; Stoker 1998: 17).

However, this criticism, which has so far been framed in general terms, would seem to be of crucial importance if the notion of governance is to be transferred or applied to social policy, since social policy differs from other (traditional) state duties and responsibilities in that the delivery of welfare has never been the sole responsibility of the state. Rather, there has always been a division of labour between various state and non-state actors. For this reason, the existence of a public – private welfare mix has always been one of the basic assumptions in social policy (Evers 1988; Kaufmann 2002).

In comparative welfare state research, it has been argued, notably by Esping-Andersen (1990, 1996) and his feminist critics (Daly and Lewis 2000; Sainsbury 1999), among others, that the elements of the public – private mix vary considerably from one welfare state regime to another. As a result, the specific division of labour between the welfare state, the market, the third sector and families in the provision of welfare has become a key characteristic in distinguishing between various types of welfare state. This applies not only to the role allocated to the various actors responsible for welfare provision in the individual social policy areas, that is at the policy level, but also to the participation of non-state actors in the political decision-making processes, that is at the political level. Thus the starting positions for the changes that have taken place in welfare states and governance differed considerably from country to country. This being so, it would be of interest to ascertain whether regime-specific governance structures have remained in place or whether a trend towards convergence based on hybrid forms can be discerned.

In social policy, therefore, governance denotes a differentiated mix of various forms of governance at both the policy and political level. In order to provide a basis for detailed analysis of this mix, therefore, we intend to adopt an interactive approach to governance that draws on the steering theory approach that itself emerged out of actor-related institutionalism (Mayntz and Scharpf 1995; Scharpf 2000) and the notion of governance developed by Kooiman (2003, 2005). In particular, we will make a distinction between the various actors and modes of governance.

The following systematisation is based on precisely this approach to governance; it distinguishes between actors and modes of governance, while at the same time making it possible to characterise both the wide range of forms taken by the division of labour between the different actors and the various forms of interaction. Listing the diversity of state and private actors involved in social policy is also intended to show that duties and responsibilities are being transferred for reasons other than denationalisation and privatisation and that these transfers may indicate a change in the nature of statehood, with competences being devolved to regional or local actors or transferred to different departments. In addition, different forms of privatisation can be identified as transfers of responsibility to, for example, market actors, the social partners, families or individuals, together with the corresponding forms of interactions, such as competition, co-governance or enabling of self-management. However, the list is not intended to provide a specific analytical framework but is to be further substantiated and extended in accordance with the specific conditions in the individual policy areas.

This approach to governance weakens, or at least modifies, the view – long dominant in dynamic analyses – that the direction of change has been 'away from the state'. Not least, it makes provision for identifying the possible 'backsourcing' or return of duties and responsibilities to the state in social policy as well.

At the same time, however, changed forms of political decision-making or the participation of non-state actors can also be identified and systematically analysed, within the framework of an interactive approach to governance, as the governance of welfare state reform. For example, the forms of interaction and the actors involved (market actors, social partners, government representatives, etc.) can serve as a basis for detailed descriptions of various forms of networks. The influence of international actors and/or the importance of new ideas as they are disseminated through various types of discourse and, in turn, impact on decision-making can also be revealed.

1. Governance Actors

- State/Public Actors
  - o Central government
  - o Regions/Länder
  - o Municipalities
  - o Parafiscal agencies
  - o Functional differentiation
    in form of various ministries
    and departments

- Private Actors
  - o Professionals, expert groups
  - o Market oriented actors
    (companies)
  - o Interest groups
  - o Third sector organisations
  - o Families
  - o Individuals
  - o ...

- International Organisations
  - o having regulatory competencies
  - o drawing legitimacy by
    scientific analysis
  - o market oriented
  - o quangos etc.

2. Modes of Governance

- Hierarchy
- Market competition
- Co-governance
  (Co-production and co-operation); Networks
- Discourse/moral
  persuasion
- Solidarity
- Enabling of self
  management
- ...

Source: Dingeldey 2009; applied

Figure 1.1   Interactive governance approach

Examination of the change in governance structures in several countries also raises the question of whether common changes or even trends towards convergence can be identified. Thus over and above clarification of the notion of governance, it is also necessary to clarify how the change in governance can be understood in configurative terms and what role the concepts of convergence and divergence can play in this regard.

COMPARING CHANGES IN DIFFERENT COUNTRIES: LEVEL AND RANGE EFFECTS

Even in the 'golden age' of the welfare state, national welfare systems varied, reflecting what has been termed the different 'worlds of welfare capitalism' (Esping-Andersen 1990) or 'varieties of capitalism' (Hall and Soskice 2001). Assuming that each specific national configuration can be plotted on a one-dimensional continuum between private and public, each country will be represented by one point on this scale. The *distribution* of countries could then be characterised by the mean value and a measure of dispersion, for example the variance. Overall change could then refer to both the spread of regime types (for example as variance around the mean in a continuum of types) and the mean (for example mean of public share of total expenditure), as measured for a set of countries, for example the OECD member states of the 'golden age'. Generally speaking, this approach could be used for single social policy fields such as pension policy, health policy, etc. It could also be used for welfare states as a whole if trends were the same in each field of welfare provision.

Table 1.1   Potential transformative changes in the structure of the welfare state

In any given set of countries (for example old OECD) for a given field of social policy		LEVEL of state intervention (mean)		
		Rising	Remains the same	Falling
RANGE Spread of policy regimes	Widening	1 Divergence, with an increased level of intervention	4 Divergence	7 Divergence, with a lower level of intervention
	Remains the same	2 Rise	5 Status-quo	8 Fall
	Narrowing	3 Convergence, with an increased level of intervention	6 Convergence	9 Convergence, with a lower level of intervention

Source: Rothgang et al. 2006a

So what is happening now, if the public – private mix is changing over time as a result of the reforms? Obviously, the answer depends on the direction of change, and – from a comparativist's point of view – on the uniformity of the movement among countries. Table 1.1 represents the different possible outcomes if changes in a number of countries are considered simultaneously.

If, for example, public pension systems were being privatised to the same extent in all countries such that the differences between countries remained constant – the range of regimes neither widened nor narrowed – a simultaneous decrease in the amount of state spending would simply lead to a decrease in the level of intervention, as in cell 8. If all countries adopted a similar public-private mix for their pension systems – narrowing the range – and the level of state intervention stayed the same, as in cell 6, there would be a simple *convergence*. But if the level of state intervention also decreases, then we have *convergence with a reduced level of intervention*, as in cell 9.[5]

Generally speaking, every reform leading to a change in the dispersion of the distribution can be referred to as a *range effect*, while shifts in the mean of the distribution are *level effects*. If both occur together this is described as a *positioning effect* (Rothgang et al. 2006a).

For the purposes of this reader, this means that comparative analyses of the governance of welfare state reform in different social policy fields should aim to capture both level and range effects, i.e. convergence and divergence.

OUTLINE OF THE BOOK

One of the aims of the present volume is to do justice to the specific conditions that prevail in social policy and also to draw attention to changes within the public sector other than privatisation, such as changes in the relationship between the state and individuals and the 'backsourcing' or return of duties and responsibilities to the state. Furthermore, it seems essential to analyse changes in the influence of international actors and in the dissemination of new ideas and discourses on the evolution of welfare states. Last but not least, the observed changes will be examined in order to identify possible trends towards convergence or divergence in the evolution of welfare states.

In order to capture as broad a spectrum of developments as possible, we investigate the change in governance in various policy fields and in various types of welfare state. In the case of health and pensions, we have selected two time-honoured and particularly important policy areas, not least in terms of the volume of expenditure devoted to them. In the case of labour market policies and education, on the other hand, the focus is on those policy areas that are regarded as key areas in the reconceptualisation of the welfare state, such as the social investment state (Giddens 1998) or the enabling state (Gilbert 2002; Gilbert and Gilbert 1989). All the contributions to the book are based on international comparisons and take account of developments in various types of welfare state.

One of our declared aims in this book is to analyse the governance of welfare state reform from an institutionalist and interactive perspective with regard both to the policies and the politics of the welfare state. In order to be able to capture trends emerging in different policy areas, our first group of chapters analyse specific aspects of the change in governance in policy implementation. Thus in Chapters 2 to 5 by Rothgang, Hippe, Dingeldey and Martens and Jakobi, the change in governance is traced through developments in health, pensions, labour market and education policy. Chapter 6 by Starke and Obinger, finally, uses data from 21 OECD countries to examine the question of system convergence.

The subsequent set of Chapters 7 to 10 by Gerlinger (health), Bonoli (pensions), Cox (labour market) and Klitgaard (education) examine political and reform processes with reference to policies in each area.

These various analyses are, as it were, the pieces of a jigsaw puzzle, which have to be fitted together to form a picture. By way of conclusion, therefore, Rothgang and Dingeldey try to ascertain whether the governance of welfare state reform, namely processes of internationalisation, regionalisation, privatisation or re-regulation, is linked to single policy fields or to certain countries. Moreover, they investigate whether homogeneous trends in welfare state transformation or other range effects can be observed.

NOTES

1. Further specific uses of the term can be found in the literature on international relations ('global governance') and political economy ('corporate governance' and the normative term 'good governance'). They will not, however, be given any further consideration here.
2. Our survey of the current state of research, which differentiates the various studies on the basis of their academic approach, diverges from a systematisation, published in 2003 (Daly 2003), of the studies of governance and social policy that had been carried out up to that point, which differentiates the various strands primarily according to thematic area.
3. In line with Mayntz (2005: 16f.), steering theory is seen in the German context ultimately as a precursor of or complement to the governance debate.
4. Both the old typologies – whether characterised as 'models of social order' (Streeck and Schmitter 1985a, Streeck and Schmitter 1985b) or as 'forms of the institutionalisation of action-coordination' (Kaufmann 2002: 190; Kaufmann, et al. 1986) – and the governance typologies have a number of variants in which both the basic and additional regulatory forms differ depending on the policy or regulatory sphere under investigation (for example Bevir and Rhodes 2003; Lütz 2004) or the basic forms themselves vary (for example different types of networks) (Rhodes 1997: 38).
5. The underlying concept of convergence thus refers to 'sigma-convergence' as Sala-i-Martin (1996: 1020–1022) defined it. *Sigma*-convergence is measured with respect to the *variance of a distribution* (denoted as σ). *Beta*-convergence on the other hand relates to the *parameter of change in a regression model* (β). With processes of growth over time beta convergence is given if the laggards are catching up, i.e. if β is higher for laggards in a regression with time

as a regressor. As long as the laggards are still behind the forerunners beta-convergence implies sigma-convergence.

REFERENCES

Armingeon, Klaus and Michelle Beyeler (eds) (2004), *The OECD and European Welfare States*, Cheltenham, UK and Northampton, MA: Edward Elgar.

Barnes, M., J. Newman and H. Sullivan (2004), 'Power, Participation, and Political Renewal: Theoretical Perspectives on Public Participation under New Labour in Britain', *Social Politics*, **11** (2), 267–279.

Benz, Arthur (1997), 'Kooperativer Staat? Gesellschaftliche Einflußnahme auf staatliche Steuerung', in Ansgar Klein and Rainer Schmalz-Bruns (eds), *Politische Beteiligung und Bürgerengagement in Deutschland. Möglichkeiten und Grenzen der Demokratisierung*, Bonn: Bundeszentrale für politische Bildung, pp. 88–113.

Benz, Arthur (2003), 'Mehrebenenverflechtung in der Europäischen Union', in Markus Jachtenfuchs and Beate Kohler-Koch (eds), *Europäische Integration*, Opladen: Leske & Budrich, pp. 317–351.

Benz, Arthur (2004), 'Einleitung: Governance – Modebegriff oder nützliches sozialwissenschaftliches Konzept?', in Arthur Benz (ed.), *Governance – Regieren in komplexen Regelsystemen. Eine Einführung*, Wiesbaden: Verlag für Sozialwissenschaften, pp. 11–29.

Bevir, Mark and Rod A.W. Rhodes (2003), *Interpreting British Governance*, London: Routledge.

Börzel, Tanja A. (2005), 'European Governance – Nicht neu, aber anders', in Gunnar Folke Schuppert (ed.), *Governance-Forschung. Vergewisserung über Stand und Entwicklungslinien*, Baden-Baden: Nomos, pp. 72–95.

Clarke, John (2004), *Changing Welfare Changing States. New Directions on Social Policy*, London: Thousand Oaks, New Delhi: Sage.

Clarke, John and Janet Newman (1997), *The Managerial State. Power, Politics and Ideology in the Remaking of Social Welfare*, London: Thousand Oaks, New Delhi: Sage Publications.

Cox, R.H. (2001), 'The Social Construction of an Imperative. Why Welfare Reform Happened in Denmark and the Netherlands but Not in Germany', *World Politics,* **53**, (April), 463–498.

Daly, M. (2003), 'Governance and Social Policy', *Journal of Social Policy,* **32** (1), 113–128.

Daly, M. and J. Lewis (2000), 'The Concept of Social Care and the Analysis of Contemporary Welfare States', *British Journal of Sociology,* **51** (2), 281–298.

de la Porte, C. and P. Pochert (2001), 'Social Benchmarking, Policy Making and New Governance in the EU', *Journal of European Social Policy*, **11** (4), 291–307.

Dingeldey, I. (2006), 'Aktivierender Wohlfahrtsstaat und sozialpolitische Steuerung', *Aus Politik und Zeitgeschichte*, **8–9**/2006, 20 February, 3–9.

Dingeldey, Irene (2009), *Auf dem Weg zum aktivierenden Wohlfahrtsstaat? Eine vergleichende Analyse zum Wandel von Staatlichkeit und Governance in der Arbeitsmarktpolitik*, forthcoming.

Esping-Andersen, Gösta (1990), *The Three Worlds of Welfare Capitalism*, Cambridge: Polity Press.

Esping-Andersen, Gösta (ed.) (1996), *Welfare States in Transition. National Adaptions in Global Economies*, London: Thousand Oaks: Sage.

Evers, Adalbert (1988), 'Shifts in the Welfare Mix – Introducing a New Approach for the Study of Transformations in Welfare and Social Policy', in Adalbert Evers and Helmut Wintersbergert (eds), *Shifts in the Welfare Mix. Their Impact on Work, Social Services and Welfare Policies*, Vienna: Europäisches Zentrum für Ausbildung und Forschung auf dem Gebiet der sozialen Wohlfahrt, pp. 7–30.

Falkner, Gerda, Oliver Treib, Miriam Hartlapp and Simone Leiber (2005), *Complying with Europe: EU Harmonisation and Soft Law in the Member States*, Cambridge: Cambridge University Press.

Ferrera, M., M. Matsagangis and S. Sacchi (2002), 'Open Coordination Against Poverty: The New EU "Social Inclusion Process" ', *Journal of European Social Policy*, **12** (3), 227–239.

Finn, Dan (2005), 'The Role of Contracts and the Private Sector in Delivering Britain's 'Employment First' Welfare State', in Els Sol and Mies Westerveld (eds), *Contractualism in Employment Services*, Amsterdam: University Press, pp. 101–119.

Giddens, Anthony (1998), 'Equality and the Social Investment State', in Ian Hargreaves and Ian Christie (eds), *Tomorrow's Politics. The Third Way and Beyond*, London: Demos, pp. 25–40.

Gilbert, Neil (2002), *Transformation of the Welfare State. The Silent Surrender of Public Responsibility*, Oxford: Oxford University Press.

Gilbert, Neil and Barbara Gilbert (1989), *The Enabling State. Modern Welfare Capitalism in America*, New York, Oxford: Oxford University Press.

Hall, Peter A. and David Soskice (eds) (2001), *Varieties of Capitalism. The Institutional Foundations of Comparative Advantage*, New York: Oxford University Press.

Hartlapp, Miriam (2005), *Die Kontrolle der nationalen Rechtsdurchsetzung durch die Europäische Kommission*, Frankfurt, New York: Campus.

Hay, Colin (1999), *The Political Economy of New Labour. Labouring under False Pretences?*, Manchester: Manchester University Press.

Hemerijck, Anton and Kees van Kersbergen (1999), 'Negotiated Policy Change: Towards a Theory of Institutional Learning in Tightly Coupled Welfare States', in Dietmar Braun and Andreas Busch (eds), *Public Policy and Political Ideas*, Cheltenham, UK and Northampton, MA: Edward Elgar, pp. 168–185.

Hillyard, P. and S. Watson (1996), 'Postmodern Social Policy: A Contradiction in Terms?', *Journal of Social Policy*, **25** (3), 321–346.

Hoffmann-Riem, Wolfgang (2000), 'Von der Erfüllungs- zur Gewährleistungsverantwortung – Eine Chance für den überforderten Staat', in Wolfgang Hoffmann-Riem (ed.), *Modernisierung von Recht und Justiz*, Frankfurt: Suhrkamp, pp. 195–219.

Jann, Werner and Kai Wegerich (2004), 'Governance und Verwaltungspolitik', in Arthur Benz (ed.), *Governance – Regieren in komplexen Regelsystemen. Eine Einführung*, Wiesbaden: Verlag für Sozialwissenschaften, pp. 193–214.

Jessop, Bob (1991), 'The Welfare State in the Transition from Fordism to Post-fordism', in Bob Jessop, Hans Kastendiek, Klaus Nielsen and Ove K. Pedersen (eds), *The Politics of Flexibility. Restructuring State and Industry in Britain, Germany and Scandinavia*, Brookfield: Edward Elgar, pp. 82–104.

Jessop, Bob (1994), 'Veränderte Staatlichkeit', in Dieter Grimm and Evelyn Hagenah (eds), *Staatsaufgaben*, Baden-Baden: Nomos, pp. 43–75.

Jessop, Bob (2004), 'From Thatcherism to New Labour. Neo-liberalism, Workfarism and Labour-market Regulation', in Henk Overbeck (ed.), *The Political Economy of European Employment. European Integration and the Transnationalization of the (un)employment Question*, London, New York: Routledge, pp. 137–152.

Kaufmann, Franz-Xaver (ed.) (2002), *Sozialpolitik und Sozialstaat: Soziologische Analysen*, Opladen: Leske & Budrich.

Kaufmann, Franz-Xaver (2002), 'Sozialstaatlichkeit unter den Bedingungen moderner Wirtschaft', in Franz-Xaver Kaufmann (ed.), *Sozialpolitik und Sozialstaat: Soziologische Analysen*, Opladen: Leske & Budrich, pp. 261–284.

Kaufmann, Franz-Xaver, Giandomenico Majone, Vincent Ostrom and Wolfgang Wirth (eds) (1986), *Guidance, Control and Evaluation in the Public Sector*, Berlin, New York: Walter de Gruyter.

Kohler-Koch, Beate (1999), 'The Evolution and Transformation of European Governance', in Beate Kohler-Koch and Rainer Eising (eds), *The Transformation of European Governance*, London, New York: Routledge, pp. 14–35.

Kooiman, J. (1999), 'Social-political Governance. Overview, Reflections and Design', *Public Management*, **1** (1), 68–92.

Kooiman, Jan (2005 (2003)), *Governing as Governance*, London: Thousand Oaks, New Delhi: Sage.

Kühnlein, Gertrud and Birgit Klein (2003), 'Bildungsgutscheine – Mehr Eigen-verantwortung, mehr Markt, mehr Effizienz? – Erfahrungen bei der Neuaus-richtung der beruflichen Weiterbildung', *Arbeitspapiere der Hans Böckler Stiftung*, Bd.74.

Leisering, Lutz (2006), *From Redistribution to Regulation. Regulating Private Old-age Pensions as a New Challenge in Ageing Societies*, paper presented at: 4th International Research Conference on Social Security, Antwerp, 5–7 May 2003

"Social Security in a Long Life Society", May 2003 (revised version January 2005).

Lister, R. (1998), 'From Equality to Social Inclusion: New Labour and the Welfare State', *Critical Social Policy*, **18** (2), 215–225.

Lister, Ruth (2002), 'Citizenship and Changing Welfare States', in Jørgen Goul Andersen and Per Jensen (eds), *Changing Labour Markets, Welfare Policies and Citizenship*, Bristol: Policy Press, pp. 39–59.

Lister, R. (2003), 'Investing in the Citizen-worker of the Future: Transformations in Citizenship and the State under New Labour', *Social Policy & Administration*, **37** (5), 427–443.

Lütz, Susanne (2004), 'Governance in der politischen Ökonomie', in Arthur Benz, (ed.), *Governance – Regieren in komplexen Regelsystemen. Eine Einführung*, Wiesbaden: Verlag für Sozialwissenschaften, pp. 147–172.

Marin, Bernd and Renate Mayntz (eds) (1991), *Policy Network: Empirical Evidence and Theoretical Considerations*, Frankfurt, New York: Campus.

Mayntz, Renate (1997), 'Verwaltungsreform und gesellschaftlicher Wandel', in Edgar Grande and Rainer Prätorius (eds), *Modernisierung des Staates?*, Baden-Baden: Nomos, pp. 65–74.

Mayntz, Renate (2004), 'Governance im modernen Staat', in Arthur Benz (ed.), *Governance – Regieren in komplexen Regelsystemen. Eine Einführung*, Wiesbaden: Verlag für Sozialwissenschaften, pp. 65–76.

Mayntz, Renate (ed.) (2005), *Governance Theory als fortentwickelte Steuerungstheorie?*, Baden-Baden: Nomos.

Mayntz, Renate and Fritz Scharpf (1995), 'Der Ansatz des akteurzentrierten Institutionalismus', in Renate Mayntz and Fritz Scharpf (eds), *Gesellschaftliche Selbstregelung und politische Steuerung*, Frankfurt, New York: Campus, pp. 39–72.

Newman, Janet (2001), *Modernising Governance*, London: Thousand Oaks, New Delhi: Sage Publications.

Newman, J., M. Barnes, H. Sullivan and A. Knops (2004), 'Public Participation and Collaborative Governance', *Journal of Social Policy*, **33** (2), pp. 203–223.

Pierre, Jon (ed.) (2000), *Debating Governance*, Oxford: Oxford University Press.

Pierre, Jon and Guy Peters (2000), *Governance, Politics and the State*, Houndmills, London: Macmillan Press.

Rhodes, R.A.W. (1994), 'The Hollowing out of the State: The Changing Nature of the Public Service in Britain', *The Political Quarterly*, **65** (2), 138–151.

Rhodes, Rod A.W. (1997), *Understanding Governance. Policy Networks, Governance, Reflexivity and Accountability*, Buckingham, Philadelphia: Open University Press.

Rhodes, Rod A.W. (2000), 'Governance and Public Administration', in Jon Pierre (ed.), *Debating Governance*, Oxford: Oxford University Press, pp. 54–91.

Rhodes, R.A.W. (2000a), 'The Governance Narrative: Key Findings and Lessons from the ESRC's Whitehall Programme', *Public Administration*, **78** (1), 345–363.

Rhodes, Rod A.W. (ed.) (2000b), *Transforming British Government*, Vol. I, Changing Institutions, New York: St. Martin's Press, LLC.

Ritter, E.-H. (1979), 'Der kooperative Staat', *Archiv des öffentlichen Rechts*, **104**, 389–413.

Rothgang, H., H. Obinger and S. Leibfried (2006), 'The State and its Welfare State: How do Welfare State Changes Affect the Make-up of the Nation-state?', *Social Policy and Administration*, **40** (3), 250–266.

Rothgang, Heinz (2006), 'Die Regulierung von Gesundheitssystemen in vergleichender Perspektive. Auf dem Weg zur Konvergenz?', in Claus Wendt and Christof Wolf (eds), *Soziologie der Gesundheit. Sonderheft 46 der Kölner Zeitschrift für Soziologie und Sozialpsychologie*, pp. 298–319.

Sainsbury, Diane (ed.) (1999), *Gender and Welfare State Regimes*, Oxford: Oxford University Press.

Sala-i-Martin, X.X. (1996), 'The Classical Approach to Convergence Analysis', *The Economic Journal*, **106** (437), 1019–1036.

Scharpf, Fritz (1987), *Sozialdemokratische Krisenpolitik in Europa. Das 'Modell Deutschland' im Vergleich*, Frankfurt, New York: Campus.

Scharpf, Fritz (1988), 'Inflation und Arbeitslosigkeit in Westeuropa: Eine spieltheoretische Interpretation', *Politische Vierteljahresschrift*, **29** (1), 6–41.

Scharpf, Fritz (2000), *Interaktionsformen Akteurzentrierter Institutionalismus in der Politikforschung*, Opladen: UTB.

Scharpf, Fritz and Vivien A. Schmidt (2000a), 'Introduction', in Fritz Scharpf and Vivien A. Schmidt (eds), *Welfare and Work in the Open Economy: From Vulnerability to Competitiveness*, Oxford: Oxford University Press, pp. 1–21.

Scharpf, Fritz and Vivien A. Schmidt (eds) (2000b), *Welfare and Work in the Open Economy: Diverse Responses to Common Challenges*, Oxford: Oxford University Press.

Schmid, Günther (2004), *Gewährleistungsstaat und Arbeitsmarkt. Neue Formen von Governance in der Arbeitsmarktpolitik*, WZB Discussion Paper SP I 2004–107, Berlin: Wissenschaftszentrum Berlin.

Schmid, Günther and Silke Kull (2004), 'Die Europäische Beschäftigungsstrategie. Perspektiven der Offenen Methode der Koordinierung', in Hartmut Kaelble und Günter Schmid (eds), *Das europäische Sozialmodell. Auf dem Weg zum transnationalen Sozialstaat*, Berlin: Edition Sigma, pp. 317–346.

Schmidt, V.A. (2002a), 'Does Discourse Matter in the Politics of Welfare State Adjustment?', *Comparative Political Studies*, **35** (2), 168–193.

Schmidt, V.A. (2002b), 'How, Where and When does Discourse Matter in Small States' Welfare State Adjustment?', *The New Political Economy*, **8** (1), 127–146.

Schulte, Bernd (2002), 'Die 'Methode der offenen Koordinierung' – Eine neue politische Strategie in der europäischen Sozialpolitik auch für den Bereich des sozialen Schutzes', *Zeitschrift für Sozialreform*, **48** (1), 1–28.

Schuppert, Gunnar Folke (1997), 'Vom produzierenden zum gewährleistenden Staat: Privatisierung als Veränderung staatlicher Handlungsformen', in Klaus König and Angelika Benz (eds), *Privatisierung und staatliche Regulierung: Bahn, Post und Telekommunikation, Rundfunk*, Baden-Baden: Nomos, pp. 539–575.

Schuppert, Gunnar Folke (1999), 'Zur notwendigen Neubestimmung der Staatsaufsicht im verantwortungsteilenden Verwaltungsstaat', in Gunnar Folke Schuppert (ed.), *Jenseits von Privatisierung und 'schlankem' Staat*, Baden-Baden: Nomos, pp. 299–329.

Schuppert, Gunnar Folke (2003), *Staatswissenschaft*, Baden-Baden: Nomos.

Schuppert, Gunnar Folke (2005), 'Der Gewährleistungsstaat – Modisches Label oder Leitbild sich wandelnder Staatlichkeit?', in Gunnar Folke Schuppert (ed.), *Der Gewährleistungsstaat – Ein Leitbild auf dem Prüfstand*, Baden-Baden: Nomos, pp. 11–53.

Sol, Els and Mies Westerfeld (eds) (2005), *Contractualism in Employment Services. A New Form of Welfare State Governance*, The Hague: Kluwer Law International.

Steuerle, C. Eugene, Van Doorn Ooms, George Peterson and Robert D. Reischauer, (2000), *Vouchers and the Provision of Public Services*, Washington D.C.: Brookings Institution.

Stoker, G. (1998), 'Governance as Theory: Five Propositions', *International Social Science Journal*, **155**, 17–28.

Streeck, W. and P.C. Schmitter (1985a), 'Community, Market, State – And Associations?', *European Sociological Review*, **1** (2), 119–138.

Streeck, Wolfgang and P.C. Schmitter (1985b), 'Gemeinschaft, Markt und Staat – Und die Verbände? Der mögliche Beitrag von Interessenregierungen zur sozialen Ordnung', *Journal für Sozialforschung*, **25** (2), 133–157.

Torfing, J. (1999), 'Towards a Schumpeterian Workfare Postnational Regime: Path-shaping and Path-dependency in Danish Welfare State Reform', *Economy and Society*, **28** (3), 369–402.

Wendt, Claus, Heinz Rothgang and Uwe Helmert (2005), *The Self-regulatory German Health Care System between Growing Competition and State Hierarchy*, Transtate Working Papers No. 32, Bremen, Collaborative Research Centre 597.

Weymann, A. and K. Martens (2005), 'Bildungspolitik durch internationale Organisationen – Entwicklung, Strategien und Bedeutung der OECD', *Österreichische Zeitschrift für Soziologie Sonderband: Bildungspolitik*, 68–86.

Williamson, O.E. (1979), 'Transaction-cost Economics: The Governance of Contractual Relations', *Journal of Law and Economics*, **22**, 233–261.

Windzio, Michael, Reinhold Sackmann and Kerstin Martens (2005), *Types of Governance in Education – A Quantitative Analysis*, TranState Working Papers, No. 25, Bremen, Collaborative Research Centre 597.

Part I
Changes of Policy and Regulatory Structures

2. Converging Governance in Healthcare Systems?

Heinz Rothgang

INTRODUCTION

One of the possible aims of an international comparison of healthcare systems is to look for common trends in all the systems under investigation; on the other hand, it is also possible to investigate the extent to which the variance between systems is changing. For a long time, the emphasis in comparative welfare state research has been on the search for *common trends* such as 'retrenchment' or 'privatisation' (for example Pierson 1994; Huber and Stephens 2001; Gilbert 2002; cf. Starke 2006 for a survey); however, there are good reasons to suppose that it is at least equally important to investigate whether the various institutional arrangements in different countries are converging (Rothgang, Obinger and Leibfried 2006). Thus the question – already posed in the introduction to the present volume – of whether convergence trends in governance can be observed in addition to or instead of common trends can also be asked of healthcare systems. It is this question that will be addressed in this chapter.

Our investigation begins with a presentation of the conceptual framework. In the empirical section that follows, changes in governance structures in three countries – Germany, Britain and the US – representing one healthcare system type each will be outlined. The chapter concludes with a discussion of how far it is possible to speak of convergence in the governance structures of healthcare systems.

CONCEPTUAL FRAMEWORK

Before any attempt can be made to evaluate possible convergence in governance structures of healthcare systems, several conceptual questions have to be clarified:

- Which healthcare systems are to be compared?
- On the basis of which aspects are these systems to be compared?
- How are governance structures in healthcare systems to be conceptualised?
- How can the notion of convergence be conceptualised in this regard?

Types of Healthcare Systems and the Countries under Investigation

Comparisons of healthcare systems require detailed examination of institutional arrangements. As a result, they are necessarily restricted to a small number of countries. In order, nevertheless, to be able to draw more general conclusions, attempts can be made to cluster healthcare systems into *types* characterised by as low a level of internal variance as possible. If representatives of these types are then compared with each other, the developments observed can be interpreted as indications of general trends that transcend individual cases.

It is common practice in health policy to make a distinction between three types of healthcare system: national health services, social insurance systems and private healthcare systems (cf. Wendt et al. 2009 for a detailed investigation of the existing typologies). In selecting Britain, Germany and the USA for investigation, therefore, we have chosen one country with a national health service, one country with a social insurance system and one country with a private healthcare system to represent each of these types of healthcare system.

The Various Dimensions of Healthcare Systems

Healthcare systems can be differentiated from each other on the basis of financing, service provision and regulation (in this regard, cf. for example Rothgang et al. 2005 and 2008). In order to answer comprehensively the question of convergence among healthcare systems, it would be necessary to analyse all the relevant dimensions simultaneously. However, it is not possible to do this in the required depth in this chapter. Consequently, the following remarks are confined to the question of which actors take the decisions in the healthcare system in question and how they interact with each other, in short to the *governance structures*.

Governance in Healthcare Systems

Healthcare systems are fully differentiated societal subsystems, in which various actors interact with each other regularly and on a continuing basis (Mayntz 1990). Their interactions can be 'regulated' in various ways. The *objects* of regulation are the relations between three sets of actors: service providers, financing bodies and the (potential) beneficiaries of the health services provided. These relate in particular to:

- coverage, i.e. the inclusion of (parts of) the population in public and/or private health care systems;
- the financing of health care by public (taxes, social insurance contributions) and/or private (private insurance contributions, out-of-pocket payments) sources;
- specific systems of remuneration for service providers;
- access of (potential) providers to healthcare markets and to remuneration by financing agencies;
- patient access to service providers, i.e. doctors and other healthcare workers; and
- the content of the benefit package.

A further distinction has to be made between regulatory *instruments*, which will not be discussed in this chapter (on this subject cf. Schmid et al. 2008) and regulatory structures. Regulatory *structures* provide information on *who* regulates and what *forms of interaction* characterise the relationship between the actors. As far as the actors are concerned, a basic distinction can be made between state, social and private actors, with the last named involved in healthcare systems primarily in their role as private market participants. As far as the interactions between the actors are concerned, a multiplicity of forms is discussed, particularly in the political science and economic literature on governance (cf. Kaufmann, Majone and Ostrom 1986; Mayntz and Scharpf 1995; Mayntz 2004; Williamson 1985, 1998). With regard to healthcare systems, three forms are commonly identified: 1) hierarchy, i.e. a clear domination-subordination relationship, 2) collective negotiations as a form in which actors operating on equal terms enter into long-term agreements and (3) market transactions, in which a competitive relationship between the actors prevails[1]. Cross-tabulating the actors and forms of interaction produces the combinations depicted in Table 2.1.

The 'pure' regulatory types are located on the main diagonal. In these types, the actors are combined with the respected form of interaction, namely state-hierarchical regulation (in national health services), social self-regulation (in social insurance systems) and private-competitive regulation (in private healthcare systems)[2]. From bottom right to top left on the main diagonals, an increasing level of state control can be observed.

Table 2.1   Types of regulation

Form of interaction \ Actors	State	Self-governing actors	Market participants
Hierarchy	STATE-HIERARCHICAL REGULATION		
Collective negotiation		SOCIAL SELF-REGULATION	
Competition			PRIVATE-COMPETITIVE REGULATION

Source: own representation

The pure forms identified here have strong similarities, for example, with the terminology used by Giaimo and Manow (1999). However, their conceptual 'triad' of 'state-led', 'corporatist-governed' and 'market-driven' does not distinguish between the configurations of actors and the forms of interaction. Rico, Saltman and Boerma (2003), on the other hand, refer only to the forms of coordination and make the standard distinction between 'market', 'hierarchy' and 'networks' but without taking any account of the actors involved. The advantage of the nine-field matrix depicted above is that other forms, such as the hierarchical interactions between private-competitive actors that are characteristic of health maintenance organisations in the USA, can be captured in the fields not located on the angle bisectors.

Convergence of Healthcare Systems

In recent years, the question of the possible convergence of healthcare systems has been increasingly debated by researchers in the area (Saltman 1997; Comas-Herrera 1999; Field 1999; Nixon 1999, 2002; Leidl 2001; Wendt, Grimmeisen and Rothgang 2005; Rothgang and Schmid 2006). Generally speaking, however, the dimensions, concepts and indicators deployed in the convergence debate differ considerably, which leads to inconsistent results (Heichel, Pape and Sommerer 2005). Consequently, before the empirical findings of any comparison of healthcare systems can be presented, it is necessary to clarify which dimensions are being tested for signs of convergence, which concepts of convergence are used and how they are being measured (for a more detailed discussion see Rothgang and Schmid 2006).

Each of the dimensions that constitute a healthcare system – financing, service provision and regulation – can be investigated for convergent trends, as can the values that prevail in the population at large (Marmor, Okma and Latham 2006) or among elites (Taylor-Gooby 1996). In fact, a large share of the studies cited here are concerned solely with financing, which is not further investigated here (Comas-Herrera 1999; Nixon 1999, 2002). These differences in the dimension under investigation may explain part of the variance in results.

The same applies to the *concepts of convergence*. In this regard, a distinction is made between beta, delta and sigma convergence, the last-named being the most frequently used (cf. Heichel, Pape and Sommerer 2005). Sigma convergence refers to a reduction in the variance between different systems with regard to one parameter and accordingly is usually measured in quantitative analyses by the variance or the variation coefficients. Beta convergence, on the other hand, attempts to measure catch-up processes among 'laggard' countries and uses the ß parameter in regression models (Sala-i-Martin 1996). So long as the 'laggards' do not overtake the frontrunners, beta convergence implies sigma convergence. The converse, however, does not apply. Delta convergence, finally, is a measure of whether and to what extent systems are evolving relative to a reference model.

The existing studies of the *regulatory dimension*, which is what concerns us here, focus exclusively on sigma and delta convergence. As far as sigma convergence is concerned, the studies have sought to ascertain whether similar changes and trends can be observed (with positive results: Abel-Smith 1992; Abel-Smith and Mossialos 1994; van de Ven 1996) and whether there has been a reduction in the level of dissimilarity (with positive results: Ham and Brommels 1994; Field 1999; Wendt, Grimmeisen and Rothgang 2005; with negative results: Taylor-Gooby 1996; Saltman 1997; Jacobs 1998). Since qualitative indicators are used here, statistical indicators are dispensed with altogether. With regard to delta convergence, Hurst (1991), in particular, found it in the 'public contract model' that served as his reference model, while Bernardi-Schenkluhn (1992) even observed diverging reactions (cf. Rothgang and Schmid 2006 for a survey of the studies and their findings).

As even this brief survey of the current state of research suggests, only sigma or delta convergence have been used as a basis for investigating convergence trends in governance structures. The latter implies one of two things. The first is that one of the three system types may be becoming dominant; as a result, the representatives of the two other types are drawing closer to it, thereby transcending the boundaries of their system type. Alternatively, a new type may be emerging, towards which the representatives of all system types are converging. Sigma convergence, on the other hand, does not go so far but implies at least that the healthcare systems in question are going beyond the boundaries of the framework marked out by the system type. If they draw closer to one another, this leads to a loss of discrimination among previously clearly drawn boundary lines and hence to a 'blurring of regimes' and, if elements of a different system type are adopted, to hybridisation.

In order to examine whether convergence trends as defined above are emerging in the healthcare systems, the most significant changes in governance structures in the three countries under investigation will first be outlined country by country and then examined at a more general level for possible convergence trends.

CHANGING GOVERNANCE STRUCTURES IN THE GERMAN, BRITISH AND US HEALTHCARE SYSTEMS

In order to be able to identify changes in governance structures, it is necessary first to determine the starting situation at a given point in time. For Germany and Britain, we will take as our starting point the situation at the beginning of the 1970s, thus before the period regarded in retrospect as the 'golden' age of the welfare state gave way to the period of 'permanent austerity' (Pierson 2001). In the case of the USA, we will go back another decade, because the introduction of the Medicaid and Medicare state insurance systems in 1965 already constituted an important shift away from the purely private insurance system.

Germany

Nearly 90 per cent of the population in Germany is insured against the consequences of illness through the statutory health insurance scheme (SHI). The SHI is, therefore, the dominant institution in the healthcare system. Under the SHI scheme, insurance is provided by statutory health insurance funds, which are not part of the state apparatus but are corporate bodies under public law and therefore part of the public realm. The legal framework for the SHI is laid down in federal law, and in particular the Social Law Code V (SGB V). Within this legal framework, however, the key regulatory tasks fall to the actors in the healthcare system themselves (corporatist model)[3]. This 'self-governance' takes place in the health insurance funds (self-governance by insurance funds) and in the associations representing doctors and other health professionals and in the panel doctors' associations (self-governance by doctors), as well as through the 'joint self-governance' practised by the insurance funds and the service providers (cf. for example Gäfgen 1988, Alber 1992 and Döhler and Manow-Borgwardt 1992 for the situation in the 1980s and Rothgang et al. forthcoming and Rosenbrock and Gerlinger 2006 for an updated description).[4]

Against the background of the oil price shocks of 1973/74 and the ensuing recession, cost reduction became the dominant objective of health policy. Beginning with the Health Insurance Cost Reduction Act of 1977, co-payments for insurees were introduced (cf. Perschke-Hartmann 1994) and continuously increased. However, these arrangements were driven primarily by fiscal considerations and are of little consequence in terms of governance or regulation – even though it was sometimes asserted, for reasons of legitimation, that governance was also one of the targets. In fact, two other trends are of far greater importance for the regulatory dimension: firstly, increasing state intervention, some of it direct, in the SHI and in private health insurance (PHI) and, secondly, the introduction and expansion of competition.

Examples of *increased direct state intervention in SHI*, which will be briefly examined here, include the Health Care Structure Act (Gesundheitsstrukturgesetz) of December 1992, which came into force in 1993, the Health Insurance Contribution Rate Exoneration Act (Beitragsentlastungsgesetz) of September 1996, the Case Fees Act (Fallpauschalengesetz) of April 2002 and the Statutory Health Insurance Competition Reinforcement Act (GKV-Wettbewerbsstärkungsgesetz) of 2007.

The Health Care Structure Act not only introduced competition between the health insurance funds as a new coordination mechanism (see below) but also established sectoral budgets for the major service types (in-patient and out-patient treatment, remedies and adjuvants and drugs), as well as arrangements for updating. Even though these provisions were subsequently subject to regular changes, the budgeting introduced by the 1992 Act shaped health policy in the following decade and took away a key area of responsibility from the system of self-governance, which was regarded as incapable by itself of achieving the cost reductions considered essential by policymakers.

The Health Insurance Contribution Rate Exoneration Act stipulated that the health insurance funds should reduce their contribution rates by 0.4 points. This equated in arithmetic terms to the savings it was hoped the Act would produce, although when the Act was passed it was of course not certain that this objective could be achieved. However, setting of the contributions rate has been one of the original and fundamental rights of the individual health insurance funds. Thus this direct encroachment on that right, which was repeated in the Statutory Health Insurance Competition Reinforcement Act of 2003, deprived the health insurance funds of one of their basic powers, albeit only temporarily in the first instance.

Another significant encroachment was the introduction, through legislation, of DRG-based flat rates per case for hospital treatment.[5] The 2000
Health Care Reform Act made provision for the incorporation into the Hospital Financing Act of a new norm, whereby the statutory insurance funds'
peak organisations (jointly with the association of private health insurers) and
the German Hospital Organisation were called upon 'to introduce a universal,
efficiency-oriented, flat-rate payment system organised along the lines of a
DRG-based payment system already in use internationally'. The Case Fees
Act of 23 April 2002 introduced just such a payment system. What is noteworthy about this legislation is that government not only placed the payment
system for hospital treatment on a completely new footing but also, by means
of a number of decrees (Ersatzvornahmen), overcame attempts by the actors
in the self-governance system to block implementation of the new system and
gave a decisive impetus to the whole implementation process, which again
highlights the importance of state intervention for the regulation of the German healthcare system (Rosenbrock and Gerlinger 2006).

An even more conspicuous example of direct state intervention is the introduction of the central health fund on 1 January 2009. From this date
onwards, contributions are no longer paid to the relevant health insurance
fund but rather to a central fund that then distributes risk-adjusted payments
for each insured person to the individual insurance funds. Furthermore, the
contribution rate is now set by the Federal Government by statutory order.
Even though the individual insurance funds have the option of demanding
their enrolees to pay an additional contribution, a key element of the self-
governance system, i.e. the right to set the general contribution rate, has now
been transferred to the Federal Government.

In *private health insurance* too, there have been a number of direct state
interventions, particularly with regard to premium setting. Three measures
are particularly worthy of mention. The first is the introduction of a standard
tariff for the over-65s that provides benefits at SHI level in exchange for a
premium that must not exceed the maximum SHI contribution rate. The second is the requirement that interest surpluses should be used largely to ease
the financial burden on older enrolees. The third is the establishment of an
equalisation mechanism across insurance companies, which has been put in
place in order to ensure that interest surpluses are used for the above-men-
tioned purpose (Wasem 1995a).[6] Furthermore, the Statutory Health Insurance
Competition Reinforcement Act requires private insurance providers to develop the standard tariff into a 'basic tariff', which is open to those hitherto
without insurance that are not given access to SHI. This obligation to contract
is intended to ensure that the health policy objective of insuring the entire
population will henceforth be achieved – with the assistance of the private
insurance providers.

In addition to the strengthening of the scope for state intervention, the last one and a half decades have also seen the introduction of a new coordination mechanism, in the shape of *competition*. The 1992 Health Care Structure Act extended the right to choose one's insurance fund, which had until then been granted only to those insured by the substitute funds, to virtually all SHI insurees.[7] At the same time a risk structure equalisation scheme was introduced as a prerequisite of meaningful inter-fund competition, which should increase efficiency and act as a coordination mechanism in its own right. It soon became evident, however, that a form of competition in which the insurance funds have no competitive parameters at their disposal in drawing up contracts with service providers but are obliged to conclude all contracts 'jointly and uniformly' leads above all to risk selection but not to any improvement in care (Höppner et al. 2006). Thus, the introduction of inter-fund competition set in train a process that led to an extension of the competition principle. A not inconsiderable part of the subsequent legislation attempted to improve the functionality of competition as a coordination instrument by introducing further competitive reforms. This legislation includes new regulations pertaining to the right to choose one's insurance fund (Act on the Re-regulation of the Right to Choose a Health Insurance Fund of 2001), changes to the risk structure equalisation scheme through the introduction of a risk pool, the authorisation of disease management programmes for chronic diseases and the obligation to adopt a morbidity-based risk structure equalisation scheme introduced in the 2001 Act on the Reform of the Risk Structure Equalisation Scheme in Statutory Health Insurance. Other reforms include the introduction of integrated care in the SHI reform of 2001 and its extension in the SHI Modernisation Act of November 2003, as well as regulations on GP-based care where GPs act as gatekeepers to specialist care. Disease management programmes, integrated care and GP-based care, which appear to be aimed directly at remedying known shortcomings in care provision, are not conceivable without the competitive environment. In each case, the individual insurance funds are being provided with instruments with which they compete to provide better care structures and are thereby able to put an end to the exclusive concentration on the dysfunctional competition for the best enrolee risk structure. In fact, with the introduction of integrated care, in which the insurance funds (as with GP-based care) bypass the panel doctors' associations in order to conclude selective contracts with (groups of) service providers, a second pillar, organised on a competitive basis, has been put in place alongside the corporatist pillar (Rosenbrock and Gerlinger 2006). In this way, competition has also become established as a coordination mechanism in the relationship between the health insurance funds and service providers – even though in quantitative terms healthcare services organised on a competitive basis are as yet of little significance.

Britain

In Britain, all residents are entitled in the event of illness to treatment provided by the tax-funded National Health Service (NHS). This treatment includes outpatient medical care provided by general practitioners (GPs) as
well as specialist treatment (in-patient and outpatient) provided in hospitals
and is in principle free at the point of delivery. Since the NHS is funded out
of the general government budget, it competes with other state activities for
its share of the budget, so that each government decides on the level of the
resources to be made available to the NHS. Until the beginning of the 1990s,
once this budget had been distributed among the various parts of the country,
it was divided strictly into sectoral budgets for GPs and hospitals. The budgets for the various parts of the country are still distributed among the regions
and districts, using a formula that was developed in 1975 by a resource allocation working party. This top-down resource allocation process has its
counterpart in a planning process that combines bottom-up needs assessments
with top-down reviews.

Until the 1984 Griffith Reform, all health authorities were managed by
multidisciplinary teams, which generally included doctors and nurses. Consequently, these professions exerted considerable influence (Baggot 2004:
102ff.). The Griffith Reform transferred the management function at all levels from the multidisciplinary teams to general managers. For the first time, a
chain of command was established, in which a general manager at a higher
level was authorised to issue instructions to a general manager at a lower
level. While the reform conjured up a new managerialism that weakened the
professional autonomy of doctors in particular, it actually carried the hierarchical regulatory principle to extremes.

In contrast, the 1990 NHS and Community Care Act, which was based on
the 'Working for Patients' white paper of 1989, introduced a new coordination mechanism. For the first time in the history of the NHS, *competition* was
introduced as a coordination mechanism by separating funding bodies from
service providers (purchaser-provider split) and establishing internal markets
or quasi-markets. Hospitals were encouraged to change their legal status from
that of dependent establishment managed by a regional or district health authority to independent NHS trust in order to acquire greater managerial
autonomy. The health authorities lost their status as hospital operators and
henceforth had to buy in hospital services from independent hospitals operating in an 'internal market'. This reform, which drew on the ideas of the
American health economist Alain Enthoven, also empowered GPs to become
fundholders, i.e. to operate as primary care physicians with budgets at their
disposal with which to purchase hospital services for 'their' patients. Since
GP fundholders were both service providers and purchasers, they actually

contradicted the philosophy of the 'purchaser-provider split'. The result was that there were two types of commissioners (district health authorities and GP fundholders) who were able to purchase hospital services for 'their' patients (LeGrand, Mays and Mulligan 1998).

Even before New Labour came to power in 1997, the Conservative government under John Major had begun to tone down the rhetoric of competition and to prioritise improvements in public health and primary care (Ham 2004: 50). Consequently, when the newly elected Blair government declared the experiment with the internal market to be over, it met with little opposition. Apart from its pledge to increase expenditure on health services, the new government promised to establish a regulatory framework for the NHS that would constitute a 'third way' between the traditional hierarchical system and the competitive approach based on quasi-markets. A further reorganisation of the NHS led to the introduction of 381 primary care groups (PCGs) in England, which replaced the GP fundholders. Like their predecessors, GP fundholders before them, the PCGs were responsible for providing primary care services and purchasing specialist hospital services. Thus the shift of power from hospital consultants to GPs that had been triggered by the introduction of GP fundholders, continued. Even though, on the rhetorical level, purchasing had now been replaced by commissioning, the purchaser-provider split continued, de facto, to exist, as did the quasi-market relations between the purchasers and providers of specialist, hospital-based services. The importance of the PCGs was further increased when they were converted into primary care trusts (PCTs). PCTs now control 75 per cent of the NHS budget, which they can use both to purchase specialist hospital services and to improve primary care (and hence also avoid hospital stays). The competition among hospitals for the funds administered by the PCTs has even increased in intensity, since the new foundation trust hospitals enjoy greater freedom than hospitals have traditionally enjoyed to retain profits and use them as they see fit. Consequently, the profit motive now plays a greater role. Moreover, the development of healthcare resource groups, which can be seen as a British variant of DRGs (Schölkopf and Stapf-Finé 2003: 34), gave the PCTs the opportunity for the first time to purchase clearly defined medical services from competing hospitals and can thus be regarded as a prerequisite of meaningful purchasing.[8]

Thus even though it is denied in the official rhetoric, it is in fact true to say that the fundamental reforms of the 1990s have endured. Hospitals are no longer the last link in a chain of command made up of health authorities operating at various levels but have established themselves as independent actors that compete with each other for commissions from the funding bodies. Among the funding bodies, the PCTs have succeeded the health authorities and the GP fundholders. They are now the only commissioning bodies for specialist hospital services and can fulfil their remit only by concluding agreements with hospitals. Direct hierarchical regulation has unquestionably been replaced by a quasi-market form of commissioning and competition plays an important role in this regard – even though any reference to that term is deliberately eschewed. Thus, in Britain, hierarchy as the sole regulatory structure has been supplemented on a long-term basis by an additional mode of interaction, namely competition.

USA

Perhaps the most important characteristic of the US healthcare system is its fragmentation (cf. Reinhard 2005). Thus currently about a quarter of the population is insured through federal programmes, such as Medicare and Medicaid; 60 per cent have private health insurance, which their employer arranges for them or provides (in the case of employers who act as underwriters), and a further nine per cent have arranged private insurance for themselves (De Navas-Walt, Proctor and Mills 2005). Nevertheless, 16 per cent of the population have no health insurance (ibid.)[9] and millions more have to be regarded as uninsured because of the inadequacy of their insurance coverage (Stone 2000). Medical services are supplied by private service providers who compete with each other just as the insurance companies do on the other side of the market. The system has traditionally been characterised by free choice of physician and a reimbursement system in which the insurance companies simply settle the bill for the services provided but do not carry out any governance or regulatory functions. State regulation is concerned primarily with the state systems, while the private health insurance market and the market for medical goods and services are largely unregulated (Cacace 2007).

Not least because of the decentralised and fragmented nature of the USA's political system, there has not been any far-reaching reform of the country's healthcare system in the last 40 years (Hacker 2002: 22). Consequently, the introduction of Medicare and Medicaid in 1965 has to be regarded as the most important reform, which gave rise subsequently to regulations within these systems but left the dominant private insurance segment of the US healthcare system untouched.

Nevertheless, the system's regulatory structure did undergo a major change in the 1980s and 90s with the so-called '*managed care revolution*'. Managed care itself is an ambiguous concept, which has various facets (cf. Glied 2000). The common core is to be found, firstly, in the use of management principles and, secondly, in the at least partial integration of the service provision and financing functions (Amelung and Schumacher 2004). This integration can be achieved either by having the services in question provided by establishments operated by the insurance company ('classic' health main-tenance organisation) or by entering into contracts with selected providers. Various models can be identified, depending on how independent service providers are of the insurance company and how closely enrolees are tied to the service providers selected by the insurance company.[10] Thus the essential defining characteristic of managed care is that elements of hierarchical gov-ernance have gained entry into a system in which service providers previ-ously operated largely uncontrolled and unregulated. Unlike the traditional NHS, however, this hierarchical governance has been introduced in the con-text of a private system.

In order to promote managed care, two pieces of legislation were passed, one in 1970, the other in 1973. The first act placed an obligation on employ-ers to at least offer their employees with health insurance the option of a managed care contract. The second act introduced subsidies for managed care contracts concluded by Medicare enrolees. However, the regulations were so strict that neither piece of legislation initially had any effect. It was not until the late 1970s and early 1980s that deregulation led to a breakthrough (Glied 2000). Since 1981, the states have even had the right to force individuals who may be eligible for the Medicaid programme to enrol in managed care pro-grammes. As a result, the share of individuals eligible for Medicaid receiving healthcare through managed care programmes rose to 40 per cent by 1996 and as high as 58 per cent in 2002 (CMS 2003).

However, the real managed care revolution took place in the early 1990s in employer-funded health insurance. In 1988, the share of insurees with tra-ditional contracts was still 73 per cent. By 2004, this share had fallen to 5 per cent. In effect, therefore, managed care organisations have completely squeezed the traditional type of health insurance out of the market.[11]

The emergence of managed care in the US healthcare system can be seen as a reaction to shortcomings in the regulation and governance of the tradi-tion system, which have made the US healthcare system the most expensive in the world. The managed care revolution has been driven by the funders, i.e. the states, which fund Medicaid, and above all employers, who on aver-age pay 70 per cent of health insurance premiums. In managed care organi-sations, and particularly in the original form of HMO, professional auton-omy, particularly for doctors, is limited by certain elements of hierarchical governance. In contrast to the British system, however, this hierarchy is em-bedded in a *private* system. Thus while competition has been introduced into the German and British systems as an additional coordinating mechanism, the managed care revolution in the USA has established hierarchy as a coordina-tion mechanism, although not in the form of a state hierarchy but rather within a system that remains private.

CONCLUSION

By way of summary, Table 2.2 below shows the changes that have taken place in the regulatory structures of the healthcare systems of Britain, Germany and the United States. These changes may be the result of deliberate reform policies or, even more plausibly, a consequence of what Hacker (2004) calls 'drift' or 'conversion'[12] (cf. also Thelen 2005).

Table 2.2   *The changing regulatory structures in Britain, Germany and the United States*

	Competition	Bargaining	Hierarchy
Market Actors	**USA** GER	USA	USA
Corporative Actors	GER	**GER**	
State	GB		**GB** GER USA

Note: While the bold country codes refer to the original situation the country codes in small print show the additional forms of governance that have emerged since then.

Source: Own depiction.

The British NHS, firstly, is an example of a state-led healthcare system that has introduced market elements in order to improve efficiency. Furthermore, much essential decision-making on healthcare has been devolved from central government to regional and local bodies (Lewis, Alvarez Rosete and Mays 2006; Osborne and Gaebler 1992). Interestingly, the prevalence of market mechanisms in the British healthcare system has been accompanied by stronger state involvement, as indicated for example by the increasing role of the state in the regulation of service providers (Giaimo and Manow 1999: 972; Grimmeisen and Frisina forthcoming; Hacker 2004). This finding is clearly at odds with the view that regulation is a zero-sum game, i.e. that an increase in market competition necessarily leads to a loss of hierarchical state regulation. On the contrary, it has to be emphasized that the growing role of market competition strengthens rather than weakens state authority, especially as these reforms, once initiated, require further state intervention (Hacker 2004: 712).

In the case of the German social insurance system, the dominant structure of mutual self-regulation by corporatist actors was largely preserved if not expanded in the first two decades of our observation period (Alber 1992; Döhler and Manow-Borgwardt 1992; Giaimo and Manow 1999: 978). These developments, however, have to some extent been offset by the introduction of competition between health insurance funds in 1992, which led to subsequent legislation even increasing the role of competition, and an ever increasing role of the state in the governance of healthcare policy. As a result of these developments, both the state and the market now play a greater role in the governance of healthcare policy. Although there is continued reliance on corporatist self-regulation, space has been opened up in the German healthcare system for public (state) and private (market) actors, with the traditional system of self-regulation being squeezed between the two (Rothgang et al. forthcoming).

Finally, with regard to the private healthcare system of the US, hierarchical state regulation increased significantly as a result of the creation of the public programmes Medicare and Medicaid in 1965. Beyond this, the federal government uses market incentives as it employs public funds to subsidise employer-sponsored private insurance (Hacker 2002). Yet within the realm of private insurance, hierarchical state regulation remained weak, paving the way for considerable policy conversion (Stone 2000; Hacker 2004: 721). Thus at the same time, the private insurance sector saw the emergence of managed care, which proliferated quickly from the 1980s onwards; although purely private in nature, the development of managed care has led to the establishment of a number of hierarchical arrangements (Cacace forthcoming). As a consequence of the backlash against managed care, the hierarchical regulation of providers and patients was amended by bargaining elements. Due to the spill-over of managed care to the private programmes, and as private insurers adopt remuneration methods borrowed from the Medicare programme, the boundaries between the public and the private have blurred (Cacace 2007).

Thus in all three healthcare systems, the regulatory structure has changed profoundly. Although each system inevitably retains its basic character, i.e. state hierarchy in Britain, corporatist self-regulation in Germany and market competition in the US, we now find more complex regulatory structures, in which the dominant regulatory mechanism is supplemented by mechanisms that were originally absent. As a result, the systems are moving towards hybrid forms of governance and in doing so illustrate one of the roles played by convergence tendencies.

NOTES

1. Market and competition can be differentiated analytically: 'competition' can be defined in general terms as rivalry between individuals, groups or nations that occurs when more than one party seeks to obtain something that not all can possess simultaneously (Stigler 1987: 531). Thus competition is an action principle that can occur inside as well as outside markets (Schneider 1994: 159). The 'market', on the other hand, is a level at which competition can take place. In healthcare systems, 'competition' is used both in markets and in quasi-markets specially created for the purpose.

2. In reality, of course, combinations of these pure forms are also conceivable and in some cases their existence can be substantiated, such as the negotiations (between self-governing actors) that take place under the shadow of (state) hierarchy (Scharpf 1993; Mayntz and Scharpf 1995: 28).

3. However, these regulatory activities take place in the knowledge that the state can always intervene. One fundamental development over the last two decades is precisely that the state has made increasing use of its options for intervention.

4. One exception here is hospital service planning, which is undertaken by the *Länder* and to a large extent lies beyond the control of the self-governance system.

5. DRG-based payment systems are a reimbursement method for inpatient treatments. They are calculated prospectively by splitting all illnesses into groups and estimating costs per case within each group.

6. Even more evident is the utilisation of private health insurance for social purposes in private mandatory long-term care insurance, in which the private insurance industry had to accept a number of obligations. These include, in particular, an obligation to enter into contracts with older individuals (over 60) and those already in need of care, compulsory unisex tariffs, coverage for children at no extra cost and the restriction of premium levels to the highest rate payable under the social long-term care insurance scheme or to 1.5 times that rate when a spouse is jointly insured (Wasem 1995b).

7. The original exceptions, which applied to those insured by the Seamen's Accident Prevention and Insurance Association and the schemes for agricultural workers and miners and mine employees, have now been abolished.

8. Even the establishment of the National Institute for Clinical Excellence (now the National Institute for Health and Clinical Excellence) in 1999 and the simultaneous introduction of treatment guidelines (National Service Frameworks) and the creation of the Healthcare Commission had the effect of promoting competition. These institutions are evidence of the growing interest in establishing uniform national quality standards. However, the homogenisation of services that can be achieved in this way is also a means of intensifying competition.

9. The figures quoted here are based on the population census and permit double counting, for example in the case of individuals who have entitlements under Medicare but at the same time also have a private health insurance policy. Consequently, the numbers do not sum to 100 per cent.

10. A broad distinction can be made here between health maintenance organisations (HMOs), point-of-service organisations (POSs) and preferred provider organisations (PPOs). The staff model HMO, with its employed doctors, can be regarded as the purest form. However, in other forms of HMO (group models, independent practice associations, network HMOs), a 'gatekeeper' is responsible for managing claims and the free choice of physician is restricted. In POS organisations, on the other hand, enrolees in need of medical treatment decide themselves whether they wish to be treated by their insurance provider's contractual partner or would prefer to seek another service provider and make the corresponding co-payments. Preferred provider organisations go a stage further and almost conform to the classic model (without gatekeeper). Virtually the only way in which they differ from the traditional model is that service providers offer discounts to their contractual partners on the insurance side (cf., for example, Newbrander and Eichler 2001).

11. At the same time, however, the share of the more restrictive forms of MC organisations (HMOs) relative to that of the less restrictive forms (POS and PPO) shifted. True, HMOs initially increased their market share from 16 per cent in 1988 to 31 per cent in 1996, but by 2004 it had fallen back to 25 per cent (the so-called 'managed care backlash'). At the same time, PPOs expanded dramatically, from a market share of 11 per cent in 1988 to 55 per cent in 2004 (Kaiser/HRET 2004). These shifts show that very restrictive forms of MC, in which the free choice of physician is severely curtailed, meet with less approval, although considerably lower premiums are required.

12. While policy conversion denotes the decentralised adjustment process driven by actors empowered under the existing regime, policy drift denotes system transformation caused by a failure to adapt policies to changing circumstances (Hacker 2004: 722).

REFERENCES

Abel-Smith, Brian (1992), *Cost Containment and New Priorities in Health Care. A Study of the European Community*, Aldershot, UK: Avebury.

Abel-Smith, Brian and Elias Mossialos (1994), 'Cost Containment and Health Care Reform: A Study of the European Union', *Health Policy*, **28**, 89–132.

Alber, Jens (1992), *Das Gesundheitswesen der Bundesrepublik Deutschland. Entwicklung, Struktur und Funktionsweise*, Frankfurt am Main: Campus.

Amelung, Volker Eric and Harald Schumacher (2004), *Managed Care*, Wiesbaden: Gabler.

Baggot, Rob (2004), *Health and Health Care in Britain*, Basingstoke, UK: Palgrave Macmillan.

Bernardi-Schenkluhn, Brigitte (1992), 'Politischer Problemdruck und aktuelle Reformstrategien im Vergleich', in Jens Alber and Brigitte Bernardi-Schenkluhn (eds), *Westeuropäische Gesundheitssysteme im Vergleich. Bundesrepublik Deutschland, Schweiz, Frankreich, Italien, Großbritannien*, Frankfurt am Main: Campus, pp. 623–700.

Cacace, Mirella (2007), *The Changing Public/Private Mix in the American Health Care System*, TranState Working Paper No. 58, Bremen: TranState Research Center.

Cacace, Mirella (forthcoming), 'The Coexistence of Market and Hierarchy in the US Healthcare System', in Heinz Rothgang, Mirella Cacace, Simone Grimmeisen, Uwe Helmert and Claus Wendt (eds), *The Changing Role of the State in OECD Health Care Systems. From Heterogeneity to Homogeneity?*, Houndsmills, Basingstoke, UK: Palgrave Macmillan.

CMS (Centers for Medicare and Medicaid) (2003), *Health Care Industry Market Update*, online source http://cms.hhs.gov/reports/hcimu/hcimu_03242003.pdf (9 June 2005), Vol. 2005.

Comas-Herrera, Adelina (1999), 'Is There Convergence in the Health Expenditures of the EU Member States?', in Julian Le Grand (ed.), *Health Care and Cost Containment in the European Union*, Aldershot, UK: Ashgate, pp. 197–218.

De Navas-Walt, Carmen, Bernadette D. Proctor and Robert J. Mills (2004), *Income, Poverty, and Health Insurance Coverage in the United States: 2003*, U.S. Census Bureau, Current Population Reports, Washington DC: US Government Printing Office.

Döhler, Marian and Philip Manow-Borgwardt (1992), 'Korporatisierung als gesundheitspolitische Strategie', *Staatswissenschaften und Staatspraxis*, **3**, 64–106.

Field, Mark G. (1999), 'Comparative Health Systems and the Convergence Hypothesis. The Dialectics of Universalism and Particularism', in Albert F. Wessen (ed.), *Health Care Systems in Transition. An International Perspective*, London: Thousand Oaks: SAGE Publications, pp. 35–44.

Gäfgen, Gérard (ed.) (1988), *Neokorporatismus und Gesundheitswesen*, Baden-Baden: Nomos.

Giaimo, Susan and Philip Manow (1999), 'Adapting the Welfare State – The Case of Health Care Reform in Britain, Germany, and the United States', *Comparative Political Studies*, **32**, 967–1000.

Gilbert, Neil (2002), *Transformation of the Welfare State: The Silent Surrender of Public Responsibility*, Oxford: Oxford University Press.

Glied, Sherryl (2000), 'Managed Care', in Anthony J. Culyer and Joseph P. Newhouse (eds), *Handbook of Health Economics*, Amsterdam: North Holland Press, pp. 707–753.

Grimmeisen, Simone and Lorraine Frisina (forthcoming), 'The Role of the State in the British Health Care System – Between Marketization and Statism', in Heinz Rothgang, Mirella Cacace, Simone Grimmeisen, Uwe Helmert and Claus Wendt (eds), *The Changing Role of the State in OECD Health Care Systems. From Heterogeneity to Homogeneity?*, Houndsmills, Basingstoke, UK: Palgrave Macmillan.

Hacker, Jacob S. (2002), *The Divided Welfare State: The Battle over Public and Private Social Benefits in the United States*, Cambridge, UK: Cambridge University Press.

Hacker, Jacob S. (2004), 'Dismantling the Health Care State? Political Institutions, Public Policies and the Comparative Politics of Health Care Reform', *British Journal of Political Science*, **34**, 693–724.

Ham, Chris (2004), *Health Policy in Britain: The Politics of Organisation of the National Health Service*, London: Palgrave MacMillan.

Ham, Chris and Mats Brommels (1994), 'Health Care Reform in the Netherlands, Sweden, and the United Kingdom', *Health Affairs*, **13**, 106–119.

Heichel, Stephan, Jessica Pape and Thomas Sommerer (2005), 'Is there Convergence in Convergence Research? An Overview of Empirical Studies on Policy Convergence', *Journal of European Public Policy*, **12**, 817–840.

Höppner, Karin, Stefan Greß, Heinz Rothgang and Jürgen Wasem (2006), 'Instrumente der Risikoselektion – Theorie und Empirie', in Dirk Göpffarth, Stefan

Greß, Klaus Jacobs and Jürgen Wasem (eds), *Jahrbuch Risikostrukturausgleich 2006 - Zehn Jahre Kassenwechsel*, St. Augustin: Asgard, pp. 119–144.

Huber, Evelyne and John D. Stephens (2001), *Development and Crisis of the Welfare State*, Chicago: University of Chicago Press.

Hurst, Jeremy W. (1991), 'Reforming Health Care in Seven European Nations', *Health Affairs*, **10** (3), 7-22.

Jacobs, Alan (1998), 'Seeing Difference: Market Health Reform in Europe', *Journal of Health Politics, Policy and Law*, **23**, 1–33.

Kaiser and HRET (2004), 'The Kaiser Family Foundation' and 'Health Research and Educational Trust', Employer Health Benefits 2004, Annual Survey, online source: http://www.kff.org/insurance/7148/index.cfm (6 June 2005).

Kaufmann, Franz-Xaver, Giandomenico Majone and Vincent Ostrom (1986), *Guidance Control and Evaluation in the Public Sector*, Berlin: De Gruyter.

LeGrand, Julian, Nicholas Mays and Jo-Ann Mulligan (eds) (1998), *Learning from the NHS Internal Market – A Review of the Evidence*, London: King's Fund.

Leidl, Reiner (2001), 'Konvergenz der Gesundheitssysteme in der Europäischen Union', *Gesundheitsökonomie und Qualitätsmanagement*, **6**, 44–53.

Lewis, Richard, Arturo Alvarez Rosete and Nicholas Mays (2006), *How to Regulate Health Care in England? An International Perspective*, London: King's Fund.

Marmor, Theodore R., Kieke G. Okma and Stephen R. Latham (2006), 'Comparative Perspectives on National Values, Institutions and Health Policies', in Claus Wendt and Christof Wolf (eds), *Soziologie der Gesundheit*, Sonderheft 46 der Kölner Zeitschrift für Soziologie und Sozialpsychologie, Wiesbaden: VS Verlag, pp. 383–405.

Mayntz, Renate and Fritz W. Scharpf (1995), *Gesellschaftliche Selbstregelung und politische Steuerung*, Frankfurt am Main: Campus.

Mayntz, Renate (1990), 'Politische Steuerbarkeit und Reformblockaden. Überlegungen am Beispiel des Gesundheitswesens', *Staatswissenschaft und Staatspraxis*, **1**, 283–307.

Mayntz, Renate (2004), 'Governance im modernen Staat', in Arthur Benz (ed.), *Governance–Regieren in komplexen Regelsystemen*, Wiesbaden: VS Verlag, pp. 65–76.

Newbrander, William and Rena Eichler (2001), 'Managed Care in the United States: its History, Forms, and Future', in Aviva Ron and Xenia Scheil-Adlung (eds), *Recent Health Policy Innovations in Social Security*, New Brunswick: Transaction Publishers, pp. 83–106.

Nixon, John (1999), *Convergence Analysis of Health Care Expenditure in the EU Countries Using Two Approaches*, Discussion Papers in Economics, 1999/03, York: University of York.

Nixon, John (2002), *Convergence: An Analysis of European Union Health Care Systems 1960–95*, Submission for the degree of PhD, September, York: Department of Economics and Related Studies, University of York.

Osborne, David and Ted Gaebler (1992), *Reinventing Government. How the Entre-preneurial Spirit is Transforming the Public Sector*, Reading, MA: Addison-Wesley.

Perschke-Hartmann, Christiane (1994), *Die doppelte Reform. Gesundheitspolitik von Blüm zu Seehofer*, Opladen: Leske & Budrich.

Pierson, Paul (2001), 'Coping with Permanent Austerity: Welfare State Restructuring in Affluent Democracies', in Paul Pierson (ed.), *The New Politics of Welfare State*, Oxford: Oxford University Press, pp. 410–456.

Pierson, Paul (1994), *Dismantling the Welfare State? Reagan, Thatcher, and the Politics of Retrenchment*, New York: Cambridge University Press.

Reinhard, Uwe E. (2005), 'The Mix of Public and Private Payers in the US Health System', in Alan Maynard (ed), *The Public-private Mix for Health*, Oxford: The Nuffield Trust, pp. 83–117.

Rico, Ana, Richard B. Saltman and Wienke G.W. Boerma (2003), 'Organizational Restructuring in European Health Systems: The Role of Primary Care', *Social Policy & Administration*, **37**, 592–608.

Rosenbrock, Rolf and Thomas Gerlinger (2006), *Gesundheitspolitik. Eine systematische Einführung*, Bern: Verlag Hans Huber.

Rothgang, Heinz, Mirella Cacace, Loraine Frisina and Achim Schmid (2008), 'The Changing Public-private Mix in OECD Healthcare Systems', in Martin Seeleib-Kaiser (ed.), *Welfare State Transformations*, Basingstoke, UK: Palgrave MacMillan, pp. 132–146.

Rothgang, Heinz und Achim Schmid (2006), *Convergence in Health Care Systems: Blurring of Regimes in Germany and Britain*, Paper prepared for the 56th Political Studies Association Annual Conference to be held at the University of Reading, URL: http://www.psa.ac.uk/2006/pps/Rothgang.pdf.

Rothgang, Heinz, Herbert Obinger and Stephan Leibfried (2006), 'The State and its Welfare State – How do Welfare State Changes Affect the Make-up of the Nation State', *Social Policy and Administration*, **40**, 250–266.

Rothgang, Heinz, Mirella Cacace, Simone Grimmeisen and Claus Wendt (2005), 'The Changing Role of the State in OECD Health Care Systems', *European Review*, **13**, 187–212.

Rothgang, Heinz, Achim Schmid and Claus Wendt (forthcoming), 'The Self-regulatory German Health Care System Between Growing Competition and State Hierarchy', in Heinz Rothgang, Mirella Cacace, Simon Grimmeisen, Uwe Helmert and Claus Wendt (eds), *The Changing Role of the State in OECD Health Care Systems. From Heterogeneity to Homogeneity?*, Houndsmills, Basingstoke, UK: Palgrave Macmillan.

Sala-i-Martin, Xavier (1996), 'The Classical Approach to Convergence Analysis', *The Economic Journal*, **106**, 1019–1036.

Saltman, Richard B. (1997), 'Convergence, Social Embeddedness, and the Future of Health Systems in the Nordic Region', in Joshua Cohen (ed.), *Governments and*

Health Systems: Implications of Differing Involvements, Chichester: Wiley, pp. 69–74.

Scharpf, Fritz W. (1993), 'Positive und Negative Koordination in Verhandlungssystemen', in Adrienne Héritier (ed.), *Policy Analyse. Kritik und Neuorientierung*, PVS Sonderheft 24/1993, Opladen: Westdeutscher Verlag, pp. 57–83.

Schmid, Achim, Ralf Götze, Mirella Cacace and Heinz Rothgang (2008), *The Role of Ideas and Problem Pressure in Healthcare System Change,* Paper to be presented at the 6th Annual ESPAnet Conference "Cross-border Influences in Social Policy" in Helsinki (Finland), 18–20 September, 2008. URL: http://www.etk.fi/Binary.aspx?Section=61331&Item=63309.

Schneider, Werner (1994), *Der Risikostrukturausgleich in der gesetzlichen Krankenversicherung*, Berlin: Schmidt.

Schölkopf, Martin and Heinz Stapf-Finé (2003), *Die Krankenhausversorgung im internationalen Vergleich: Zahlen, Fakten, Trends*, Düsseldorf: Deutsche Krankenhaus Verlagsgesellschaft mbH.

Starke, P. (2006), 'The Politics of Welfare State Retrenchment: A Literature Review', *Social Policy & Administration*, **40**, 104–120.

Stigler, Georg J. (1987), 'Competition', in John Eatwell, Murray Milgate and Peter Newman (eds), *The New Palgrave: A Dictionary of Economics*, Vol. I, New York: Norton, pp. 531–535.

Stone, Deborah (2000), 'United States', *Journal of Health Politics, Policy and Law*, **25**, 953–958.

Taylor-Gooby, Peter (1996), 'The Future of Health Care in Six European Countries: The Views of Policy Elites', *International Journal of Health Policy*, **26**, 203–219.

Thelen, Kathleen and Wolfgang Streeck (2005), 'Introduction: Institutional Change in Advanced Political Economies', in Wolfgang Streeck and Kathleen Thelen (eds), *Beyond Continuity. Institutional Change in Advanced Political Economies*, Oxford: Oxford University Press, pp. 1–39.

van de Ven, Wynand P.M.M. (1996), 'Market-oriented Health Care Reforms: Trends and Future Options', *Social Science & Medicine*, **43**, 655–666.

Wasem, Jürgen (1995a), 'Gesetzliche und private Krankenversicherung – auf dem Weg in die Konvergenz?', *Sozialer Fortschritt*, **44**, 621–634.

Wasem, Jürgen (1995b), 'Zwischen Sozialbindung und versicherungstechnischer Äquivalenz – Die private Krankenversicherung und die Pflege-Pflichtversicherung', in Uwe Fachinger and Heinz Rothgang (eds), *Die Wirkungen des Pflege-Versicherungsgesetzes*, Berlin: Duncker & Humblot, pp. 263–278.

Wendt, Claus, Lorraine Frisina and Heinz Rothgang (2009), 'Healthcare System Types – A Conceptual Framework for Comparison', *Social Policy and Administration*, **75** (1), 70–90.

Wendt, Claus, Simone Grimmeisen and Heinz Rothgang (2005), 'Convergence or Divergence in OECD Health Care Systems?', in Bea Cantillon and Ive Marx (eds), *International Cooperation in Social Security: How to Cope with Globalization?*, Antwerpen: Intersentia, pp. 15–45.

Williamson, Oliver E. (1998), 'The Institutions of Governance', *The American Review*, **88**, 75–79.

Williamson, Oliver E. (1985), *The Economic Institutions of Capitalism: Firms, Markets, Relational Contracting*, New York: Free Press.

3. Vanishing Variety? The Regulation of Funded Pension Schemes in Comparative Perspective

Thorsten Hippe

THE REGULATION OF FUNDED PENSIONS – TOWARDS NEO-LIBERALISM OR HYBRIDISATION?

Since the 1990s, pay-as-you-go (PAYGO) pension systems have been under increasing political pressure. In particular, so-called Bismarckian countries with hitherto extensive PAYGO schemes (Austria, Belgium, France, Germany and Sweden) – embodying high collective responsibility for status maintenance in old age – have considerably reduced PAYGO benefit levels. As a result, the function of unfunded pensions is increasingly restricted to preventing poverty in old age. Individuals are encouraged to take out funded pensions in order to achieve status maintenance. Thus the difference between Bismarckian and Beveredgian countries – which have always restricted the benefit levels of unfunded pensions to poverty prevention (Australia, the Netherlands, New Zealand, Switzerland and the UK) – seems to be eroding. Consequently, the cross-national mean level of state intervention seems to be falling while the spread of national pension policies seems to be narrowing. Pension systems in OECD countries seem to converge on a subsided state intervention plateau, cell 9 (Chapter 1, Table 1.1).

However, theories of pension policy change that focus solely on the financial dimension neglect the regulatory aspect of funded pension provision (Leisering 2006). Regulation is important because funded pension provision can be embedded in different institutional governance structures. These structures may exhibit a high degree of *collective* responsibility for status maintenance in old age (cf. Modigliani and Muralidhar 2004) or a high degree of *individual* responsibility for status maintenance (cf. Littlewood 1998). Other authors propose various regulatory measures that balance collective and individual responsibility (James 2005; Le Grand 2003: 139;

Sunstein and Thaler 2003). Hence, the shift from PAYGO towards funding does not necessarily indicate a process of neo-liberal convergence towards unfettered markets.

Instead, some authors (Leisering 2006; Nullmeier 2001) suggest that the regulation of funded pension schemes will be based on a mixture of governance elements, as is the case with health policy (see Rothgang, Chapter 2), thereby producing intermediate levels of collective intervention. This 'hybridisation hypothesis' suggests that social policy structures and market mechanisms will become increasingly intertwined. The hierarchical structures of the old provider welfare state are likely to be replaced by market mechanisms because of cultural individualisation, but public pressure on political actors to ensure financial security for pensioners will encourage the establishment of *socially* regulated markets.

In order to examine the hybridisation hypothesis, I propose a theoretical concept of funded pension regulation and differentiate between three ideal types of regulatory governance (the next section). In the following section, the development of the regulation of funded pensions in three groups of Western countries that had structurally different pension systems in the 1980s is investigated empirically. The developments will be analysed with reference to the ideal typology in order to enable genuine comparisons. The chapter concludes with an analysis of the extent to which funded pension regulations converged towards hybridization or a particular ideal type between 1980 and 2005.

AN IDEAL TYPOLOGY OF FUNDED PENSION REGULATION

Following Leisering (2006), the regulation of funded pension provision is conceptualised here as encompassing all responses to the (anticipated) failure of financial markets by normative, legal, organisational and financial means institutionalised by collective actors (state/social partners). The following four central potential market failures jeopardising the security, efficiency and equity of funded pension provision are particularly intensively debated in the current literature:

a. *Myopia.* Individuals may undervalue future needs in old age compared to present desires (hyperbolic discounting) (Mitchell and Utkus 2003). This raises the question of whether saving in funded schemes should be collectively enforced, promoted by state subsidies, etc.
b. *Volatility risk.* Financial markets are quite volatile, not only in the short term but even over retirement saving periods of 40 years (Burtless 2000).

Such volatility can undermine the security of retirement planning and produce artificial inequalities between different birth cohorts. Legal minimum guarantees or forms of intergenerational solidarity can be instituted to give savers more security (Modigliani and Muralidhar 2004).

c. *Choice risk.* The average pension consumer is overwhelmed by choice overload (Iyengar et al. 2003), and often chooses investment products that are inappropriate (Cronqvist 2003; James 2005; Kahneman et al. 2005). As financial education hardly helps (Erturk et al. 2005; Mitchell and Utkus 2003), this raises the question of whether individual freedom of choice should be collectively guided or even abolished in favour of collective asset pooling in a common investment portfolio.

d. *Administration charges.* Administration costs in decentralised funded pension schemes with individual accounts are considerably higher than in PAYGO and centralised funded pension schemes (Döring 2002: 115), thereby reducing accumulated pension savings considerably (Furman 2005; Murthi et al. 2001).

This raises the question of whether provider charges should be legally capped or whether the accumulation process should be centralised in order to exploit economies of scale (Kotlikoff 1999: 20 f.), etc.

Examination of the different theoretical recommendations for best practice in the economic literature reveals three ideal-type regulatory strategies for funded pension provision (see also Table 3.1):

a. The neo-liberal governance strategy, which emphasises competition and exit, relegates responsibility for status maintenance primarily to the individual, implying a low level of collective intervention (for example Littlewood 1998). This approach relies on consumer sovereignty to overcome myopia. Trusting the market's 'invisible hand' (Smith) as a masterful 'discovery device' (Hayek), it regards the enforcement of unfettered provider competition and market transparency as sufficient to provide protection against financial market downturns, high charges and inappropriate providers/products.

b. In the social-liberal governance strategy, which balances hierarchy and competition, responsibility for securing status maintenance is to be shared between individuals and society, which implies an intermediate level of collective intervention. In order to prevent myopia without falling into the trap of paternalism, automatic enrolment with the possibility of opting out is proposed (Sunstein and Thaler 2003). This automatic enrolment may or may not be accompanied by direct state subsidies (matching contributions) (Le Grand 2003, 139). Volatility risk should be cushioned by moderate minimum return guarantees or by automatic enrolment in life-cycle funds (Munnell and Sundén 2004: 175), with the asset mix being gradually shifted from stocks towards less volatile bonds with increasing customer age. As far as choice risk is concerned, this governance strategy proposes the establishment of an 'institutional market' (James 2005) in which individual choice is restricted to a handful of broadly diversified index funds, which charge low fees because they just replicate the asset compilations of financial market indices. The providers of these funds are to be chosen by a public regulator (competitive bidding). As the institutional market reaps economies of scale via centralised contribution collection, yearly administration charges should be legally capped clearly below 1 per cent of assets per account.

Table 3.1   Three ideal types of funded pension regulation

IDEAL TYPE ⟍ Issue/problem	SOCIAL-DEMOC-RATIC GOVERN-ANCE STRATEGY	SOCIAL-LIBERAL GOVERNANCE STRATEGY	NEO-LIBERAL GOVERNANCE STRATEGY
Responsibility for status maintenance	Collective actors (state and/or social partners)	Individual citizen and the state (shared responsibility)	Individual citizen
Myopia	Mandatory participation	Automatic enrolment (with possibility of opting out) and/or state subsidies	Voluntary participation (individual must opt in)
Volatility risk	Defined benefit via intergenerational risk-sharing	Moderate minimum return guarantees or automatic enrolment in life-cycle funds	Defined contribution
Choice risk	Pooling of members' assets in a collective portfolio; no provider competition; collective voice via member councils instead of individual exit	Individual choice in an 'Institutional Market' is restricted to a handful of broadly diversified index funds chosen by a public regulator	Unrestricted provider competition; unrestricted individual choice
Administration charges	Reaping economies of scale by collective pooling of assets in monopolist corporatist funds or a public fund	Charge cap below 1 per cent of assets per account - made possible by centralised contribution collection in an 'Institutional Market'	Fostering competition

c. The social-democratic governance strategy, which stresses hierarchy and voice, relegates responsibility for status maintenance to the state and/or the social partners, which implies a high degree of collective intervention. This approach stipulates compulsory participation in funded schemes, with a collective actor paying contributions for the unemployed and those caring for children. A defined benefit level, stipulated as a certain percentage of the average net wage, is determined and guaranteed via intergenerational sharing of financial market risks (Bovenberg 2002; Modigliani and Muralidhar 2004). The scheme is established on a centralised (nation or industry-wide) level and members' assets are pooled in a single collective portfolio and managed by monopolist actors, i.e. corporatist or public agencies (legally independent from the government), so as to reduce administration costs by exploiting economies of scale. Members can express their concerns by collective voice, i.e. via elected representatives on member councils.

THREE WAYS OF ACHIEVING STATUS MAINTENANCE IN OLD AGE IN THE 1980s

In the 1980s, the pension systems in OECD countries could be divided into three groups depending on their policy toward status maintenance in old age.

The first group comprised the 'Anglo-american early funders' (Australia, Canada, Ireland, New Zealand, the UK and the US). Here, average earners had always been dependent on funded pension schemes for securing status maintenance, because the replacement rate of the unfunded pillar(s) was too low to achieve status maintenance. In accordance with the economically liberal culture in these countries, funded schemes were rather loosely regulated (participation was not collectively enforced; no collectively standardised replacement target levels were set, etc.).

The second group was made up of the 'European early funders' (Finland, the Netherlands and Switzerland). Here, (partially[1]) funded schemes with mandatory participation explicitly designed to ensure the status maintenance of average earners were established by the state and/or the social partners much earlier than in other European countries, i.e. in 1985 at the latest. These schemes were quite strictly regulated (participation was (quasi)mandatory; collectively standardised replacement target levels were established, etc.).

The third group consists of the 'European late funders' (Austria, Belgium, France, Germany and Sweden). Here, until the end of the 1990s, average earners were able to rely on mandatory PAYGO schemes for achieving status maintenance.

Have these three country groups, located at different points of the pension policy field in the 1980s, now converged towards a common policy path with regard not only to the financial dimension (funded pensions are indispensable for status maintenance in all these countries nowadays) but also with regard to the regulation of these funded pensions? Or are there different varieties of funded pension regulation? The next three sections examine these questions by investigating one country in each group (the US, the Netherlands and Sweden). I also examine briefly the extent to which the developments outlined in each case study are representative of the group as a whole.

REGULATORY DEVELOPMENTS IN ENGLISH-SPEAKING EARLY FUNDER COUNTRIES (1980–2005)

The US: Reinforcing the Neo-liberal Features of Regulation

The US pension system comprises 1) a mandatory PAYGO pillar (Social Security), 2) a means-tested programme for poor pensioners (Supplementary Security Income) and 3) funded pension plans, especially in the occupational sector. Social security provides average earners with a full career with a prospective net replacement rate of a mere 51 per cent (VDR 2005: 155), which is insufficient for status maintenance.

Myopia regulation in the US

Employers have never been obliged to offer occupational pension plans. Until the early 1980s, employers who voluntarily offered plans usually enrolled their employees automatically in what were predominantly defined benefit (DB) plans with prescribed contribution rates. In contrast, only 14 per cent (2002) of the now dominant defined contributions (DC) plans have adopted automatic enrolment. Moreover, employees choose their personal contribution rate. Thus the prevention of myopia is now more than ever an individual issue. Although the coverage rate for the private workforce did not decline, it remained at a rather low level of about 40 per cent between 1980 and 2000 (Munnell and Sundén 2004: 7). Empirical evidence for myopia is strong: 60 per cent of employees have not calculated how much they have to save for retirement, 40 per cent appear unlikely to achieve status maintenance by age 65 and many experience an unexpected decline in their living standard after retirement (Mitchell and Utkus 2003: 3). Whereas high earners benefit strongly from tax exemptions offered under regressive EET[2] taxation, there are no direct state subsidies for low or moderate income earners with negligible or zero income tax liabilities.

Clearly, myopia regulation in the US reflects a reinforced neo-liberal governance strategy.

Volatility risk regulation in the US

Volatility risk has been shifted from employers to employees since 1980. In the 1970s, the majority of occupational pension schemes were DB plans. However, some workers lost a huge part of their promised benefits when their company went insolvent. For example, the automobile factory Studebaker went bankrupt in 1963 when its DB pension plan was 80 per cent in deficit. The US legislature eventually reacted to those problems with the passing of the Employees' Retirement Income Security Act (ERISA) in 1974. This act introduced mandatory minimum vesting standards, minimum funding requirements and insolvency insurance.

However, ERISA not only increased the security of employees' pensions but also raised employers' costs (for example bankruptcy insurance premiums) and their investment risk. Between 1981 and 1996, these costs tripled as a percentage of the payroll (Munnell and Sundén 2004: 27). As a result, new companies have increasingly resorted to DC plans, which were granted tax advantages under Section 401(k) of the Internal Revenue Code, passed into law in 1980. These 401(k) plans are not subject to ERISA regulation and employers bear no investment risk. Whereas only 30 per cent of all contributions to funded pensions went into DC plans in 1975, these plans received over 80 per cent of all contributions in 1998 (Munnell and Sundén 2004: 19).

The shift from DB to DC shows that volatility risk regulation in the US reflects a reinforced neo-liberal governance strategy.

Choice risk regulation in the US

In contrast to DB plans, which are dwindling in number, the increasing number of 401(k) plans offer employees a wide range of investment choice options, which are not statutorily restricted. As long ago as 1995, 50 per cent of 401(k) participants had a choice between at least 16 alternatives (Munnell and Sundén 2004: 70). However, many savers still lack the skills required to make sensible investment choices (Mitchell and Utkus 2003: 21). Moreover, a representative investigation by Elton et al. (2004) showed that the investment options offered by employers were inadequate in 62 per cent of cases.

Furthermore, 401(k) plan members are exposed to the risk of under-diversification that heavy investment in employer stock entails. Whereas DB plan participants are sheltered by ERISA, which stipulates that not more than 10 per cent of plan assets may be invested in the employer's company, 401(k) plan legislation contains no such restriction. Approximately 20 per cent of 401(k) plan participants hold over 20 per cent of their portfolio in employer stock. The share of employer stock in total 401(k) plan assets can reach staggering heights, ranging between 66 per cent and 96 per cent in large companies (Kaplan 2004: 72 f.). One reason is that employers are allowed to make their matching contributions in the form of company stock. Age-related selling restrictions regarding employer stock are also permitted. Enron employees could not sell their Enron equities in their 401(k) account until they reached the age of 50 or left the company.

Legislative initiatives before and in the wake of the Enron crisis to put caps on employer stock in 401(k) plans have failed. Employer organisations threatened that employers' matching contributions – an important savings incentive for employees – would decrease:

> If employers are prohibited from requiring their contributions to defined contribution plans to be invested in employer stock, they are likely to curtail their contributions, thereby reducing employees' retirement saving (ERIC 2002).

Moreover, such caps are not popular among US employees. Many of them like having a high slice of their pension portfolio invested in their company, because a familiarity bias ('invest in what you know') makes them believe (falsely) that investment in employer stock is safer than diversified funds (Kaplan 2004: 75). Even the meltdown of 401(k) plan assets at Enron, WorldCom and Global Crossing – all heavily invested in employer stock – did not affect the popularity of employer stock among US employees (Choi et al. 2005). Clearly, choice risk regulation in the US reflects a reinforced neo-liberal governance strategy.

Administration charge regulation in the US
The charges levied on 401(k) plans are not statutorily regulated and – despite fierce provider competition – are very high. Annual average fees amount to 1.44 per cent of assets (Thompson 2002: 30), reducing total pension capital at retirement by roughly 30 per cent. Administration charge regulation in the US exemplifies the neo-liberal governance strategy.

Funded Pension Regulation in Other English-speaking Early Funder Countries

The other English-speaking countries can be divided into three groups with regard to the development of funded pension regulation: North America, where neo-liberal governance has persisted, Australia, Ireland and New Zealand, where governance takes a hybrid form, and the UK, where there is the prospect of a switch to social-liberal governance. Hence, the average level of state intervention in the Anglo-american group has increased somewhat.

As in the US, the regulation of Canadian occupational registered pension plans (RPPs) and private registered retirement savings plans' (RRSPs) still follows a neo-liberal governance strategy.

In Australia, New Zealand and, especially, in Ireland, the regulation of funded pensions has become more mixed. In 1992, Australia introduced the mandatory superannuation scheme. While charges in these DC plans remain unregulated and individual investment choice options have been extended, the Australian state has inaugurated subsidies (superannuation co-contribution) for additional voluntary retirement savings by low wage earners in 2002. The amount of these subsidies was expanded in 2005.

Table 3.2   *The regulation of funded pensions in English-speaking countries: the current situation*

ISSUE / COUNTRY	Governance strategy				Overall governance strategy
	Myopia	Volatility risk	Choice risk	Administration charges	
Australia (Super-annuation)	Social-democratic + Social-liberal	Neo-liberal	Neo-liberal	Neo-liberal	Pre-dominantly neo-liberal
Canada (RPP and RRSP)	Neo-liberal	Neo-liberal	Neo-liberal	Neo-liberal	Neo-liberal
Ireland (PRSA)	Neo-liberal (but social-liberal reform suggested)	Social-liberal	Neo-liberal	Neo-liberal + Social-liberal	Hybrid
New Zealand (Kiwi Saver)	Social-liberal	Neo-liberal	Neo-liberal	Social-liberal	Hybrid
United Kingdom (NPSS – as currently planned)	Social-liberal	Social-liberal	Social-liberal	Social-liberal	Social-liberal
United States (401k plans)	Neo-liberal	Neo-liberal	Neo-liberal	Neo-liberal	Neo-liberal

New Zealand has opted to go down the social-liberal route by automatically enrolling employees in the Kiwi Saver scheme established by act of parliament in 2005, coupled with universal start-up subsidies. Moreover, the government subsidizes and negotiates downwards the charges levied by default providers.

Ireland established personal retirement savings accounts (PRSAs) in 2002. Saving in these DC schemes is voluntary, but those who participate are automatically enrolled in a life-cycle fund. Moreover, annual charges have been statutorily capped – albeit at the fairly high level of >1 per cent of assets, because there is no institutional market. Furthermore, the public regulator of funded pension schemes, the Irish Pensions Board (on which sit representatives from all relevant ministries and interest groups), has recently unanimously suggested replacing regressive indirect tax relief for contributions (EET taxation) by direct, equal matching contributions of € 1 for each € 1 invested by individuals (Pensions Board 2005, 15).

The British government has recently released a white paper (DWP 2006) suggesting the establishment of a national pension savings scheme (NPSS) as proposed by the Pensions Commission (2005). This scheme features automatic enrolment, a life-cycle fund as the default fund and centralised collection of contributions by a public agency with the aim of reducing annual charges to 0.3 per cent of assets (institutional market). Moreover, tempering its former stance on financial education and information, the government has explicitly conceded (DWP 2006: 56) that many Britons suffer from cognitive choice overload when it comes to financial investments. Thus the commission's recommendation that the number of investment choices in the NPSS should be limited to six to ten suitable funds (Pensions Commission 2005, 376) has been acknowledged (DWP 2006, 56). Of course, final legislation is still awaited.

REGULATORY DEVELOPMENTS IN EUROPEAN EARLY FUNDER COUNTRIES (1980–2005)

The Netherlands: Defying Neo-liberalism, but Nibbling at Inter-generational Solidarity

Besides its first pillar, a residence based, flat-rate citizens' pension (AOW), the Dutch pension landscape is dominated by a funded occupational pillar. These monopolist pension funds – predominantly organised on an industry-wide basis – are managed by the social partners. The two pillars provide average earners with a full career with a comparatively generous prospective net replacement rate of 84.1 per cent (VDR 2005, 123).

Myopia regulation in the Netherlands

Myopia is prevented in a collective, neo-corporatist manner. The social partners in an industry can apply to the Ministry of Social Affairs and Employment to issue a declaration that employer (and employee) participation in an industry-wide fund should be mandatory. Such applications are usually successful. Whereas the significance of the third, private pillar is very limited (Bieber and Schmitt 2004), the coverage rate for occupational pensions has steadily risen to 94 per cent of the workforce (Lutjens 2005). Contribution rates are set by the social partners with a total minimum net replacement rate of 70 per cent in mind (VDR 2005: 122). Since 1990, coverage gaps have been systematically reduced. Employers have been forbidden to discriminate between part-time and full-time employees. A mandatory pension fund for employees of temporary employment agencies has been established. A special fund managed by the social partners pays contributions on behalf of unemployed people aged 40 years and over, provided they are in receipt of unemployment insurance benefits. Discrimination against workers with fixed-term jobs has also been legally prohibited (Bieber and Schmitt 2004). The social partners aim to reduce the coverage gap to 3.5 per cent by 2006. Otherwise, the government has threatened to introduce appropriate legislation (EU Social Protection Committee 2005: 27).

Clearly, Dutch myopia regulation is part of a reinforced social-democratic governance strategy.

Volatility risk regulation in the Netherlands

Volatility risk in the Netherlands has traditionally been prevented on a collective basis. Although legal regulations are missing, almost all occupational pension funds (95 per cent) follow the DB principle (Bieber and Schmitt 2005), with intergenerational sharing of financial market risks. In average salary schemes, yearly accrual rights are usually fixed at 2.25 per cent of the nominal individual wage (VDR 2005: 122). Although not legally mandated, accrued pension rights and current pensions are usually indexed to wage growth (Dutch Ministry of Social Affairs and Employment 2002: 15).

In its National Strategy Report on Pensions of 2002, the ministry praised the solidarity and efficiency of intergenerational risk-sharing in the Dutch funded DB system:

In such a system, younger generations partially compensate [the retiring generations, T.H.] for lower returns when investment results are disappointing by paying higher contributions. When returns are healthier, surpluses can be passed on to the next generation. (…) The solidarity in the second pillar also delivers efficiency gains. In its report entitled 'Generationally-aware Policy', the Advisory Council on Government Policy (WRR) compared DB plans with intergenerational solidarity to DC plans without this form of solidarity. The WRR calculated that in the latter schemes people have to pay 25 per cent more contributions to cover the same risk of a decline in the pension result. The WRR concluded that pension accrual on the basis of solidarity is more efficient than individual accrual. (...) This solidarity makes it possible to achieve good investment returns at a relatively low risk for the participants because the risks can be borne collectively (ibid. 19 and 32).

The efficiency advantages of intergenerational solidarity have also been stressed by Dutch economists (Bovenberg 2002: 311). However, the stock market slump after 2000 revealed how badly regulated intergenerational risk-sharing had in fact been. During the 1990s, Dutch occupational pension plans accumulated large book surpluses because calculations of liabilities were based on a capital yield of 4 per cent, whereas actual asset yields were much higher at that time. However, instead of building up reserves to provide a cushion against future market slumps, a large part of the surpluses was consumed by granting contributions holidays and transferring money from pension funds to companies:

> the social partners themselves are responsible for the current problems because they set the contribution levels too low in the preceding years. These low contributions – in some cases culminating in exemptions from paying contributions for employers and employees, or even pay-outs from the pension funds – often served to lubricate collective bargaining (Van Het Kaar 2004).

Dutch governments – keen on reining in non-wage labour costs and tax-exempt pension contributions – reinforced this myopic behaviour:

> This distorted image helped to create the opportunity, in 1989, for a draft act to be sent to parliament, a draft act that was withdrawn only last year, which intended to counter the creation and maintenance of structural solvency surpluses by pension funds. Those were the days! Yet it put pension funds under pressure to avoid the creation of (substantial) solvency surpluses and to reduce pension contributions. Apart from impending government measures to skim off pension funds' solvency surpluses, contribution policies also came under pressure from agreements between the government and the social partners. (...) They might now have many billions of euros at their disposal if contribution discounts had been limited (Witteveen 2005).

Thus the buffers required to cushion the market slump after 2000 were often not available. Consequently, the average contribution rate had to be increased from 8.2 per cent (1997) to 14 per cent (2004) (EU Social Protection Committee 2005: 20). Pension indexation was sharply reduced (Bieber and Schmitt 2004). Employers, employees and pensioners became embroiled in protracted distributional conflicts:

The construction company HBG is one of a number of companies against which retired employees have instituted legal proceedings in the hope of forcing the company to redeposit into its pension fund money previously transferred for other purposes. Over the past few years, HBG has reportedly taken surplus profits from the fund, but now finds itself facing a shortfall of dramatically lower share prices. The former employees are demanding a supplementary deposit of no less than €76 million over and above the extra 14 million the company has already paid into the fund. For the time being, HBG is refusing to do so. (…) Pensioners now claim that the company's transfer out of the fund of positive investment results has left insufficient leeway for the creation of much needed reserves. (…) Sharply declining capital reserves have made it impossible to pay out annual pension adjustments in line with price increases (Grünell 2002).

Nevertheless, industry-wide occupational funds in the Netherlands have preserved intergenerational solidarity. The strong increase in the average contribution rate in response to the slump shows that losses have been shared between active and retired generations instead of the burden being borne solely by retirees, which is typical of DC systems.

However, some observers (Noorman 2004) argue that the introduction of the International Financial Reporting Standards (IFRS) for publicly listed EU companies will lead large Dutch companies listed on the stock market to switch to DC pension plans. While the latter do not have to be included in companies' balance sheets as they imply no liabilities, IFRS prescribe that the market value of the assets and liabilities of DB company pension funds must be included in companies' balance sheets, thereby making company results more volatile. Listed companies want to avoid this. A shift to DC is indeed what is happening currently in some Dutch company schemes, but not in industry-wide schemes:

At a number of companies pension risk is being shifted towards the employees. Akzo Nobel (chemicals) has reached agreement with trade unions to switch completely to a DC occupational pension scheme. The desire has been amplified as a consequence of the recent introduction of International Financial Reporting Standards (IFRS), obliging companies to offer more insight into their financial risks, including potential pension obligations. Similar schemes have been introduced at SNS Reaalgroep (banking/insurance) and Philips (electronics). (…) It is noteworthy that this appears to be the case only with company-level pension funds for the time being (Van Het Kaar 2004).

The most likely future development regarding volatility risk regulation is a polarisation between Dutch company and industry-wide funds (with more than 75 per cent of Dutch employees belonging to the latter):

Rabobank anticipates a shift from DB to DC schemes, but this may not sit too easily with the pension culture in the Netherlands. (…) In general, there is a lot of consensus about the idea that DB is superior to DC as it allows having a longer-term investment horizon, translating into higher returns. (...) Mr van den Brink foresees a shift to DC, but only for company, not for industry-wide, pension funds.[3]

Thus the mode of volatility risk regulation in the Netherlands has shifted from being exclusively social-democratic in nature to being merely predominantly social-democratic today.

Choice risk regulation in the Netherlands
Members of Dutch pension funds cannot choose between different investment providers and products. Instead, contributions are invested in a common portfolio by expert advisers employed by the social partners on behalf of fund members. Contrary to 401(k) plans in the US, investments in companies affiliated with an occupational plan are legally restricted to 10 per cent of assets (Lutjens 2005). Members cannot quit the pension fund of the industry or company in which they are employed. Hence there is no provider competition for members. Instead, members can express their concerns via their representatives on members' councils, which have the right to take legal action if the plan's board does not follow its recommendations (Bieber and Schmitt 2004). Seventy-five per cent of the Dutch population prefer the current DB system without individual choice to a competitive DC system with individual choice (Van Rooij et al. 2004: 15). Provider competition is rejected:

> There is in the Netherlands no competition between pension funds. And there is also no need for competition. (...) The social partners in these branches or companies decide on the premium schemes, they pay the premiums and administer the pension fund. Because they pay the premiums themselves, they have the best incentive for effective and efficiently governed pension funds' (Peter Stein, Pension Expert in the Dutch Ministry of Social Affairs and Employment) (Stein 2004: 202).

Thus choice risk regulation in the Netherlands has maintained the social-democratic governance strategy, which favours collective voice over individual exit.

Administration charge regulation in the Netherlands
Administration charges are minimised in the Dutch pension system by an emphasis on centralised, non-profit-making schemes. These schemes are organised on an industry-wide basis in the form of mutually owned financial conglomerates providing all services to member companies in-house. This mode of organisation is preferred to decentralised, profit-making schemes. Administrative costs in industry-wide occupational funds are considerably

lower than in commercial schemes (Döring 2002: 115). Dutch governments have not been keen on promoting individualised pension saving in the third pillar, because the second pillar has no upper ceiling on the wage from which contributions are deducted and in 2001 legislation was passed that restricted tax exemptions to those contributions aimed at reaching a total net replacement rate of not more than 70 per cent (Lutjens 2005) – the social partners' official target (Bieber and Schmitt 2004).

Clearly, administration charge regulation in the Netherlands adheres to the social-democratic governance strategy.

Funded Pension Regulation in Other European Early Funder Countries

As in the Netherlands, the regulation of funded pension schemes in other European Early Funder countries remains dominated by social-democratic governance strategies. Participation in (partially) funded second pillars in both Finland and Switzerland remains mandatory. Neither offers any investment choice for employees but both feature provider competition for *employers*, who negotiate collective contracts on behalf of their workforces. Assets are still pooled at (multi-)company level in order to keep administration costs down.

The Swiss and Finnish systems have evolved differently as far as volatility risk is concerned. In the wake of the global financial market slump after 2000, the Swiss occupational pillar has been transformed from a de facto DB system into a DC system with a minimum interest guarantee that varies with financial market developments. In contrast, the Finnish statutory earnings-related pillar adheres to the DB principle. To be sure, the Finnish pension reform in 2005 introduced a life expectancy coefficient so that the future benefit level of a retirement cohort will be dependent on its life expectancy. However, the Finnish Government does not promote private pensions to compensate for the expected benefit reductions resulting from the life-expectancy factor. Instead, it is encouraging workers to remain in employment for longer and has strongly increased the financial incentives to delay retirement. The Finnish state has retained its responsibility for status maintenance:

> The earnings-related pension scheme provides earnings-adjusted, insurance-based pensions, which ensure to a reasonable degree that all wage and salary earners and self-employed persons retain their level of consumption after retirement (Finland's National Pensions Strategy Report 2005: 5).

However, because intergenerational risk-sharing has been abolished in Swiss occupational plans and its coverage has been reduced in the Netherlands, the average level of collective intervention in this group has decreased somewhat.

Table 3.3   The regulation of funded pensions in European early funder countries: the current situation

ISSUE / COUNTRY	Governance strategy				Overall governance strategy
	Myopia	Volatility risk	Choice risk	Administration charges	
Finland (TEL)	Social-democratic	Social-democratic	Social-democratic	Social-democratic	Social-democratic
Netherlands (Pensioen Polder)	Social-democratic	Social-democratic (Industry-wide schemes) Neo-liberal (company schemes)	Social-democratic	Social-democratic	Predominantly social-democratic
Switzerland (BVG)	Social-democratic	Social-liberal	Social-democratic	Social-democratic	Predominantly social-democratic

REGULATORY DEVELOPMENTS IN EUROPEAN LATE FUNDER COUNTRIES (1980–2005)

Sweden: Mixing Individual and Collective Responsibility

Until the mid-1990s, the Swedish pension system comprised a universal flat-rate citizens' pension, an earnings-related PAYGO system (ATP) and quasi-mandatory, funded occupational DB schemes administered by the social partners. The pension reform of 1998 transformed the first pillar into a means-tested one, converted the ATP into a notional defined contribution system and added a new funded pillar named 'Premium Pension' (PP).

Myopia regulation in Sweden

Despite the reform, myopia is still largely prevented at the collective level. The mandatory ATP, the mandatory PP (with a statutory contribution rate of 2.5 per cent) and the quasi-mandatory occupational pension schemes provide average earners with a full working career with a total prospective net replacement rate of 68.2 per cent (VDR 2005: 135). Furthermore, the state pays contributions into the PP on behalf of those caring for children and individuals receiving unemployment benefits (Sunden 2004: 5).

Swedish myopia regulation adheres to the social-democratic mode of governance.

Volatility risk regulation in Sweden
The new PP scheme is a DC system without minimum benefit guarantees with regard to the investment accumulation process. However, when account balances are converted into annuities at retirement, retirees do benefit from a minimum interest guarantee:

> In order to reduce interest rate risk, the Swedish government guarantees a minimum rate of return of 2.7 per cent for converting account balances to annuities (Turner 2005, 2).

In 1998, the STP, the occupational pension scheme for blue-collar employees, was replaced by the SAF-LO, a DC system. Very recently, the occupational pension scheme for white-collar employees (ITP) was also changed into a DC system, although employees have to invest half of their contributions into funds with guaranteed minimum returns (SSA 2006).

Thus as far as volatility risk is concerned, Sweden has shifted from a social-democratic governance strategy (DB) to a mixture of neo-liberal and social-liberal governance (DC with partial minimum return guarantees).

Choice risk regulation in Sweden
The Premium Pension offers 705 funds managed by 82 providers (Premium Pension Committee 2005: 45). A representative survey revealed that 52 per cent of participants complained about having insufficient knowledge and expertise to choose appropriate funds (ibid., 38). This critical self-estimation was confirmed by a detailed empirical investigation of PP savers' investment behaviour:

> The Swedish experience shows that many individual investors (indeed, many more than expected) paid attention to non-informative fund advertising, made an active choice, and chose portfolios with the opposite characteristics of those most economists would find attractive (Cronqvist 2003, 31).

Moreover, despite the fact that their investments have often performed very badly, most participants have been reluctant to restructure their portfolios: by the spring of 2005, only 12 per cent of premium pension savers had switched once or more (Premium Pension Committee 2005: 36). However, without sophisticated investors, provider competition cannot function well.

The Swedish government recognised that average citizens have considerable difficulties in making appropriate choices in the face of such a proliferation of investment offers and commissioned an academic evaluation:

> The Swedish National Audit Office notes that in many cases pension savers have found it difficult to cope with their role as managers. The sheer variety of funds to choose between is felt by some pension savers to be a problem.[4]

However, the evaluation report broadly approved the wide array of choices:

> The committee's basic stand is that a fund category or type of fund cannot in itself be considered unnecessary or impractical in a well compiled portfolio for pension investments. To reduce the risk of systematically poor outcomes one solution might be to develop a better decision-making support to help pension savers evaluate their choices instead of excluding certain categories of funds. (...) Pension savers that elect to be guided throughout the process should be presented with a limited selection of broad, cost-effective funds, which means they are guided to a highly diversified fund portfolio managed at low fees (Premium Pension Committee 2005, 46 ff.).

However, the choice problem has been partially solved by scheme participants themselves, as many of them (90 per cent of new entrants) nowadays renounce active investment choice so that they are automatically enrolled in a high-quality default fund (Cronqvist and Thaler 2004) managed by the Premium Pension Authority. The importance of this central default fund can be seen when the Swedish system is compared with the Australian superannuation scheme, where employers usually determine default funds, which are of varying and often questionable quality.

Thus, Swedish choice risk regulation mixes elements of neo-liberal (high number of products and providers) and social-liberal governance (a central default fund of high quality).

Administration charge regulation in Sweden

The institutional structure of the new PP scheme shows its creators were especially concerned to keep administration charges down through administrative centralisation. Individual accounts are not administered on a decentralised basis by commercial providers, but by a public authority, the Premium Pension Authority (PPM). After Swedish citizens have notified the PPM of their preferred fund(s), the PPM collects the contributions and distributes them on an aggregated, anonymous basis to commercial providers. This institutional market reduces administration costs by centralising paperwork, enabling the bulk trading of fund switches and eliminating commissions to sales agents.

Providers have to pass these efficiency gains on to their customers. A statutory formula determines the permitted maximum level of charges. Funds attracting a small amount of mandatory PP contributions may charge up to 0.85 per cent of assets (annually), whereas large funds may charge not more than 0.15 per cent (Whitehouse 2000). Switching charges are prohibited (Weaver 2005). The current average fee amounts to 0.43 per cent (Sunden 2004). To this must be added a levy of 0.27 per cent for the PPM's administrative work, making a total average charge of 0.7 per cent – half of the US level. Moreover, this level is expected to fall to 0.25 per cent in the future as the system matures (Weaver 2005).

Administration charge regulation in Swedish occupational pension funds resembles that in the PP scheme. Here, equivalent organisations (Fora in the SAF-LO scheme, SPP in the ITP scheme) established by the social partners fulfil similar functions to those of the PPM.

Administration charge regulation in Sweden is consistent with a social-liberal governance strategy, i.e. an institutional market with a charge cap.

Funded Pension Regulation in Other European Late Funder Countries

Like Sweden, other European late funder countries mix neo-liberal, social-liberal and social-democratic governance strategies, though in different ways. Germany and Austria combine elements of neo-liberal governance (no charge caps) with elements of social-liberal governance. Both have introduced matching contributions paid by government into their schemes (Riester Rente and Prämienbegünstigte Zukunftsvorsorge), and both guarantee non-negative returns. One element of social-democratic governance is that, in both countries, the investment fund provider in *new* occupational pension schemes is chosen by the social partners at company (Austria) or industry level (Germany).

Belgium also combines elements of neo-liberal (voluntary participation), social-liberal (minimum interest rate guarantee, statutory charge cap) and social-democratic governance (promoting occupational plans with collective investment at industry and company level and granting members collective voice facilities for expressing discontent).

Only France pursues a quite neo-liberal governance strategy with regard to its individual 'plan d'épargne retraite populaire' (PERP) and its occupational 'plan d'épargne pour la retraite collectif' (PERCO) established by the Fillon Act in 2003. While those citizens who save are automatically enrolled in a life-cycle fund in the PERP (social-liberal element), participation in these plans is voluntary, the state grants no matching contributions and neither individual investment options nor charges are regulated (neo-liberal elements) (Chanu 2004).

*Table 3.4   Funded pension regulation in European late funder countries:
the current situation*

ISSUE / COUNTRY	Governance strategy				Overall governance strategy
	Myopia	Volatility risk	Choice risk	Administration charges	
Austria (Prämienbegünstigte Zukunftsvorsorge)	Social-liberal	Social-liberal	Neo-liberal New occupational pensions (Abfertigung Neu): social-democratic	Neo-liberal	Hybrid
Belgium (Vandenbroucke Act of 2003: Social Pension Schemes)	Neo-liberal	Social-liberal	Social-democratic	Social-liberal	Hybrid
France (PERP + PERCO)	Neo-liberal	Neo-liberal (PERCO) + Social-liberal (PERP)	Neo-liberal	Neo-liberal	Neo-liberal
Germany (Riester-Rente)	Social-liberal	Social-liberal	Neo-liberal New occupational pensions: social-democratic	Neo-liberal	Hybrid
Sweden (Premium Pension)	Social-democratic	Neo-liberal and social-liberal	Neo-liberal and social-liberal	Social-liberal	Hybrid

CONCLUSION

Firstly, taking all national developments together, the average level of collective responsibility for status maintenance has decreased.

(A) European late funder countries have considerably reduced the degree of collective responsibility by shifting the task of status maintenance from PAYGO systems with high degrees of collective responsibility to funded systems with either intermediate levels of collective responsibility, as in Sweden, Belgium, Germany and Austria or, as in France, a low level of collective responsibility.

(B) Four out of the six English-speaking countries have increased, or plan to increase, the degree of collective responsibility by shifting from funded systems with low degrees of collective responsibility to systems with low-to-intermediate or intermediate degrees of collective responsibility. This applies particularly to Ireland and, prospectively, the UK and to a lesser extent to Australia and New Zealand.

(C) Two out of the three European early funder countries (Switzerland and the Netherlands) have slightly decreased the degree of collective intervention by (partially) abolishing the intergenerational sharing of financial market risks.

If we assume that the opposed trends in (B) and (C) roughly offset each other, the decrease of collective responsibility in group (A) remains.

Secondly, the comparison shows that the absolute spread of regulatory regimes has remained constant. The US, which has the lowest degree of collective responsibility for status maintenance, shows no signs of increasing intervention, while Finland, which has the highest degree of collective responsibility, has not lessened the social-democratic character of its regulatory system. At the same time, however, the average level of state intervention in the English-speaking group has increased slightly, while the average extent of collective intervention in the European Early Funder group has decreased slightly. Thus the average variance of regulatory regimes has declined somewhat: the variety has not disappeared but it has been reduced to some degree.

Taken together, the reduced total average level of collective intervention and the reduced total average variance of regulation show that, even if both the financial dimension and the regulatory dimension of pension policy are taken into account, we indeed end up in cell 9 (convergence towards a reduced level of intervention), (Rothgang and Dingeldey, Chapter 1, this volume).

Nevertheless, it would be inappropriate to speak of a neo-liberal race to the regulatory bottom. To be sure, neo-liberal recommendations have found their way into the regulation of funded pensions in European late funder countries, despite their doubtful adequacy. Neo-liberal beliefs about superior regulation and concomitant, overly simplistic notions of self-responsibility propagated by economic elites have often been influential. Thus the regulatory frameworks for the new funded systems that have been put in place in European late funder countries do not have the same high degree of collective responsibility that was and is characteristic of their previous PAYGO systems and the mature funded systems in Finland, Switzerland and the Netherlands.

However, the new funded pension systems in European late funder countries have not adopted the neo-liberal governance strategy in toto. Rather, Sweden in particular and most of the other countries have chosen a mix of neo-liberal, social-liberal and social-democratic governance elements, thereby opting for intermediate degrees of collective responsibility for status maintenance. Moreover, Australia, Ireland, New Zealand and the UK have begun to depart from the purely neo-liberal governance path and are now – to a greater or lesser extent – adopting elements of social-liberal governance. At the same time, the Netherlands and especially Switzerland have somewhat reduced their high level of collective responsibility for status maintenance by partially abolishing the intergenerational sharing of financial market risks.

Thus a certain cross-national, albeit not ubiquitous, trend towards intermediate degrees of collective responsibility for status maintenance can be discerned. This finding shows that the hybridisation hypothesis, which predicts convergence towards mixed regulatory frameworks based on market mechanisms that stress individual responsibility as well as towards social policy structures that promote collective responsibility, is indeed supported by recent developments to some extent. However, this is not the case in all countries. It does not apply to Canada, Finland, France or the US and in some countries, including Australia, the Netherlands and Switzerland, hybridisation remains quite limited. Moreover, a distinction has to be made between different kinds of mixed frameworks that combine markets and social policy structures. They can be established either by adopting a social-liberal governance strategy, as currently proposed in the UK, which is a governance type in its own right, or by mixing governance elements from all three governance strategies, as in Sweden.

ACKNOWLEDGEMENTS

Thanks to Prof. Lutz Leisering and my other colleagues Frank Berner, Petra Buhr, Christian Marschallek and Uwe Schwarze for helpful discussions within the research project 'The Regulatory Welfare State – State Regulation of Private and Occupational Pensions in Europe' (REGINA) at the University of Bielefeld (Germany). Funding was provided by the German Research Foundation (DFG) and is gratefully acknowledged. All remaining errors are mine.

NOTES

1. Finland's second pillar combines PAYGO (roughly 75 per cent) and funding (roughly 25 per cent).
2. EET means that saving contributions are deducted from taxable income (E = exempt), investment yields are not taxed (E = exempt) while pension benefits are taxed (T = taxed).
3. See FT Mandate: 'Dutch legislation shake-up', http://www.ftmandate.com/-news/fullstory.php/aid/751/Dutch_legislation_shake-up.html.
4. 'Evaluation of the premium pension system', Swedish Finance Ministry press release of June 23, 2004. See www.sweden.gov.se/sb/d/586/a/26809/m/wai.

REFERENCES

Bieber, U.V. Schmitt (2004), ' "De pensioenpolder"– Einführung in die betriebliche Altersversorgung in den Niederlanden', *Deutsche Rentenversicherung*, **59**, 486–511.

Bovenberg, Lans (2002), 'Comment', in Martin Feldstein and Horst Siebert (eds), *Social Security Pension Reform in Europe*, Chicago: University of Chicago Press, pp. 307–14.

Burtless, Gary (2000), *Social Security Privatization and Financial Market Risk. Lessons from U.S. Financial History*, Center on Social and Economic Dynamics, Working Paper No. 10.

Chanu, Pierre-Yves (2004), 'Les Dispositions sur l'éparge retraite de la Loi Fillon', *Analyses et Documents Économiques*, **96**, 18–23.

Choi, J., D. Laibson and B. Madrian (2005), 'Are Empowerment and Education Enough? Under-diversification in 401(k) plans', *Brookings Paper on Economic Activity*, **2**, 151–213.

Cronqvist, Henrik (2003), *Advertising and Portfolio Choice*, University of Chicago, Graduate School of Business, see http://lcb.uoregon.edu/finance/conference/papers/cronqvist.pdf.

Cronqvist, H. and R. Thaler (2004), 'Design Choices in Privatized Social-security Systems: Learning from the Swedish Experience', *American Economic Review*, **4** (2), 424–28.

Döring, Dietmar (2002), *Die Zukunft der Alterssicherung*, Frankfurt: Suhrkamp.

Dutch Ministry of Social Affairs and Employment (2002), *National Strategy Report on Pensions*, The Netherlands.

DWP (Department for Work and Pensions) (2006), *Security in Retirement*, Norwich: The Stationery Office.

Elton, Edwin, Martin Gruber and Christopher Blake (2003), *The Adequacy of Investment Choices Offered by 401(k) Plans*, see http://www.reish.com/publications/pdf/401kchoices.pdf.

ERIC (ERISA Industry Committee) (2002), *Statement on Investments in Employer Stock*, Submitted to the Committee on Health, Education, Labor, Pension, US Senate on February 7.

Erturk, Ismail, Julie Froud, Sukhdev Johal, Adam Leaver and Karel Williams (2005), *The Democratisation of Finance? Centre for Research on Socio-cultural Change*, University of Manchester, Working Paper No. 9.

EU Social Protection Committee (2005), *Report on Privately Managed Pension Provision*, see http://www.eu.int/comm/employment_social/social_protection/docs/private_pensions_en.pdf.

Finland's National Pensions Strategy Report (2005), see http://ec.europa.eu/employment_social/social_protection/docs/2005/fi_en.pdf.

Furman, Jason (2005), *The Financial Costs of Individual Accounts. Testimony Before the Subcommittee on Securities and Investment of the U.S. Senate Committee on Banking, Housing and Urban Affairs*, see http://www.cbpp.org/6–14–05socsectest.pdf.

Grünell, Marianne (2002), *Supervisory Body for Occupational Pension Funds Offers More Stringent Rules*, see www.eiro.eurofound.eu.int.feature/nl0210102f.html.

Iyengar, Sheena, Wei Jiang and Gur Huberman (2003), *How Much Choice is Too Much?*, Pension Research Council, The Wharton School, University of Pennsylvania, Working Paper 2003–10.

James, Estelle (2005), *Reforming Social Security: Lessons from Thirty Countries*, Dallas: National Center for Policy Analysis, Policy Report No. 277, see http://www.estellejames.com/downloads/30Countries.pdf.

Kahneman, Daniel, Terrance Odean and Brad Barber (2005), *Privatized Pensions: An Irrational Choice*, see www.globalagendamagazine.com/2005/danielkahneman terranceodeanbradbarber.asp.

Kaplan, Richard (2004), *Enron, Pension Policy, and Social Security Privatization*, University of Illinois, College of Law, Law and Economics Working Paper No. 16.

Kotlikoff, Laurence (1999), *The World Bank's Approach and the Right Approach to Pension Reform*, Working Paper, Boston University, see http://people.bu.edu/kotlikof/adb.pdf.

Le Grand, Julian (ed.) (2003), *Motivation, Agency, and Public Policy*, Oxford: Oxford University Press.

Leisering, Lutz (2006), 'From Redistribution to Regulation. Regulating Private Old-age Pensions as a New Challenge in Ageing Societies', in Roland Sigg and Bea Cantillon (eds), *Social Security in a Life-long Society*, International Social Security Association, NY: Transaction Publishers.

Littlewood, Michael (1998), *How to Create a Competitive Market in Pensions: The International Lessons*, IEA Health and Welfare Unit, London: St Edmundsbury Press.

Lutjens, Erik (2005), 'Die kapitalgedeckte zusätzliche Altersversorgung in den Niederlanden', in Monika Schlachter, Ulrich Becker and Gerhard Igl (eds), *Funktion und rechtliche Ausgestaltung zusätzlicher Alterssicherung*, Baden-Baden: Nomos, pp. 23–34.

Mitchell, Olivia and Stephen Utkus (2003), *Lessons from Behavioral Finance for Retirement Planning Design*, University of Pennsylvania, Wharton School, Pension Research Council Working Paper 2003–20.

Modigliani, Franco and Arun Muralidhar (eds) (2004), *Rethinking Pension Reform*, Cambridge: Cambridge University Press.

Munnell, Alicia and Annika Sundén (eds) (2004), *Coming Up Short. The Challenge of 401(k) Plans*, Washington, DC: Brookings Institution Press.

Murthi, Mamta, Michael Orszag and Peter Orszag (2001), 'Administrative Costs under a Decentralized Approach to Individual Accounts', in Robert Holzmann and Joseph Stiglitz (eds), *New Ideas about Old Age Security*, Washington, DC: The World Bank, pp. 308–35.

Noorman, Jitzes (2004), *FTK and IFRS to Shake-up Dutch Pension Funds. Financial Markets Research*, Rabobank International, see http://corporates-public.rabobank. nl/research/specials/ftk_ifrs_shake_up_dutch_pension_funds.pdf.

Nullmeier, F. (2001), 'Sozialpolitik als marktregulative Politik', *Zeitschrift für Sozialreform*, **47**, 645–68.

Pensions Board (2005), *National Pensions Review*, see http://www.pensionsboard.ie/ index.asp?locID=61&docID=-1.

Pensions Commission (2005), *A New Pension Settlement for the 21st Century*, see http://www.pensionscommission.org.uk/publications/2005/annrep/main-report.pdf.

Premium Pension Committee (2005), *Difficult Waters? Premium Pension Savings On Course*, see http://www.sweden.gov.se/sb/d/574/a/52265.

SSA (US Social Security Administration) (2006), *International Update: Recent Developments in Foreign Public and Private Pensions*, July, see http://www.ssa.gov/policy/docs/progdesc/intl_update/2006–07/2006–07.html#sweden.

Stein, Peter (2004), 'The Dutch Pension System: Risks and Reform', in OECD (ed.), *Reforming Public Pensions*, Paris, pp. 199–205.

Sunden, Annika (2004), *The Future of Retirement in Sweden*, Pension Research Council, University of Pennsylvania, Working Paper 2004–16.

Sunstein, C. and R. Thaler (2003), 'Libertarian Paternalism is Not an Oxymoron', *The University of Chicago Law Review*, **70**, 1159–1202.

Thompson, Lawrence (2002), *Policy Approaches to Promote Private and Occupational Old-age Provision in the United States*, Bertelsmann Vorsorgestudien 9.

Turner, John (2005), *Private Accounts in Sweden*, AARP Public Policy Institute, Fact Sheet No. 109, see www.aarp.org/ppi.

Van Het Kaar, Robbert (2004), *Occupational Pensions Issues Place Increasing Pressure on Industrial Relations*, see www.eiro.eurofound.eu.int/2004/09/feature/nl0409104f.html.

Van Rooij, Marten, Clemens Kool and Henriette Prast (2004), *Risk-return Preferences in the Pension Domain: Are People Able to Choose?*, De Nederlandsche Bank, Working Paper No. 025/2004.

VDR (Verband Deutscher Rentenversicherungsträger) (2005), *Renten auf einen Blick: Staatliche Politik im OECD-Ländervergleich*, Bad Homburg. (German edition of OECD (2005): Pensions at a Glance.)

Weaver, Kent (2005), *Design and Implementation Issues in Swedish Individual Pension Accounts*, Center for Retirement Research at Boston College, Working Paper 2005–05.

Whitehouse, Edward (2000), *Administrative Charges for Funded Pensions: An International Comparison and Assessment*, The World Bank, Social Protection Discussion Paper No. 0016.

Witteveen, D.E. (2005), *Towards a Healthy Pension Sector*, Speech at the Congrescentrum Orpheus in Apeldoorn on September 12, 2005, see http://www.dnb.nl/dnb/detail.jsp?lang=en&pid=tcm:13-61463-64.

4. Changing Forms of Governance as Welfare State Restructuring: Activating Labour Market Policies in Denmark, the UK and Germany

Irene Dingeldey

INTRODUCTION

Most recent welfare state research highlights a paradigm shift in welfare state development. Depending on the underlying normative concepts, the new model is described as a 'workfare'(Jessop 1991; Torfing 1999a), an 'enabling' (Gilbert and Gilbert 1989; Gilbert 2002), a 'social investment' (Giddens 1998) or an 'activating' state (Mezger and West 2000; OECD 1990; Trube and Wohlfahrt 2001).[1] Although there are slight differences between these concepts, all of them refer implicitly or explicitly to changes in the goals of welfare state policies linked to structural and qualitative changes in the governance of welfare states (Bandemer 2001). The most prominent of these changes are the introduction of new public management techniques, including the privatisation of services, and a shift in the balance of responsibilities between the state and the individual towards the latter. Thus the normative concepts suggest a withdrawal on the part of the state and an increase in privatisation which, taken together, may be described as welfare state retrenchement (Pierson 1996).

Activating labour market policy (activating LMP) plays a prominent role in all of these concepts. Its central goal of 'employability' is promoted by the EU and the OECD.[2] Empirical studies have already confirmed that many countries have moved towards an activating approach to labour market policy (Barbier and Ludwig-Mayerhofer 2004; Bredgaard and Larsen 2005; Hvinden 2004; Serrano Pascual and Magnussen 2007). As a result, organisational changes arising out of new public management strategies such as the partial privatisation or contracting out of employment services have been observed in this policy field (Bruttel and Sol 2006; Knuth, et al. 2004; Konle-

Seidl and Walwei 2001). To date, however, there has been a dearth of analyses with a broader perspective on governance, one that encompasses the changing forms of public intervention with respect to the individual, or rather the regulation of individuals' labour market participation by the welfare state.

From this broader perspective, however, activating policies cannot simply be regarded as the means whereby the right to decommodification is withdrawn (Allan and Scruggs 2004; Korpi and Palme 2003) and the Keynesian welfare state dismantled, because in many respects the new goals imply an expansion of public intervention. First, increasing state activity can be expected in order to guarantee employability and/or labour market access for all citizens. Achievement of this goal is likely to require not only active LMP measures, such as placement services and further training, but also the provision of additional infrastructure and services, such as child care, for example. Second, the workfare aspects suggest an increase in enforcement and control. Furthermore, the implementation of mandatory work experience requires the state to act as employer of last resort, at least to some extent.

Against this background, this chapter advances the argument that the changing forms of governance in activating LMP involve a combination of welfare state retrenchment and expansion and can therefore be classified as restructuring. Furthermore, it is assumed that the new paradigm may be channelled along path dependent trajectories, so that convergent and divergent trends in welfare state development can be expected to develop at the same time.

In order to provide evidence for these hypotheses, a comparative and systematic analysis of changing forms of governance in activation LMP is conducted for Denmark, the UK and Germany, each country representing a different type of welfare state and gender regime (Esping-Andersen 1990; Sainsbury 1999).

GOVERNANCE IN SOCIAL POLICY

If an actor-based interactive perspective on governance, as developed by Scharpf (2000) or Kooiman (2005 (2003)), and described in the introduction, is applied to labour market policy, changing forms of governance can be understood either as a shift in the balance of responsibilities between different actors and/or a change in the mode of interaction. Within that approach, a number of different public actors are identified, including central government, regional authorities, municipalities and independent, intermediate-level financial organisations, such as some of the social insurance funds. The private actors include collective, market-based actors and third-sector organisations, as well as families and individuals. The modes of interaction include the standard ones, such as hierarchy, competition and solidarity, as well as co-governance, which denotes the co-production of services by different actors and/or the establishment of networks. Thus the actor-based interactive approach provides a basis for detailed analysis of the changes in country-specific governance mixes in labour market policy, making it possible to distinguish national variants within the general trend of privatisation.

However, since the relation between the welfare state and the individual and, more specifically, the regulation of individuals' labour market participation, plays a key role in labour market policy, we also need to be more precise about the various forms of state intervention. According to (Marshall (1949) 1963), the welfare state can be said to grant social rights to the individual. However, these rights may be withdrawn and may vary in scope. Thus a re-interpretation of social rights following changes in the modes of governance may cast a spotlight on the regulation of individuals' labour market participation, which in particular is based on an understanding of the welfare state that regulates the particular tension between commodification and decommodification (Knijn and Ostner 2002; Lenhardt and Offe 1977).

Thus social rights to decommodification can be regarded as a form of public intervention mediated by transfer payments that offer temporary compensation for social risks and allow individuals to subsist without labour market participation. In contrast, the provision of social services may be regarded as social enablement, in which enablement to take part in the labour market, i.e. commodification, is a central element. In order to be effective, this mode of governance requires individuals to cooperate in the co-production of the service; consequently, the process of enablement is closely linked to the increased conditionality of rights to transfers or to mandatory activation, i.e. enforcement, which must be regarded as another standard form of state intervention. The weight each of the various forms of intervention carries is a matter of political choice and the various possible combinations of intervention may give rise to a number of different types of activating LMP (Dingeldey 2007).

The following empirical analysis begins with a brief outline of the context and timing of activating LMP in Denmark, the UK and Germany. Two dimensions of governance in the welfare state will then be analysed. The first of these is the changing relationship between the welfare state and the individual with respect to the right to decommodification, enablement and the enforcement of commodification. The second is the shift in the balance of responsibilities between the state and collective actors with respect to the production of labour market services. Finally the findings are summarised and related to our argument concerning welfare state restructuring and its consequences for diverging and converging trends in welfare state development.

CONTEXT AND TIMING OF REFORMS

Activating LMP was introduced at different times in Denmark, the UK and Germany. The Social Democrat-dominated government in Denmark elected in 1994 was a pioneer in this regard, introducing activating LMP as part of its first labour market reform in the same year. Since then, there have been further activating reforms in 1995 and 1998. With the most recent programme, known as More People in Work, which came into force in 2003, the then newly elected conservative government changed the set of policy instruments and priorities. In particular, it sought to restrict or eliminate altogether any opportunities to remain out of the labour market while in receipt of benefits (Andersen 2001; OECD 2003).

In the UK, activating policy began with the introduction of the job seeker's allowance in 1996, when the Conservative Party was still in power. However, the introduction of activating LMP was completed under New Labour, which launched the New Deal or Welfare to Work Programme in 1998, as high unemployment was already beginning to fall. The New Deal was first targeted at the young unemployed (NDYP), the long-term unemployed (NDLTU; renamed ND25+ in 2001) and at lone parents (NDLP). Programmes for partners of the unemployed (NDPU) were introduced in 1999, followed in 2000 by a programme for the unemployed aged 50 and above (ND 50+) and finally in 2001 by one for disabled people (NDDP) (OECD 2002/1: 60). Thus there was a steady increase in target groups and changes were made to particular regulations in order to establish a more inclusive approach to activation.

As a consequence of German reunification, it was not the restructuring but the expansion of traditional instruments of active labour market policy, particularly of job creation schemes, that was on the agenda in the beginning of the 1990s (Heinelt and Weck 1998). Although unemployment benefit did suffer some cuts, labour market policy did not change direction until 1998 with the reform of the Employment Promotion Act, which had actually been drawn up under the Kohl government. The incoming SDP-Green coalition government produced two waves of rather contradictory activating policy reforms. The Job Aqtiv Act of 2002 was essentially an enabling and preventive instrument, which also promoted women's labour market participation. The Hartz Reforms, also called the First to Fourth Law for Modern Services in the Labour Market, which came into force between 2003 and 2005, have partly withdrawn these measures, facilitated flexible forms of employment, like marginal part-time jobs, and – most importantly – cut the benefits of the long-term unemployed.

THE CHANGING RELATIONSHIP BETWEEN THE WELFARE STATE AND THE INDIVIDUAL

This section begins with a brief overview of labour market performance. Activating LMP in Denmark, the UK and Germany is then discussed in order to outline the changes that have taken place in the right to decommodification, with a focus on the generosity and duration of transfers for the unemployed (1). Enforcement is analysed by examining the use of contracts between the individual and the labour market authorities, the regulations governing the duty to work and/or mandatory activation (2). Finally, the enablement of labour market participation will be discussed by examining the development of training measures and childcare facilities, since the latter in particular is a precondition for enabling women (and indeed men) with children to enter the labour market (3).

Denmark

In Denmark the high level of labour market participation that existed before the reforms, has been maintained and in some cases increased (activity rate of nearly 80 per cent, employment rate of 75.5 per cent and unemployment rate of only 4.9 per cent in 2005). In certain target groups, particularly women with children and older workers, labour market participation has risen significantly, while part-time rates for women are declining (24.9 per cent) (OECD 2006). This good labour market performance has been accompanied by an activating LMP that emphasises social enablement, although the level of decommodification has been cut and enforcement increased.

1. The compensation rate of unemployment benefit has remained unchanged at the fairly generous level of 90 per cent of the former wage. However, combined with a rather low income ceiling, unemployment benefit in fact functions almost as a flat-rate benefit (relatively lower compensation rates for higher income); between 1994 and 1999 the duration of unemployment benefit was reduced in stages from eight to four years (Torfing 1999b).

2. During the initial period of entitlement to unemployment benefit, known as the benefit period, claimants are offered 'activation measures', i.e. opportunities to re-enter the labour market. The most recent reform abolished the notion of 'occupational protection', which gave job seekers the right to decline jobs not corresponding to their formal qualification and previous occupation. Instead, any 'reasonable' job offer must be accepted from the first day of unemployment. If, after one year of unemployment (six months for those under 30), no job has been found, a so-called activation period starts, during which claimants have the right

and duty to take part in education or job training. This is followed up by a new activating programme whenever a person is 'out of touch with the labour market' for more than six months (Andersen 2002: 70 f.; OECD 2003: 182 f.).

Following the introduction of individual action plans in 1994, a contract between unemployed individuals and their personal advisers in the employment service must be set up no later than the time at which an unemployed individual receives his or her first offer of a place on an activation programme. Evaluation studies suggest that this has led to an increase in interviews in the employment offices (150,000 more per year), although individuals are still required to turn up in person only once every three months. The studies emphasise that the Danish approach to activating LMP is dominated not by the compulsory aspects but rather by the core values of Nordic social and labour market policy, namely the treatment of 'the citizen/user/clients as individual human being in his/her own right' (Olesen 2001: 104 f., 134).

3. One particularity of the Danish labour market reform was that between 1994 and 2001 the so-called job-rotation programmes offered those in employment the opportunity to take training leave for up to one year in order to create employment opportunities for unemployed workers, who would replace them temporarily (other options were sabbatical or parental leave). However, unemployed individuals could also choose the training option in order to interrupt their period of unemployment (Compston and Madsen 2001). When the programme was at its peak in 1995, more than 9,731 employed and 29,706 unemployed people were on training leave. Since then, the entire programme has been phased out because of increasing demand for labour. Nevertheless, education and training, particularly for the unemployed, continues to be promoted. Since 1995, between 10,000 and 37,000 unemployed people have taken part each year in courses designed to supplement their initial secondary education. In 2001, an apprenticeship for adults was introduced; it has attracted at least 5,000 participants per year. Additionally, some short labour market training programmes have helped to intensify job search during the activation period, and counselling or language courses are being offered to migrant workers (Statistikdatenbanken Denmark 2005; Dingeldey 2005). In sum, the great relevance of labour market training is perhaps best demonstrated by the training expenditure rate, which remains high at 0.54 per cent of GDP in 2004 (OECD 2004a) after decreasing over the last years due to changes in the programme structure and a decline in the number of unemployed participants. Furthermore, as a result of activating LMP, coverage rates for childcare facilities had risen by the year 2005 to 61.9 per cent (0–2 years), 95.2 per cent (3–5 years), 80.2 per cent (6–9

years) and 10.1 per cent (10–13 years) (Denmark Statistics: various). Half-time day-care places have been converted into full-time places, while good-quality care has been maintained (OECD 2002: 102, 162). Both these measures demonstrate that the Danish policies designed to enable labour market access and enhance employability are fairly wide in scope.

UK

Until 2005 in the UK, improved labour market performance (employment rate of 72.6 per cent, unemployment rate of 4.6 per cent) and growing labour market participation (activity rate of 76.1 per cent) had gone hand in hand with a significant decrease in long-term unemployment (from 45.4 per cent of total unemployment in 1994 to 22.4 per cent) (OECD 2006)). Furthermore, the increase in the activity rate of lone mothers to over 55 per cent in 2004 may possibly be related to activating LMP (Budget 2005). However, these broadly positive developments conceal the continued existence of large numbers of poorly paid jobs and high levels of (low-hours) part-time employment, particularly among women, who account for 77.3 per cent of all part-time employment (OECD 2006). The labour market policy that helped to produce this improved labour market performance made considerable use of work incentives and enforcement but also created and made increased use of social enablement measures.

1. A major reform of unemployment benefit had already been implemented in 1996, when the contributory unemployment benefit and non-contributory income support for unemployed claimants were replaced by the jobseekers' allowance (JSA). This retains a contributory component that lasts only six months (previously 12), so that 72 per cent of all unemployed individuals claimed the means-tested allowance in 2005 (Clasen 2007: 29). The benefit is payed as a flat rate that was £57.45 per week in 2006. This has led to a decline in net replacement rates to less than 47 per cent of former income (calculated on the basis of an average production worker's income), which provides a comparatively low level of social protection (OECD 2004b).

2. Since 1996, the actions of the unemployed have been monitored fortnightly by officials who have received new discretionary powers, enabling them to issue a jobseekers' directive, which requires individuals to look for jobs in a particular way and to take certain steps to 'improve their employability' (Trickey and Walker 2000: 188). In addition, the New Deal introduced individual action plans, which are signed when clients enter the gateway period. Non-compliance or a failure to follow up job offers is sanctioned by benefit withdrawal. Although many

programme advisers are not overly rigorous in policing the rules, many of them believe that the fear of being sanctioned motivates clients to attend client interviews and support service and training sessions (Joyce and Pettigrew 2002). By September 2002, the target of 40 per cent of participants finding unsubsidised employment during the gateway period had almost been reached, and it is assumed that these practices played an important role in this success (Clasen and Clegg 2003).

The New Deal scheme starts with a so-called gateway period (up to four months for the young unemployed), in which intensive help and support for job search are offered. This is followed by the intensive activity period, during which the various target groups are offered different activation options. In the most highly developed NDYU programmes, these are subsidised employment, working on an environmental task force or in the voluntary sector or up to twelve months' free training. The New Deal was made mandatory for the major target groups, namely the young unemployed (after six months of unemployment), for those older than 25 (after 18 months) and, since 2002, for the partners of the unemployed as well (< 45 years, no children). For lone parents, the only obligation is to attend work-focused interviews; participation in programmes is still voluntary (as it is for older workers and the disabled) (OECD 2002/1: 60).

One particular British strategy that has played an important role is the activation of so-called workless households (mainly for the low-wage sector and/or in the form of (female) part-time employment) through so called in-work benefits. 'Making work pay' is the slogan summarising what is in fact the keystone of New Labour's strategy for reducing welfare dependejoyncy. It involved a restructuring in 1999 of what was then known as the working family tax credit and its subsequent replacement in 2003 by the working tax credit (WTC), available to all adults; families with children could, in addition, claim the child tax credit (CTC). These reforms were intended to eliminate poverty traps for those on benefits and to increase disposable market income through transfer payments that vary depending on the number of children in the family (Budget 1998). In 2003 and 2004 more than 1.6 million families were claiming WTC and more than 5.5 CTC, spending on which amounted to almost £15.4, respectively £8.6 million[3] (HMRevenue & Customs Analysis Team 2006), which exaggerates the spending on active LMP measures.

3. The various New Deal programmes offer training as an option after the gateway period. Half of the young unemployed choose the training option, but there is no information on the quality of the particular programmes. In the case of the long-term employed aged over 25, it is

known that only a few find places on one-year programmes, such as Education and Training Opportunities (ETO), that work towards a recognised vocational qualification. The majority attend programmes of much shorter duration that aim to improve basic skills (BET) or to update work-related skills (LOT) and job search skills (SJFT) (Dingeldey 2005a, Sommerville and Brace 2004). For lone parents, the distribution of training programmes might be expected, at best, to be similar. In view of the comparatively low level of expenditure on labour market training (0.02 per cent of GDP) and apprenticeships (0.10) in 2002 and 2003 (OECD 2004a), it can be assumed that training and skill enhancement is still rather underdeveloped in the UK. This will not be changed easily, although in 2005 the government did introduce a New Deal for Skills programme, aimed particularly at young people (16–19 years) and intended to enable them to reach at least NVQ level 2 (HM Treasury, et al. 2004).

Largely as a result of a policy tradition of non-intervention in family matters, childcare places were available for fewer than 11 per cent of under-5s in the 1990s (Rostgard and Fridberg 1998). In order to facilitate employment for (lone) mothers in particular, the New Deal was combined with the National Childcare Strategy with a view to expanding childcare provision. As a result, approximately 90 per cent of 3 and 4-year olds now have a place in nursery schools or reception classes. In many cases, however, care is provided only for a few hours in the morning (Rake 2001). The number of places in day nurseries (9.5 places/100 children in 2001) as well as in after-school clubs (8.2 places/100 children in 2001) have also increased considerably. Given that these policies started virtually from zero, considerable efforts have been made. Nevertheless, the scope and quality of the services provided must be regarded as modest, particularly in comparison with Denmark.

Germany

The labour market in Germany is characterised by an activity rate that remains modest (73.8 per cent), a particularly low employment rate (65.5 per cent) and very high unemployment (11.3 per cent) (figures for 2005) (OECD 2006). The picture is completed by a fairly high female part-time rate (39.4 per cent) and rising long-term employment (from 44.3 in 1994 to 54.0 per cent in 2005) (OECD 2006). This situation may be described as an ongoing labour market crisis, which has been exacerbated by an indecisive labour market policy that has combined a decrease in decommodification and an increasingly punitive attitude to the long-term unemployed with a general reduction in the provision of training measures.

1. The first wave of benefit cuts was implemented in 1993, before a proper activation policy was introduced. Since then, the replacement rates for unemployment benefit have remained unchanged at 60 per cent for single claimants and at 67 per cent for recipients with dependants during the first year of unemployment. Until 2005, means-tested unemployment assistance (UA) paid 53 per cent for singles or 57 per cent for recipients with dependants of former wages to the long-term unemployed (unemployment exceeding one year). Since then, UA and social assistance (SA) have been merged into Unemployment Benefit II (UB II), which is designed as a flat-rate payment fixed close to the level of the lower benefit, offering €345 per month (no difference between West and East Germany since 2006), plus supplements for children and/or adult dependants as well as for housing costs (Bundesministerium für Arbeit und Soziales 2006). As the means testing rules have also been tightened, it is estimated that all those former UA recipients who previously had rather high earnings or still have significant savings or a working partner will face reductions in entitlement or even lose it altogether, whereas former SA recipients, particularly single parents, will be slightly better off and have access to the federal activation programmes (Koch and Walwei 2005).

2. Every unemployed person signs a so-called integration agreement, which documents his or her commitment to job-seeking activities since 1998. Labour market experts tend to take the view that the signing of this agreement is a formality that does not significantly influence relations between individuals and the employment service. The use of sanctions and/or periods of exclusion from unemployment benefit has increased considerably since the mid-1990s. Although resignation remains the main reason for the imposition of sanctions (applying in 56.9 per cent of cases in 2004), a refusal to accept a reasonable job is now the reason given in an increasing share of cases (34.7 per cent) (Bundesagentur für Arbeit 2006).

   Occupational protection has been removed in stages for all unemployed persons in Germany. In contrast to Denmark and the UK, however, mandatory activation has not been generalised. Under German law, it has always been possible for recipients of SA to be required to work for their benefit. The new legislation has maintained the possibility of recruiting UB II recipients for work in the general public interest, which means that these work opportunities are usually offered by public or third-sector employers. In the Hartz IV legislation they are called one-euro jobs. The unemployed are obliged to take up such jobs, although they do not give rise to proper employment relationships, but just provide benefit recipients with an additional income of one or two euros per hour

(Koch and Walwei 2005). It is up to employment service advisers to decide whether such compulsory job offers should be made. In 2005, 6.7 per cent of the long-term employed were working in one-euro jobs (Bundesagentur für Arbeit 2006).

3. Further vocational training was used extensively in Germany during the reunification process, so that the cutbacks in recent years have to some extent to be seen against that background. Nevertheless, Hartz I+II undoubtedly marked a change of direction. The general guidelines suggest that the only schemes that should be subsidised are those that offer individuals a good chance of finding employment. The regulations governing the duration of benefit entitlement, the level of payment and eligibility for participation in training schemes were made more restrictive (Kühnlein and Klein 2003). These changes have been accompanied by an increase in short-term schemes such as labour market training (assessment, general facilities for job applications) and programmes targeted primarily at the young unemployed (preparation for vocational training and vocational training). The number of participants in high-quality programmes such as further vocational training has decreased rapidly from more than 720,000 in 1993 to 114,350 in 2005 (Bundesagentur für Arbeit 2006; Dingeldey 2007).

The employment opportunities of women with dependent children are particularly restricted by the inadequate provision of childcare facilities. In West Germany in particular, there were virtually no places for the under-3s (9.6 per cent compared with 39.8 per cent in East Germany in 2005). For the 3–6 age group, the supply is much better (85.2 per cent in the West, 95.7 per cent in the East), but only 27 per cent were full-time in West Germany compared to 98 per cent of the places in East Germany in 2005 (BFSFJ 2006; Fuchs 2006: 66, 34). There were also very few places in after-school clubs, particularly in the West (5.0 per cent, compared with 41.0 per cent in East Germany) (Spieß, et al. 2002). This may be caused by the persistence of the idea that an increase in women's labour market participation increases unemployment. Thus for mothers on benefit the general exemption from labour market activation has been maintained, as long as the children are younger than three years or do not have access to childcare places. However, for the under-3s, the Day Care Expansion Act (*Tagesbetreuungsausbaugesetz*) has led to an increase of places since 2005, so that 9.6 per cent of the age group in the West and 39.8 per cent in the East had places in 2005 and 2006. Furthermore, the federal government's scheme to co-finance more full-time schools as a response to Germany's low ranking in the PISA Study (Gottschall and Hagemann 2002) may have the side effect of positively influencing the employability of women with dependent children.

*Table 4.1   Changing mixes of decommodification and commodification in
Denmark, the UK and Germany*

	Denmark	UK	Germany
Right to de-commodification	*- duration* *= compensation rate*	*- duration* *= compensation rate*	*= for short-term unemployment* *- compensation rate for long-term unemployed*
Unemployment benefit: -duration -compensation rate	8→ 4 years 90 per cent of former wage (quasi flat rate)	1 year → 6 months unemployment benefit flate rate of £57.45 per week in 2006 equal less than 47 per cent of former wage; means tested after 6 months	1 year 60/67 per cent (single/with dependants) of former wage Wage related (53/57 per cent) → flat rate €345 plus housing costs and family supplements, means tested, after 1 year
Enabling policies	*+ options* *+ services*	*+ options* *+ services*	*= options* *-/+ services*
Options, employment services	Various training options Increase in secondary education High, but decreasing spending on training Improvement of placement services	Subsidised employment Increase in training options, but often short-term Low spending on training Improvement of placement services (good client/counsellor ratio)	No right to training decrease in training options moderate, but decreasing spending on training Improvement of placement services (better but still low client/counsellor ratio)
Services related to infrastructure	Increase in already highly developed childcare coverage	Improvement of placement services Expansion of insufficiently developed childcare coverage, but still only part-time before school age (which at 4 is much lower than the European average)	Small increase in child care coverage (particularly for the under-3s), mostly part-time (for 3 years and school-age children)
Enforcement	*+ mandatory activation*	*+ mandatory activation*	*= selective mandatory activation*
	Universal after 1 year (6 months for < 30)	Particular target groups 18 months (6 months <25) In-work benefits for low paid	Selectively 1 year

Note: - means reduction, + means increase in responsibility of the actors in question;
             = means no significant change.

The data presented above confirm that, in all three countries, entitlement to social benefits has been restricted through cuts in the level and/or duration of unemployment benefits. This reduction in decommodification has been accompanied by increasing enforcement of labour market participation, through the introduction of contracts between the employment service and individual clients, some form of mandatory activation and increasing control and sanctions. Furthermore, public intervention in the form of social enablement has been increased, as reflected in the expansion of placement services, further (vocational) training and childcare facilities. The only exception is the decline in further vocational training in Germany. However, over and above this general convergence, major differences between the countries persist as a result of country-specific trajectories. For example, the degree of decommodification, i.e. the level and duration of unemployment benefit, has remained high in Denmark, in combination with an increase in social enablement with regard to both training opportunities and child care. One of the striking features of the German reforms is that social enablement in the form of training has been decreased, while the major increase in enforcement (cuts in benefits and mandatory activation) has been limited to the long-term unemployed. The UK, finally, is the only country to make extensive use of in-work benefits, that is supplementary benefits conditional on a minimum level of labour market participation (see Table 4.1).

Thus within the general paradigm shift towards an activating welfare state, the re-regulation of the tension between commodification and decommodification still varies considerably from country to country. In the cases of Denmark and the UK at least, the changes that have been introduced can be said to conform to the path-dependent trajectories that might be expected of a universal or liberal welfare state regime respectively. Only Germany may be regarded, in part at least, as being on the move away from a conservative towards a liberal welfare state type.

SHIFTING BALANCE OF RESPONSIBILITIES BETWEEN THE WELFARE STATE AND COLLECTIVE WELFARE PROVIDERS

In this section, we analyse activating labour market reforms in Denmark, the UK and Germany, focusing in particular on shifts in the balance of responsibilities among collective actors with respect to different objects of governance, namely regulation (1), financing (2) and service provision (3). We start with a brief introduction to the situation before the reforms.

Denmark

In Denmark the entire system of labour administration is strongly corporatist, which means that the social partners participate in regulatory and decision-making processes at all levels of public administration. The benefit system is administered by the trade unions, although public control was introduced in 1969 in order to generalise benefit levels and conditions. The Employment Service (AMS) is subordinated to the Ministry of Employment and provides job placement services and active labour market programmes. Nevertheless, at national as well as regional level, so-called labour market councils were called on to give advice to the public administration prior to reforms. Labour market training, which historically in Denmark was aimed primarily at the employed and was opened up to the unemployed only recently, is regarded as a public task. Thus vocational training programmes take place mainly in regional training centres, which form part of the public labour market training system (AMU System). The AMU is the product of cooperation between the organisations of the social partners and the public authorities, operating together within a tightly structured network.

1. With the introduction of activating LMP, regulation was decentralised while the influence of the social partners increased. Since the 1990s in particular, planning and managerial competences have increasingly been devolved to the regional labour market councils, including decisions on contracting-out and the design and scope of the tendering rounds. As the social partners are members of these councils, this has undoubtedly strengthened their influence (Arnkil and Spangar 2004: 8, 113f.).
2. The social partners have seen a slight rise in their share of the funding of labour market policy programmes, particularly with regard to labour market training. Labour market policy in Denmark has traditionally been financed by the contributions paid by members of the (voluntary) unemployment insurance scheme (about 15–20 per cent of costs) and by taxation. The labour market reforms of 1994 and 1997 introduced a so-called labour market contribution (particularly for employees), which was intended to supplement the financing of labour market training (Knuth et al. 2004). Since 2001, the social partners, or more precisely their representatives on the newly established labour market training funding council (AUF), have been responsible for raising the funding required for adult training courses provided to meet employers' skill requirements. The AUF may recommend that particular programmes should be jointly funded by employers or that participants seeking higher qualifications should pay the fees (OECD 2001).

3. The provision of labour market services still falls largely within the public domain, although elements of marketisation have been introduced. In 1990 the public employment services' monopoly on placement services was abolished in order to give 'other actors' an opportunity. The first tendering round in 2003 led to the conclusion of contracts with private enterprises (57 per cent), trade unions (25 per cent) and public institutions (18 per cent). Thus in 2004 an average of about 30 per cent of the unemployed population were referred to 'other actors' (the legal obligation is a minimum of 10 per cent). Initial evaluation studies show that the private services perform marginally better than the PES in returning the unemployed to work (Bredgaard, et al. 2005: 89). Since the introduction of a so-called taximeter system, payments to labour market training providers (AMU) has been linked to the number of participants in programmes (OECD 2001). In conjunction with the 2007 reform of local government, there are plans to devolve further responsibilities to the municipalities, to introduce greater marketisation and to merge the hitherto separate services for employment benefit and social assistant recipients and create 90 Joint Jobcentres.

UK

In the UK, the labour market administration is part of the national civil service and unemployment benefits are administered and paid out by local offices. Under Margaret Thatcher, the newly constituted Employment Service (ES) was made directly answerable to the government in the shape of the Ministry of Education and Employment. This removed all powers of codetermination from the social partners. The ES was managed by targets. In accordance with new public management theories, the provision of labour market services was privatised; the new providers included newly created networks and profit-making organisations. Thus the implementation of labour market training programmes was delegated to the training and enterprise councils (TECs), a recently established, employer-dominated network. The TECs were managed by output-related contracts and allocated budgets. The training programmes themselves were delivered by private providers (Dingeldey 1997: 250).

1. Under New Labour, the trend towards privatisation was maintained, although some regulatory responsibilities were returned to the public sector. Because of problems with inefficiency and performance, New Labour replaced the TECs with the learning and skills councils (LSCs), which are much more accountable and rooted in the public sector. The LSCs were made responsible for the distribution of resources for training and education beyond initial general education (excluding the universities).

The training programmes themselves are still delivered by private organisations under contract to the LSCs.

2. As the funding of unemployment benefits was always mainly tax based, there were hardly any changes. Furthermore, the decrease in the number of unemployed people has been offset by the relative stability of the number of recipients of income support and incapacity benefit for persons of working age, both of which are non-contributory (Knuth et al. 2004).

3. The already high level of marketisation in the provision of services has actually increased still further under the Labour government. Private placement services had always been allowed in the UK, but as recently as the 1990s the share of private providers was only about 6 per cent (Konle-Seidl and Walwei 2001). Since then, however, New Labour has privatised the implementation of labour market programmes to a considerable degree. About 10 per cent of the New Deal budget is channelled into programmes for particular target groups, which are delivered by private organisations. Thus the delivery of programmes for young unemployed people has been contracted out in 10 regions. In the year 2000, the establishment of 15 employment zones (EZ) (most disadvantaged regions with above-average unemployment) was accompanied by the privatisation of the provision of all employment programmes for the long-term unemployed in these areas. Public providers also competed in the tendering, particularly Working Links, a public-private joint venture between the ES and a private placement organisation, which competed successfully in eight cases (Finn and Knuth 2004).

Germany

In Germany, benefits and services for the unemployed are provided within the unemployment insurance system, headed by the Federal Employment Office, now named the Federal Employment Agency (BA). The unemployment insurance fund is a self-governing agency within which the social partners have rights of co-determination. Although contributions and benefits are determined politically, it enjoys considerable autonomy when it comes to implementation. Labour market programmes have always been delivered by third parties, mostly by non-public, third-sector organisations and – to a minor extent – by profit-making organisations.

1. Most recent reforms have reduced the influence of the social partners on the regulation of labour market services. Since 2003, tripartite codetermination within the BA is limited to the administrative council, which only has a controlling function, while the executive committee is appointed for a limited period only (Kannengießer and Gundel 2003; Konle-Seidl 2003).

2. As in the UK, there has been a shift from contributory to non-contributory benefits and long-term unemployment has increased. In consequence more than two-thirds of all unemployed in 2008 receive the tax-funded UB II.
3. Since the public sector's share in service provision has always been small, the trend towards further marketisation has been rather limited. When the public placement services' monopoly was broken at the end of the 1990s, private providers acquired a 5 per cent share of total provision (Konle-Seidl 2003). Since 2002, the drive to privatise has intensified but has not proved to be very successful. The introduction of vouchers for private placements services led to only about 70,000 successful placements between April 2002 and June 2004 (Hujer et al. 2005: 9). In addition, in 2004, the placement of 396,000 unemployed people was partly and of 239,000 in whole handled by third parties appointed by the employment agencies. In general, there is no evidence from evaluation studies that private agencies have a better placement record than the public services (Bundesregierung 2006: 125). The so-called PersonalServiceAgencies (PSAs) were created by a tendering procedure and regulated by contract in order to use temporary employment as a placement instrument. In 2004, the PSAs offered employment to between 27,000 and 33,000 people, which was very considerably below expectations (Bundesregierung 2006: 138).

The introduction of UB II in 2005 was combined with the creation of customer centres, which were supposed to end differences in the treatment of unemployment benefit recipients, on the one hand, and, on the other, those claiming social assistance (administered by the municipalities). Recipients of UB I and UB II are still dealt with in different offices, as UB II is administered by 434 consortia formed by local PES offices and the municipalities (in 69 cases, municipalities took over completely) (Kemmerling and Bruttel 2005). Thus municipal responsibility for implementing labour market policy has increased.

In all three countries, the responsibility for regulation remains within the public sector. The most widespread trend in changing forms of governance is a shift in the balance of responsibilities in the provision of labour market services towards private, profit-making organisations. However, the extent of private-sector involvement and the success of, for example, private placement services varies considerably from country to country. As far as the regulation and financing of labour market policy is concerned, contradictory trends can be observed. In Denmark, the role of the social partners has been strengthened, with regard to both financing and regulation – the latter being a side effect of the decentralisation of regulatory responsibilities.

*Table 4.2   Shifting responsibilities with respect to regulation, funding and
service provision in activating labour market reforms in
Denmark, the UK and Germany*

	Denmark	UK	Germany
Regulatory responsibility	*+ Social partners*	*+ State*	*+ State*
	Increased responsibilities for social partners following increase in regional labour market councils' responsibilities	(Re-)anchoring of Learning and Skills Councils within the public sector	Curtailing of tripartite codetermination within BA
Funding responsibility	*+ Social partners*	*= State*	*+ State (indirect)*
Benefits	Employees' and employers' contributions	Dominance of taxed financed benefits (state)	Employees' and employers' contributions plus taxes (state)
	+ employees	+ State indirect increase in non-contributory benefits	+ State indirect increase in tax-funded benefits
Labour market programmes	State/ + social partners	State	Contributions Social partners/state
Service provision	*+ private; profit-making organisations*	*+ private; profit-making organisations*	*+ private; profit-making organisations + municipalities*
Labour administration	Trade unions: unemployment insurance State: Employment Service (AMS)	State: Employment Service	Parafiscal agency federal agency
Placement services	State; + private profit-making organisations	State; + private profit-making organisations	Parafiscal agency federal agency, + municipalities + private profit-making organisations
Training programmes-	State; + private; profit-making organisations	Private: enterprise networks	Private: third sector organisations, profit-making organisations; networks

Note: - means reduction, + means increase in responsibility of relevant actors;
= means no significant change.

In the UK, the provision of services is increasingly dominated by market-based actors, but if inefficiencies are considerable, the example of training policy has demonstrated that a partial reversion of responsibility away from a network-based structure back to the public sector is viable. The same seems true for Germany, where co-determination within the BA has been curtailed. In both countries, the funding structure of labour market policies has remained fairly stable (Table 4.2). Thus, it may be stated that, although the general trend towards privatisation can be observed in all three welfare states, in many cases path-dependent priorities concerning the shift of responsibilities towards the social partners or market-based actors have been maintained. Again, Germany may be a slight exception in this respect, as the reduction in further training has gone hand in hand with extensive damage to the training infrastructure, which is provided mainly by third sector organisations.

COMMON CHANGES BUT CONTINUING DIVERGENCE OF GOVERNANCE IN LABOUR MARKET POLICIES

In all three countries analysed, the most recent labour market reforms are all underpinned by the notion of labour market activation, in which the promotion of employability is a major goal. Efforts to achieve that goal are reflected in various changes of governance, i.e. a shift in the balance of responsibilities between public and private actors in the production of welfare as well as changing forms of public intervention with regard to decommodification and the social enablement and enforcement of commodification.

Analysis of these two aspects of governance confirms the thesis that the transformation of the welfare state contains elements of both retrenchment and expansion and can thus be interpreted as a restructuring.

One of the most striking aspects of these findings is that although benefit cuts and, to some extent, privatisation have been justified by the alleged financial constraints to which public budgets are subject, state intervention is also increasing. This expansion has taken the form of increased state regulation and funding of placement and counselling services, training and child care. Thus the restructuring of the welfare state is closely linked to a substitution of public transfers by increased regulation and funding of service provision. This expansion of public intervention is related to increasing state influence over the way individuals live their lives, based on the assumption that labour market participation should be universal. In consequence, even absence or withdrawal from the labour market requires public regulation and financial support, which makes certain decisions like the extent of childcare to be provided by parents more and more a public issue or an object of standardised norms laid down by the welfare state.

However, although the reforms in the different countries reflect a shift 'in the same direction', a strong convergence of welfare state types cannot be observed. What can be observed is a soft blurring of regimes, as privatisation, for example, is introduced or increased in systems in which all services were previously publicly provided. The same is true when mandatory activation and benefit cuts are introduced in regimes that used to be characterised by extensive rights to decommodification or, conversely, when services such as child care or training are subjected to increasing state regulation in systems with traditionally low levels of public intervention. Thus it is becoming impossible to distinguish between welfare state regimes on the basis of clear-cut institutional principles or social values. However, because of differences in starting points and country-specific trajectories, relative differences in the use of particular forms of governance will be maintained in future. So far it is only in Germany that there has been an accumulation of path-breaking changes that may indicate a move towards the liberal regime. For Denmark and the UK, however, the transformation towards the activating welfare state can largely be regarded as a process of path-dependent change.

NOTES

1. In the following, the term 'activating state' is used to denote the new paradigm, on the grounds that it is the most general term.
2. (Jacobsson 2004; Lefresne 1999; OECD 1990; OECD 1994).
3. The numbers concerning CTC and WTC are not to be summed up as many families claim both credits.

REFERENCES

Allan, J.P. and L. Scruggs (2004), 'Political Partisanship and Welfare State Reform in Advanced Industrial Societies', *American Journal of Political Science*, **48** (3), 496–512.

Andersen, Jørgen Goul (2001), 'From Citizenship to Workfare? Changing Labour Market Policies in Denmark Since the Oil Crisis', in Axel Bolder, Walter R. Heinz and Günter Kutscha (eds), *Deregulierung der Arbeit – Pluralisierung der Bildung?*, Opladen: Leske & Budrich, pp. 73–86.

Andersen, Jørgen Goul (2002), 'Work and Citizenship: Unemployment and Unemployment Policies in Denmark, 1980–2000', in Jørgen Goul Andersen and Per H. Jensen (eds), *Changing Labour Markets, Welfare Policies and Citizenship,* Bristol: Policy Press, pp. 59–85.

Arnkil, Robert and Timo Spangar (2004), *Comparing Recent Danish, Finnish and Swedish Labour Market Policy Reforms*, WZB Discussion Paper FS I 01–204.

Bandemer, Stephan V. (2001), 'Aktivierender Staat, New Governance und Arbeitsmarkt- und Beschäftigungspolitik', in Thomas Olk, Adalbert Evers and Rolf G. Heinze (eds), *Baustelle Sozialstaat. Umbauten und veränderte Grundrisse*, Wiesbaden: Chmielorz, pp. 37–51.

Barbier, J.-C. and W. Ludwig-Mayerhofer (2004), 'The Many Worlds of Activation', *European Societies*, **6** (4), 423–37.

Bredgaard, Thomas and Flemming Larsen (eds) (2005), *Employment Policy from Different Angles*, Copenhagen: DJ øF Publishing Copenhagen.

Bruttel, O. and E. Sol (2006), 'Work First as a European Model? Evidence from Germany and the Netherlands', *Policy and Politics*, **21** (1), 69–89.

Budget (1998), *The Working Families Tax Credit and Work Incentives. The Modernisation of Britain's Tax and Benefit System*, London: Number Three.

Budget (2005), *Budget Report 2001*, see http://www.hm-treasury.gov.uk/media/AA7/bud05_chap05_209.pdf, last access 2 May 2005.

Bundesagentur für Arbeit (2006), 'Arbeitsmarkt 2005', *Amtliche Nachrichten der Bundesagentur für Arbeit* 54, Sondernummer August.

Bundesministerium für Arbeit und Soziales (2006), *Gesetz zur Fortentwicklung der Grundsicherung für Arbeitssuchende*, see http://www.bmas.bund.de/BMAS/Navigation/Arbeitsmarkt/arbeitslosengeld-2,did=146436.html, Berlin: last access 27 November 2006.

Bundesministerium für Familie, Senioren, Frauen und Jugend (2006), *Kindertagesbetreuung für Kinder unter drei Jahren. Bericht der Bundesregierung über den Stand des Ausbaus für ein bedarfsgerechtes Angebot an Kinder Tagesbetreuung für Kinder unter drei Jahren*, Berlin: BFSFJ.

Bundesregierung (2006), *Wirksamkeit moderner Dienstleistungen am Arbeitsmarkt. Bericht 2005 der Bundesregierung zur Wirkung der Umsetzung der Vorschläge der Kommission Moderne Dienstleistungen am Arbeitsmarkt*, see http://www.bundesregierung.de/Anlage955196/Hartz-Evaluation+%28Lang fassung%29.pdf, Berlin: Bundesregierung.

Clasen, Jochen (2007), *Distribution of Responsibilities for Social Security and Labour Market Policy*, Country Report: The United Kingdom. Amsterdam Institute for Advanced Labour Studies, Working Papers Number 07/50, Amsterdam: University of Amsterdam.

Clasen, J. and D. Clegg (2003), 'Unemployment Protection and Labour Market Reform in France and Great Britain in the 1990s: Solidarity Versus Activation?', *Journal of Social Policy*, **32** (3), 361–81.

Compston, H. and K.P. Madsen (2001), 'Conceptual Innovation and Public Policy: Unemployment and Paid Leave Schemes in Denmark', *Journal of European Social Policy*, **11** (2), 117–32.

Dingeldey, Irene (1997), *Britische Arbeitsbeziehungen. Gewerkschaften zwischen Konflikt, Kooperation und Marginalisierung*, Wiesbaden: Deutscher UniversitätsVerlag.

Dingeldey, Irene (2005a), *Welfare State Transformation between 'Workfare' and an 'Enabling' State. A Comparative Analysis*, TranState Working Papers, Series of the CRC 597, Nr 021/2005, Bremen: Transformations of the State.

Dingeldey, I. (2005b), 'Zehn Jahre aktivierende Arbeitsmarktpolitik in Dänemark', *WSI-Mitteilungen*, **58** (1), 18–24.

Dingeldey, I. (2007), 'Between Workfare and Enablement: The Different Paths to Transformation of the Welfare State', *European Journal of Political Research*, **46** (6), 823–851.

Esping-Andersen, Gösta (1990), *The Three Worlds of Welfare Capitalism*, Cambridge: Polity Press.

Finn, Dan and Matthias Knuth (2004), *One Stop? Joining Up Employment Assistance and Benefit Administration in Britain and Germany*, Paper presented at the annual conference of Espanet, Oxford, see http://www.apsoc.ox.ac.uk/Espanet/espanetconference/papers/ppr.11A.DF.pdf.

Fuchs, Kirsten and Christian Peucker (2006), ' "...und raus bist du!" Welche Kinder besuchen nicht den Kindergarten und warum?', in Walter Bien, Thomas Rauschenbach and Birgit Riedel (eds), *Wer betreut Deutschlands Kinder? DJI-Kinderbetreuungsstudie*, Weinheim and Basel: Belz, pp. 61–82.

Giddens, Anthony (1998), 'Equality and the Social Investment State', in Ian Hargreaves and Ian Christie (eds), *Tomorrow's Politics. The Third Way and Beyond*, London: Demos, pp. 25–40.

Gilbert, Neil (2002), *Transformation of the Welfare State. The Silent Surrender of Public Responsibility*, Oxford: Oxford University Press.

Gilbert, Neil and Barbara Gilbert (1989), *The Enabling State. Modern Welfare Capitalism in America*, New York and Oxford: Oxford University Press.

Gottschall, K. and K. Hagemann (2002), 'Die Halbtagsschule in Deutschland: Ein Sonderfall in Europa?', *Aus Politik und Zeitgeschichte*, B 41/2002, 12–22.

Heinelt, Hubert and Michael Weck (1998), *Arbeitsmarktpolitik. Vom Vereinigungskonsens zur Standortdebatte*, Opladen: Leske & Budrich.

HM Revenue & Customs Analysis Team (2006), *Child Tax Credit and Working Tax Credit. Take-up Rates 2003–4*, see http://www.hmrc.gov.uk/stats/personal-tax-credits/takeup_rates_2003-04_mar06.pdf, London: HM Revenue & Customs.

Hujer, Reinhard, Günther Klee, Werner Sörgel and Alexander Spermann (2005), *Vermittlungsgutscheine. Zwischenergebnisse der Begleitforschung 2004. Teil VIII Zusammenfassung der Projektergebnisse*, IAB Forschungsbericht 8.

Hvinden, Bjørn (2004), 'Activation in the Western Europe of the 1990s: Did it Make a Difference?', in Peter Krause, Gerhard Bäcker and Walter Hanesch (eds), *Combating Poverty in Europe. The German Welfare Regime in Practice*, Aldershot, UK and Burlington, VT: Ashgate, pp. 267–85.

Jacobsson, Kerstin (2004), 'A European Politics for Employability: The Political Discourse on Employability of the EU and the OECD', in Christina Garsten and Kerstin Jacobsson (eds), *Learning To Be Employable. New Agendas on Work, Responsibility and Learning in a Globalizing World*, New York: Palgarave, pp. 42–61.

Jessop, Bob (1991), 'The Welfare State in the Transition from Fordism to Post-fordism', in Bob Jessop, Hans Kastendiek, Klaus Nielsen and Ove K. Pedersen (eds), *The Politics of Flexibility. Restructuring State and Industry in Britain, Germany and Scandinavia*, Aldershot, UK and Brookfield, VT: Edward Elgar, pp. 82–104.

Kannengießer, C. and E. Gundel (2003), 'Der Reformprozess der Bundesanstalt für Arbeit – Vom bürokratischen Monolith zum Dienstleister am Markt', *Sozialer Fortschritt*, **52** (8), 207–13.

Kemmerling, Achim and Oliver Bruttel (2005), *New Politics in German Labour Market Policy? The Implications of the Recent Hartz Reforms for the German Welfare State*, WZB Discussion Paper SP I 2005–101.

Knijn, Trudie and Ilona Ostner (2002), 'Commodification and De-commodification', in Barbara Hobson, Jane Lewis and Birte Siim (eds), *Contested Concepts in Gender and Social Politics*, Cheltenham, UK and Northampton, MA: Edward Elgar, pp. 141–70.

Knuth, Matthias, Oliver Schweer and Sabine Siemes (2004), *Drei Menüs - Und kein Rezept? Dienstleistungen am Arbeitsmarkt in Großbritannien, in den Nieder-landen und in Dänemark*, Bonn: Friedrich Ebert Stiftung.

Koch, S. and U. Walwei (2005), 'Hartz IV: Neue Perspektiven für Langzeitarbeitslose?', *Aus Politik und Zeitgeschichte*, **16**, 10–17.

Konle-Seidl, R. (2003), 'Von der Anstalt zum ersten Dienstleister am Arbeitsmarkt? Möglichkeiten und Grenzen der Reform der Bundesanstalt für Arbeit', *Gesundheits- und Sozialpolitik*, **1** (2), 22–29.

Konle-Seidl, Regina and Ulrich Walwei (2001), *Job Placement in Europe: Trends and Impacts of Changes*, IABtopics Nr. 46, see http://doku.iab.de/topics/2001/topics46.pdf.

Kooiman, Jan (2005 (2003)), *Governing as Governance*, London: Thousand Oaks, New Delhi: Sage.

Korpi, W. and J. Palme (2003), 'New Politics and Class Politics in the Context of Austerity and Globalization: Welfare State Regress in 18 Countries, 1975–95', *American Political Science Review*, **97** (3), 425–46.

Kühnlein, Gertrud and Birgit Klein (2003), *Bildungsgutscheine – Mehr Eigenverantwortung, mehr Markt, mehr Effizienz? – Erfahrungen bei der Neuausrichtung der beruflichen Weiterbildung*, Arbeitspapiere der Hans Böckler Stiftung, Bd.74.

Lefresne, F. (1999), 'Employability at the Heart of the European Employment Strategy', *Transfer*, **5** (4), 460–81.

Lenhardt, Gero and Claus Offe (1977), 'Staatstheorie und Sozialpolitik. Politisch-soziologische Erklärungsansätze für Funktionen und Innovationsprozesse der

Sozialpolitik', in Christian von Ferber and Franz-Xaver Kaufmann (eds), *Soziologie und Sozialpolitik. Kölner Zeitschrift für Soziologie und Sozialpsychologie – Sonderheft 19*, Opladen: Westdeutscher Verlag, pp. 98–127.

Marshall, Thomas H. ((1949) 1963), 'Citizenship and Social Class', in Thomas H. Marshall (ed.), *Sociology at the Crossroads and Other Essays*, London: Heinemann, pp. 67–127.

Mezger, Erika and Klaus West (eds) (2000), *Aktivierender Sozialstaat und politisches Handeln*, Marburg: Schüren.

OECD (1990), *Labour Market Policies for the 1990s*, Paris: OECD.

OECD (1994), 'New Orientations for Social Policy', in *OECD Social Policy Studies 12*, Paris: OECD.

OECD (2001), *Thematic Review on Adult Learning. Background Report Denmark*, download 12 April 2002, Paris: OECD, see http://www.oecd.org/copyr.htm/.

OECD (2002), *Denmark*, Paris: OECD.

OECD (2002/1), *United Kingdom*, Paris: OECD.

OECD (2003), *Denmark*, Paris: OECD.

OECD (2004a), *Employment Outlook 2004*, Paris: OECD.

OECD (2004b), *Benefits and Wages. OECD Indicators*, Paris: OECD.

OECD (2006), *Employment Outlook*, Paris: OECD.

Olesen, Søren Peter (2001), 'Discourses of Activation at Danish Employment Offices', in Michael Seltzer, Christian Kullberg, Søren Peter Olesen and Illmari Rostilla (eds), *Listening to the Welfare State*, Aldershot, UK, Burlington, VT, Singapore: Ashgate, pp. 103–37.

Pierson, P. (1996), 'The New Politics of the Welfare State', *World Politics*, **48**, 143–79.

Rake, K. (2001), 'Gender and New Labour's Social Policies', *Journal of Social Policy*, **30** (2), 209–31.

Rostgard, Tine and Torben Fridberg (1998), *Caring for Children and Older People – A Comparison of European Policies and Practices*, Copenhagen: The Danish National Institute of Social Research.

Sainsbury, Diane (1999), *Gender and Welfare State Regimes*, Oxford: Oxford University Press.

Scharpf, Fritz (2000), *Interaktionsformen Akteurzentrierter Institutionalismus in der Politikforschung*, Opladen: UTB.

Serrano Pascual, Amparo and Lars Magnussen (eds) (2007), *Reshaping Welfare States and Activation Regimes in Europe,* Brussels, Bern, Berlin, Frankfurt, New York, Oxford, Vienna: Peter Lang.

Sommerville, Will and Chris Brace (eds) (2004), *The Welfare to Work Handbook Second Edition*, London: Centre for Economic & Social Inclusion.

Statistics Denmark (various), Statistical Yearbook, http://www.dst.dk/HomeUK/Statistics/ofs/Publications/Yearbook.aspx. Kopenhagen.

Spieß, K., F. Büchel and J. R. Frick (2002), *Kinderbetreuung in West- und Ost-deutschland: Sozioökonomischer Hintergrund entscheidend*, *DIW Wochenbericht*, **68** (31).

Torfing, J. (1999a), 'Towards a Schumpeterian Workfare Postnational Regime: Path-shaping and Path-dependency in Danish Welfare State Reform', *Economy and Society*, **28** (3), 369–402.

Torfing, J. (1999b), 'Workfare with Welfare: Recent Reforms of the Danish Welfare State', *Journal of European Social Policy*, **9** (1), 5–28.

Trickey, Heather and Robert Walker (2000), 'Steps to Compulsion within British Labour Market Policies', in Ivar Lødemel and Heather Trickey (eds), *An Offer You Can't Refuse*, Bristol, UK: The Policy Press, pp. 181–214.

Trube, A. and N. Wohlfahrt (2001), ' "Der aktivierende Sozialstaat" – Sozialpolitik zwischen Individualisierung und einer neuen politischen Ökonomie der inneren Sicherheit', *WSI-Mitteilungen*, **54** (1), 27–36.

5. International Organisations as Governance Actors: The OECD in Education Policy

Kerstin Martens and Anja P. Jakobi

INTRODUCTION

The OECD is today a major vehicle for education policy, and its studies attract considerable attention in national policy debates (*among others* Henry et al. 2001; Jakobi 2006; Kennedy 1995; Rinne et al. 2004). Although the organisation has embraced education policy issues since its inception, it has only recently been recognised as an important actor in this field. Our chapter will trace the rise of the OECD as one of the leading organisations in education policy and contrast its current role with its activities in the 1960s and 1970s, when it was far less widely recognised. In doing so, our aim is to examine how policy 'is made' by international organisations (IOs), such as the OECD, as governance actors that influence national reform processes in the field of education. In essence we argue that the OECD is currently making significant contributions to education policy because – unlike in the past – it has now developed a comprehensive 'package' of modes of governance that provides states not only with the definition of a problem but also with its solution.

Our theoretical premise draws on institutionalist ideas of organisational fields and policy diffusion within 'world society' (among others, DiMaggio and Powell 1983; Meyer et al. 1997). On the basis of such assumptions, we claim that the OECD acts as a policy entrepreneur, exerting influence over national education policies. However, neo-institutionalism leaves open the specific modes of governance by which IOs succeed or fail as entrepreneurs. To explore these, we suggest an analytical matrix in which a distinction is made between agenda setting (discursive elaboration of relevant policy issues), policy formulation (development of recommended courses of action) and policy coordination (harmonisation of policies).

These different modes of governance are examined by means of two examples of policy formation in the OECD: (1) dissemination of the goal of lifelong learning[1] and (2) benchmarking through education indicators. Both represent typical modes of operating at the OECD: lifelong learning is an education policy paradigm, while benchmarking takes place through quantitative data collection. The article is structured as follows: firstly, the basic premises of governance by international organisations are introduced by presenting the OECD as a policy entrepreneur. Secondly, its relevant modes of governance are described and explained. This leads thirdly to an empirical analysis of lifelong learning and education indicators, in which the 1970s and 1990s are contrasted as two different phases in the development of the OECD as an education organisation. The evolution of instruments within the OECD is outlined on the basis of semi-structured interview material and a document analysis.[2]

GOVERNANCE BY INTERNATIONAL ORGANISATIONS

We regard IOs as policy entrepreneurs that try to strengthen interaction amongst states, increase information flows and facilitate inter-organisational cooperation and communication with regard to commonly shared objectives. These are processes that constitute the conditions for the establishment of an organisational field between states (DiMaggio and Powell 1983). Our research therefore examines the OECD from the perspective of what is known in political science as 'social constructivism' and in particular 'new institutionalism'. Inspired by sociological research on world society (Meyer et al. 1997, among others), scholars have investigated the role of international organisations as sources of national policy development and policy change (Barnett and Finnemore 2004; Finnemore 1993; Finnemore and Sikkink 1999). In recent years, political scientists working in various fields, including international relations generally and the European Union more specifically (for example Börzel and Risse 2000; Finnemore 1993, 1996; Radaelli 2000), have drawn on this sociological perspective on IOs and states.

New institutionalism is attractive to political scientists because it emphasises and conceptualises the effect of international organisations on domestic activity. Moreover, it questions the mere functionality of IOs and sheds light on them as actors (Barnett and Finnemore 1999). However, institutionalists have difficulties when it comes to explaining change and the rise of new models. The literature on the conditions for policy diffusion through IOs mirrors this problem: it refers to individualistic values, certain points in time or the growing number of committed actors promoting the expansion of institutions (Finnemore and Sikkink 1999: 261). However, it leaves unresolved the question of how IOs might change in order to become more successful governance actors in an organisational field. Thus, analysing the puzzling rise of the OECD in education policy from a new institutionalist perspective only fails to explain how it has become such a significant entrepreneur in this field.

Expanding this set of literature we argue that IOs have different means at their disposal to influence nation states. The most obvious are legal regulations and financial resources – for example binding treaties in the context of the World Trade Organization or project funding from the European Union or World Bank. The OECD hardly has such means: although it has access to legally binding measures for all its member states, only 188 pieces of legislation have been adopted to date and only one eighth of them are compulsory (Marcussen 2004). Just one measure, dating from 1978, concerns education policy. Obviously, the OECD's influence is based on other governance instruments: it shapes policy by providing 'causal stories' (Stone 1989) to policy makers and by offering a vision of the future. We identify three governance instruments used by the OECD in its role as education policy entrepreneur: *agenda setting, policy formulation* and *policy coordination*:

Governance by Agenda Setting

International organisations are able to identify issues and set agendas which are later discussed at national level. Conferences hosted by international organisations are particularly important instruments for drawing attention to topics affecting global society (Lechner and Boli 2005). The OECD is able to identify issues in its different forums and draw attention to them at national level. Within its different departments, the OECD has specialists with ample professional expertise for this task (Marcussen 2004: 117). Like their counterparts in research institutions, they identify issues of current and future relevance. The OECD develops projects and focus areas for its member states. Its Centre for Educational Research and Innovation (CERI), for instance, has explicitly adopted the role of an agenda setter (Schuller 2005).

With their agenda-setting capacities, international organisations are able to steer the international debate on education policy. The OECD determines which topics are relevant to this debate, both for the present and the future. As a result, these topics are already 'framed' by the OECD, which defines cause-and-effect relationships (Snow et al. 1986; Stone 1989): international organisations' agenda-setting functions not only influence which issues will be discussed at the international level, but also *how* they will be discussed. In this way, the OECD creates a framework that can affect the direction and objective of discussions on a specific topic.

Governance by Policy Formulation

Not only do international organisations define the relevant issues, but they can also draw up and disseminate recommendations for action in their member states in order to address previously identified problems. The OECD's analyses can help countries identify relevant policy issues and also offer recommendations (Schuller 2005: 177). Such policy recommendations may influence domestic policies in the member states. In the case of the OECD, its staff prepares publications outlining a specific approach to certain issues within national political processes, such as strategies for the funding of lifelong learning initiatives (OECD 2004a). OECD material, brochures, information and statistical data identify the best approach to certain problems and suggest effective solutions. In this way, the OECD determines 'policy directions' (for example OECD 2001b: 9–40).

Thus the OECD introduces internationally generated policy formulations into national decision-making processes. National opinion formers can then draw on OECD publications to justify the adoption or rejection of a particular domestic policy. In the process of formulating policies, the OECD draws up and develops models and approaches that then influence the political behaviour of its member states. Policies discussed within the forums of international organisations already affect national policy making for the simple reason that countries frequently import policy options that were previously unknown or considered unfeasible in their particular political systems. Without the OECD's Programme for International Student Assessment (PISA), for instance, the Finnish school system would not have acquired the status of a role model and attracted the level of attention it is currently receiving from German and other foreign observers. By promoting 'best practice' models in the organisational field, the OECD provides a source for mimetic isomorphism (DiMaggio and Powell 1983).

Governance by Policy Coordination

International organisations also contribute to the diffusion of national policies by exerting a coordinating effect on the policies of their member states. Relevant actors can meet and exchange solutions at conferences initiated and held within the IO's framework, such as the OECD conference on funding issues for lifelong learning (OECD 2004a). The OECD has also launched projects in which countries' domestic policies are described and compared. It also prepares background material, submits procedural recommendations and drafts international agreements.

With this capacity for coordination, the OECD can provide incentives for member countries to adjust their education policies in the light of developments in other countries. This gives rise to competing policy options: different approaches can suddenly be compared with each other, which in turn creates a need for justification and may even lead to the imposition of new action programmes. In the course of this process, international organisations also develop standards for the evaluation and mutual assessment of policies. As a result, the OECD can collectively commit its member states to a common set of goals, draw attention to positive examples and ultimately promote greater convergence between member states.

This set of instruments will be used as a basis for comparing the OECD's work in education policy in the 1970s with its work in the 1990s.

EDUCATION POLICY AT THE OECD[3]

Although education was not mentioned explicitly in its founding convention, the OECD has been involved in this policy field since its inception in 1961. In its early phases, the OECD, strongly influenced by modernisation theory, gave priority to the promotion of technology, mathematics and the natural sciences (for example OECD 1963, 1964). Consequently, in developing an education policy, it sought to promote the human factor as a prerequisite for technological and economic progress. Education planning was seen as a condition for producing an adequate supply of scientists and technicians (Interview OECD 26, 2004; Papadopoulos 1994: 21). At several of the conferences held under the organisation's auspices, speakers argued for an expansion of education; education itself was largely considered an economic investment (Papadopoulos 1994: 37, 40). The 1961 Economic Growth and Investment in Education conference is seen as paradigmatic in this regard (Papadopoulos 1994: 39).

The creation of the Centre for Educational Research and Innovation in 1968 furthered institutionalised education policy within the OECD. Two years later the Committee for Scientific and Technical Personnel was renamed the Education Committee; this gave education policy its own committee within the OECD structure and formally legitimised it as an OECD activity (Papadopoulos 1994: 63). In 1975, the Education Committee was transferred to the newly established Directorate for Social Affairs, Manpower and Education.[4] In the 1970s, education policy was closely linked to the labour market (Papadopoulos 1994: 68). At the same time, social objectives and education ideals were moving to the fore, with debates on equality of opportunity becoming an established part of politics. Several education programmes were launched at that time, broadening the scope of the OECD's activities (Papadopoulos 1994: 74–91).

The onset of the oil crisis ended the expansion of education policy. In 1978, the first ministerial conference of education ministers on the future of education policy emphasised the changing social and economic context (Henry et al. 2001: 64). Rising unemployment rates (especially among adolescents), a lack of public funds and demographic changes increasingly dominated the OECD programmes relating to education policy in the 1980s (OECD 1985, 1989). Likewise, increased attention was being paid to the links between education and economic growth (Henry et al. 2001: 64). A number of programmes from that period are still part of the current OECD portfolio (Rinne et al. 2004: 460–1). With the demise of the Soviet Union, the Eastern European states approached the OECD, which welcomed several as new members. As a result, OECD programmes – including those on education policy – became yet more diverse in the 1990s, with non-OECD states also increasingly being included in OECD projects.

By now the OECD had acquired the status of 'éminence grise' in international education policy (Rinne et al. 2004), surpassing even such renowned education organisations as UNESCO in reputation and policy influence. Despite the comparatively limited financial and legal options available to it, the OECD has grown to become one of the most important organisations in the area of education policy. Internally, education was strengthened in 2002 with the creation of an education directorate.

Two OECD initiatives that were launched in the 1970s but only received wide recognition in the 1990s are crucial to its current status as an international education organisation. The first of these is dissemination of the notion of lifelong learning. It was during an OECD conference of education ministers in 1996 that the notion of recurrent education was revived as lifelong learning for all and it has remained a seminal topic in OECD member countries. The second is benchmarking by means of education indicators. In this case, a programme that had been in existence for some time was developed further and has become one of the most influential of the OECD's programmes. The organisation's growing influence on education policy in its member states will be illustrated in the following section with some examples.

Lifelong Learning

From a policy perspective, lifelong learning involves state facilitation of learning processes throughout life. It is less a clearly defined work programme than a guideline for reform in education policy. Aside from broader education opportunities, the cornerstones of a reform geared towards lifelong learning include the creation of needs-based curricula and the recognition of previously acquired qualifications as a basis for further studies. The OECD was one of the first IOs to promote the concept of lifelong learning as early as the 1970s. Whereas its early work in the area met with little acclaim, the OECD has since become highly effective in the dissemination of this policy objective and its implementation.

Early OECD activities related to lifelong learning

Early OECD discussions on lifelong learning were linked to the idea of recurrent education. The concept was introduced at the OECD towards the end of the 1960s in a speech by Olof Palme. Recurrent education was interpreted by the OECD to mean alternating periods of education and work over the life course. Recurrent education was the first systematic attempt to improve education policy in industrialised nations (Papadopoulos 1994: 112–3). Prompted by Palme's speech, the OECD devoted considerable efforts to making a systematic and empirical assessment of the topic in subsequent years. Between 1972 and 1977, the OECD compiled country reports on the state of recurrent education in the member states and outlined options for the future (Papadopoulos 1994: 113, 119). By and large, these reports were comparatively brief and very descriptive. In some cases, they included a highly critical analysis of the problems associated with recurrent education in individual member states (Cantor 1974: 23–5; Hansen 1976: 32), but they neither identified best practices nor directly compared countries.

A high point of the OECD's involvement in recurrent education was the publication in 1973 of a study entitled Recurrent Education – A Strategy for Lifelong Learning (OECD 1973). Based on the proceedings of a conference and referred to internally as a 'clarifying report', this study proposed limiting the duration of secondary education and instead creating opportunities for periods of learning over the life course. Education was seen in the context of personal development, equal opportunities and employment. The report also addressed the implications of recurrent education and pointed to the need for further research. Moreover, it made reference to the links between education policy and employment policy (Schuller et al. 2002). Nevertheless, the report was intended merely as a trigger for further debate and not as a package of concrete policy measures (OECD 1973: 6). Accordingly, it contained few ideas for specific changes and confined itself to advancing some proposals for future education policy guidelines.

At the 1973 conference of European education ministers, the presentation of ideas outlined in the clarifying report met with harsh criticism and rejection, in particular from the UK. By way of compromise, the follow-up conference in 1975 was to be devoted to the theme of recurrent education. On that occasion, the OECD adopted a declaration on lifelong learning that described recurrent education as a long-term strategy for restructuring education systems. Despite this political success, implementation efforts were very limited (Papadopoulos 1994: 114), even though the OECD included more specific proposals in the report that it had compiled for the meeting, such as the establishment of commissions and changes to the enrolment requirements for certain phases of education, etc. (OECD 1975: 40–9). A further international meeting on recurrent education took place in 1977 but made only sporadic progress: there was little evidence of large-scale implementation (Papadopoulos 1994: 115). OECD activities in the area of recurrent education ended that year with the last country reports; with a few exceptions (for example OECD 1986) the issue did not reappear in OECD publications or discussions until the 1990s.

In developing the notion of recurrent education, the OECD had defined an objective but neglected to outline specific measures for realising that objective. It concerned itself little with policy formulation and failed completely to promote policy coordination. In the 1970s, the OECD's 'toolbox' did not include instruments for identifying countries with particularly successful models and bringing them together with other countries, on the assumption that positive experiences could be transferred from one country to another. Instead, the country reports remained purely descriptive and representational. Rather, the organisation assumed that member states would recognise the need for reform and implement all the required measures by themselves. It made no effort to harness a group dynamic based on national comparisons for the purpose of identifying best practices.

Lifelong learning since the 1990s

After a period of silence, the international debate on lifelong learning resumed in the 1990s. For the OECD, the 1996 ministerial conference served as a platform for renewal of the five-year CERI mandate and the formulation of a new research programme. The 1994 Jobs Study had already focused attention on employees' skills and qualifications (OECD 1995: 15). Moreover, the results of the Adult Literacy Survey had revealed significant deficiencies in adult literacy and numeracy in OECD countries, thereby highlighting the need for adult education (OECD 1996: 237–8). In the wake of these events, members of the OECD actively lobbied for the European year of lifelong learning, thereby creating awareness of the importance of this topic beyond the OECD's institutional boundaries (Interview OECD 16, 2004). At the 1996 summit education, ministers unanimously emphasised the significance of lifelong learning and international cooperation. Their communiqué is explicit: 'Lifelong learning will be essential for everyone as we move into the 21st century and has to be made accessible to all [...]' (OECD 1996: 21).

The meeting also drew up strategies for the promotion of lifelong learning processes, addressing four sets of issues: the role of school and pre-school education as a means of preparation for learning processes, a stronger connection between work and learning, the role of different stakeholders and the creation of incentive systems. Following this meeting, lifelong learning became firmly established as an issue within the OECD, its member states and beyond. Moreover, no other issue could have been a better advertisement for the activities of CERI (Interview OECD 16, 2004), which now coordinates various reform projects. These include the evaluation of educational infrastructure – notably school buildings – with regard to their role in fostering lifelong learning (OECD 2002c), the analysis of individuals' motivation to engage in lifelong learning (OECD 2000) and the role of schools in this process (Istance 2003; OECD 2002a). Research on new fields in lifelong learning was also stimulated: in 2001 the OECD put in place the Lifelong Learning Network, which brings together educational science and neurological brain research (Hinton 2005). A conference on funding issues for lifelong learning was organised as well (OECD 2004a).

Again, the OECD publishes on national implementation of lifelong learning but, in contrast to the 1970s, these reports are no longer purely descriptive but contain specific recommendations. In 1999, the OECD analysed the Hungarian education system (OECD 1999) and between 2000 and 2002 it compiled a country report on lifelong learning in Norway (OECD 2002b); both reports revealed shortcomings in these education systems and suggested possible improvements. What is more, countries are now explicitly being compared to each other. In 2001, the OECD published comparative analyses of the developments in lifelong learning in member countries, including participation in pre-school or adult education (OECD 2001b: 43–71).

Between 2000 and 2005, a wide-ranging project on the role of qualification systems in promoting lifelong learning was conducted, with the aim to analyse the success of different education systems and their respective instruments. This resulted in the establishment of thematic working groups and the publication of 15 country reports encouraging the transfer between member states of know-how pertaining to the design and management of qualification systems. Along with the 24 participating countries, this project also involved other IOs such as the EU Commission, the World Bank and the ILO. Particular emphasis was placed on the creation of so-called national qualification frameworks (OECD 2004b). These have been introduced in several countries since the 1990s and provide a domestic framework for the evaluation of individual learning progress and shortcomings, similar to the credit point systems widely used in universities (Jakobi 2006: 77).

The OECD has highlighted the role of lifelong learning in various contexts and argued that it should become an integral part of member countries' education policies. At the 2001 conference of education ministers, the OECD was given a mandate to focus on the issue of funding for lifelong learning

(OECD 2001a). The objective of lifelong learning for all has since become widely accepted and is considered a guiding principle of education policy in several OECD countries (Czech Ministry of Education Youth and Sport 2004: 2; UK Education Policy Report 2004).

Lifelong learning will remain a central issue in OECD education policy for the foreseeable future. In 2003, education ministries agreed on a strategic objective, directing the OECD to disseminate the concept of lifelong learning and address its connections to other policies. The 2005–2006 Working Programme provides for OECD involvement in the facilitation of lifelong learning for all in member and partner states (OECD 2005a: 6, 10–11). Increased cooperation with other IOs is another aspect of this growing influence. OECD delegates have given presentations on lifelong learning at World Bank workshops, for instance (Wurzburg 2003), and at the last Bologna Process summit in Bergen in 2005 lifelong learning featured on the agenda and was the subject of a presentation by the head of CERI.

In brief, there are many differences between the OECD's current policy and that of the 1970s. The OECD was highly successful in launching lifelong learning as a new topic at the 1996 summit. Coordination with other organisations has helped the topic gain even wider acceptance. Very much in contrast to its earlier approach, the OECD now advises countries on the implementation of education policies and explicitly compares national strategies. It draws on the group dynamics of policy transfer between states and has thus markedly contributed to the coordination of domestic policies. Projects mostly encourage the coordination and exchange of expertise between states. Reports on lifelong learning are part of an external review process with systematic proposals resulting in concrete recommendations. They clearly differ from the descriptive studies of the 1970s in that they offer specific advice.

The Indicator Programme

In recent years, the OECD has become particularly well known as an international education organisation through its work on educational statistics. Its annual publication 'Education at a Glance' and the results of its triennial PISA studies attract worldwide attention. In some countries – and particularly in Germany – the results of the 2000 PISA study triggered a huge debate on the objectives and quality of education. Encouraging appropriate use of education statistics is part of one of the OECD's oldest projects. However, its work in this field has only recently received worldwide attention.

The OECD's early education statistics

The OECD was already beginning to develop indicators for the international comparison of education systems in the early 1960s. The importance of making available more reliable and accessible data on students, teachers, school buildings and finances was pointed out at the 1961 Conference on Economic Growth and Investment in Education. Such education indicators were intended mainly to serve one purpose, namely to provide a basis for efficient education planning (Papadopoulos 1994: 39). The collection and international comparison of education data would provide policy makers with the necessary information they needed to develop the appropriate measures.

The education ministers' need for internationally comparable education indicators was emphasised once again at the 1964 conference of education ministers, held in London. It was suggested that the OECD should develop a special handbook of education data that would serve as a basis for calculating the efficiency of political inputs into the education system (Papadopoulos 1994: 50). This suggestion led to the so-called Green Book, which served as a model handbook for education statistics among OECD countries until the 1970s. These quantitative indicators were intended to provide a basis for forecasting the level and pattern of pupil and student numbers in the various levels of national education systems. They were also intended to help education ministers in planning how to fund the expected expansion of education, particularly higher education. Plans for development were to be drawn up on the basis of mathematical models in order to ensure the efficient use of resources (Papadopoulos 1994: 50–51). Later, the OECD also established the Working Party of the Education Committee on Educational Statistics and Indicators to help with the development of a model that would capture the connection between education and society.

Over the years, however, it became clear that the gathering of internationally comparable data on various education systems presented a challenge that was too big for the OECD (Papadopoulos 1994: 190): data quality was only moderate. This was due mainly to the fact that the OECD did not generate its own data but rather assembled data sent to it by national authorities. The OECD used the data exactly as it had been sent to it, without subjecting it to further scrutiny or amendment, even if the data contained obvious errors (Interview OECD 25, 2004). The fact that there were no uniform international standards made work in the field of education statistics even more difficult. Even though the OECD asked its member states as early as 1966 to compile their education statistics according to the handbook, there was no binding declaration and each country submitted data compiled on the basis of its own methods of data collection. Nor had the OECD ever put in place a standardised data gathering system. Consequently, the statistics were unreliable and did not allow any comparison between countries (Interview OECD 20, 2004).

Moreover, the OECD collected input data only; since there was no corresponding output data, however, it was impossible to make any judgements as to the efficiency of a particular education system. Such judgements or indirect comparisons were not a priority for the OECD in the 1970s. On the contrary: projects that allowed direct comparisons between countries or simple cost-benefit calculations were actually avoided (Interview OECD 14, 2003). Because of these shortcomings, the OECD's work in this field was only a marginal activity at this point: the OECD produced only three sets of education indicators, in 1974, 1975 and in 1981 (Papadopoulos 1994: 190). Despite these shortcomings, the education data that were collected on the basis of the Green Book remained the only statistical source in this field for a long time. In the end, work in this field came to a partial halt (Rinne et al. 2004: 460).

Thus, in the 1960s and 1970s, the OECD pointed to problems in individual member countries but did not suggest any solutions. The aim of the education indicators was to facilitate the planning of education inputs and the OECD processed the necessary information. In this way, the OECD was dealing with an important issue by working on questions relevant to politicians. Nevertheless, its aim was not to make recommendations or to coordinate a series of uniform decisions in its member states that would determine the further policy measures to be taken.

Benchmarking through education indicators since the 1990s
The OECD today is one of the leading generators of education data. In the course of the 1990s, Education at a Glance was increasingly acknowledged as pointing the way forward. The OECD's studies in the field of education indicators are perceived more positively than those of 'real' education organisations, such as the International Association for the Evaluation of Educational Achievement (IEA), which has conducted many international comparative studies (for example TIMSS) or UNESCO, which in its early days developed the Manual of Educational System Classification (known as ISCED). The gathering of data and the development of indicators are nowadays the 'first priority of the member states' in their OECD work on education (Interview OECD 9, 2003). Moreover, the education indicators have now become a central piece of OECD activities – for which the organisation has received considerable attention, acknowledgement and praise.

The OECD's breakthrough as an international education organisation can be attributed mainly to the PISA survey, which constitutes a standardised instrument for the evaluation of 15-year-old pupils in participating countries. The survey aims to assess the extent to which pupils are able to apply the knowledge they have acquired (OECD 2005b). It tests their reading and mathematical and scientific literacy at three-yearly intervals. Data on family backgrounds and educational institutions are also gathered. It is by no means just OECD countries that take part in the survey. No fewer than 43 countries were involved in the first assessment cycle in 2000 (the OECD has 30 member states) and 41 in 2003; 57 countries have taken part in the third cycle in 2006. Besides the major industrialised countries, participants include such countries as Brazil, Azerbaijan, Qatar and Thailand.

In implementing the PISA project, the OECD has developed its own standardised instrument for gathering information on education systems and making it internationally comparable. The OECD's aim in education policy is 'to create a framework for assessing educational systems where we can look at them in the light of other educational systems' (Interview OECD 9, 2003). Work on the PISA project began in 1995 and the instruments required were developed by the OECD in cooperation with scientists from all over the world over the next five years (Interview OECD 9, 2003; Interview OECD 20, 2004). Despite occasional criticism, PISA has been acknowledged as an instrument for the internationally comparable measurement of achievement in education and receives wide political recognition for its high scientific standards (Interview OECD 9, 2003).

The so-called PISA shock triggered by the unexpectedly weak results obtained by some countries hit Germany, whose results were moderate indeed, particularly hard. The chief shortcomings of the German system were identified as the failure of immigrant children to integrate and the poor achievement levels of children from less socially privileged backgrounds. Germany's relatively poor showing gave rise to intensive public and political debates about the country's education system. However the PISA results have also been vigorously debated in Denmark, Austria and Spain. The Danish system, for example, achieved only moderate results, although Denmark is the country that invests most in education (Interview OECD 6, 2003). In the United Kingdom, the PISA results became a political issue as well: because of its bad results the government insisted on withholding the British results, on the grounds that the sample size for the UK was too small.

The esteem that the OECD's education statistics now enjoy can be attributed to the relaunch of the indicator project in the mid-1980s. Under the overall leadership of the USA, a group of countries (France, Austria and Switzerland) put forward proposals for a project that would seek to assess the quality of national education systems in an internationally comparable way. The reason for this request was the publication in 1983 of a report entitled 'A Nation at Risk: Imperatives for Educational Reform' (National Commission for Excellence in Education 1983), which revealed considerable shortcomings in the American education system and triggered what became known as the Great School Debate (Gross and Gross 1985) in the US. The Reagan administration turned to the OECD and requested that a programme be developed that would examine the poor performance of America's schools from an international perspective. This programme was put together at a number of conferences (Washington 1987 and Poitiers 1988) and agreement was reached on a set of identical indicators. In 1988, the indicator project was institutionalised within the OECD with the establishment of the International Indicators of Educational Systems (INES) project.

The establishment of INES meant that data were gathered and indicators developed on a regular basis and to a high standard, unlike in the 1970s. One result of this work is the publication *Education at a Glance*, which has been published annually since 1992. Based on 36 standardised indicators, *Education at a Glance* allows comparability of the data across countries (Interview 21, 2004). It is not only the quality but also the focus of the indicators that has changed. The development of outcome indicators (education and work, effects of employment) as well as of the usual income indicators (private and public spending on education, personnel costs, pupil and student numbers) is now also part of the INES project. The PISA study is a particularly typical example of this change of focus, in that it tests the outcomes of education by assessing how well students at the end of compulsory school have been prepared to face the challenges of the knowledge society.

In the 1990s, in brief, the OECD managed with its indicator programme, PISA in particular, to identify and pursue topics of relevance to policy in the field of education. Its initiating and coordinating function gives the OECD opportunities to implement programmes whose content has been agreed and accepted by all member states. On the basis of the international standards of comparability, which it creates through its standardised survey methods, the OECD can carry out benchmarking exercises and ascertain which countries should serve as examples. By identifying 'best practices' it shows countries with weaker results how to improve and therefore makes indirect recommendations for action. The OECD today not only defines the problem, it also offers the solution, in contrast to its practice in the 1970s.

SUMMARY AND OUTLOOK

In sum, the increased attention paid to the OECD's work, as demonstrated by the examples of lifelong learning and education indicators, went hand in hand with the application of specific instruments by the OECD. Table 5.1 summarises the results.

Table 5.1   Development of OECD instruments in respect to lifelong learning and indicators

	Year	Activity	Instrument
Lifelong Learning	1969	Conference (Versailles)	A
	1972–1977	Descriptive country studies on 'recurrent education'	A
	1973	Conference and publication on 'recurrent education'	A
	1975	Conference and publication	A, B
	1996	Conference (Paris) and publication	A, B, C
	2000–2005	'The Role of Qualification Frameworks in Promoting Lifelong Learning'	C
	2001	Conference	A
	2003	Conference on Co-financing of lifelong Learning	B, C
	2003	Work programme 2003–2006	A
	1999; 2002	Country Reviews in Hungary und Norway	B
Benchmarking through Indicators	1961	Conference on Economic Growth and Investment in Education	A
	1964	Conference of education ministers (London)	A
	1966	Demand on educational data	A
	1967	Preparation of Greenbook for the collection of educational (input) data	A
	1974; 1975; 1981	Publication of input indicators on the basis of the Greenbook	A
	1988 (until today)	Initiation and elaboration of INES project throughout several international conferences (Washington, Semmering, Lugarno, Lahti, Tokyo)	A, C
	Since 1992	Annual publication of indicators with output indicators and the following 'benchmarking' and 'best practices'	A, B, C
	Since 2000	Assessment of knowledge of 15-year-olds every three years	A, B, C
	2004	Country Review on Denmark and 'Pisa-lesson'	B

Note: A: Governance by Agenda Setting; B: Governance by Policy Formulation; C: Governance by Co-ordination.

Source: own account

In the early days of its involvement with education policy, the OECD was merely setting the agenda; since the 1990s, however, it has extended its activities to include policy formulation and the coordination of evaluation on an international scale.

The examples presented in this chapter have shown how the OECD sets the education policy agenda (lifelong learning) and determines best practice (indicator programme) through the use of internationally comparable statistics. In contrast to its earlier activities, the organisation now uses a much broader set of modes of governance. It not only lists tasks to be carried out and raises specific issues but also provides a comprehensive package of definitions of and solutions to problems (agenda-setting, policy formulation and policy coordination). Thus the OECD not only identifies common problems but also offers solutions for them. This package of problems and solutions has contributed considerably to the OECD's success and to the international diffusion of policy models.

The example of the OECD shows that the role of governmental IOs as policy entrepreneurs is crucial. The OECD has achieved its respected position by adopting 'soft' modes of governance rather than through 'hard' legal regulations. The OECD approach has been taken up by other organisations, some of which even have legal means at their disposal. Thus the EU's open method of coordination, for example, is very similar to the OECD's methods of peer reviewing (Martens 2005; Schäfer 2004). The modes of governance adopted by IOs, such as agenda-setting, policy formulation and policy coordination and, most importantly, combinations thereof, need to be given increasing attention in future research.

NOTES

1. For reasons of readability, the term 'lifelong learning' is written without quotation marks throughout this article.
2. Interviews cited in this article were held with former and current OECD employees between December 2003 and August 2004. They have been identified with codes to safeguard the anonymity of the interviewees. This interview data was ascertained as part of a research project on 'International Education Politics' at the Collaborative Research Centre 597 'Transformations of the State'. The centre is funded by the German Research Foundation (DFG).
3. The empirical part of this chapter is based on Jakobi and Martens (2007).
4. In 1991 it was renamed as the Directorate for 'Education, Employment, Labour and Social Affairs'.

REFERENCES

Barnett, M. and M. Finnemore (1999), 'The Politics, Power and Pathologies of International Organizations', *International Organization*, **53** (4), 699–732.

Barnett, Michael and Martha Finnemore (2004), *Rules of the World. International Organizations in Global Politics*, Ithaca and London: Cornell University Press.

Börzel, T. and T. Risse (2000), 'When Europe Hits Home: Europeanization and Domestic Change', *European Integration Online Papers*, **4** (15).

Cantor, Leonard M. (1974), *Recurrent Education. Policy Development in OECD Member Countries. United Kingdom*, Paris: OECD.

Czech Ministry of Education, Youth and Sport (2004), *Report on the Development of Education*, see http://www.ibe.unesco.org/international/ice47/english/natreps/nrep _main.htm, last access: July 2005.

DiMaggio, P.J. and W.W. Powell (1983), 'The Iron Cage Revisited: Institutional Isomorphism and Collective Rationality in Organizational Fields', *American Sociological Review*, **48**, 147–160.

Finnemore, M. (1993), 'International Organizations as Teachers of Norms: The United Nations Educational, Scientific, and Cultural Organization and Science Policy', *International Organization*, **47** (4), 565–597.

Finnemore, Martha (1996), *National Interest in International Society*, Ithaca and London: Cornell University Press.

Finnemore, Martha and Kathryn Sikkink (1999), 'International Norm Dynamics and Political Change', in Peter J. Katzenstein, Robert O. Keohane and Stephen D. Krasner (eds), *Exploration and Contestation in the Study of World Politics*, Cambridge, MA: MIT Press, pp. 247–277.

Gross, Ronald and Beatrice Gross (eds) (1985), *The Great School Debate*, New York: Touchstone.

Hansen, Berrit (1976), *Recurrent Education: Policy and Development in OECD Member Countries. Denmark*, Paris: OECD.

Henry, Miriam, Bob Lingard, Fazal Rizvi and Sanda Taylor (2001), *The OECD, Globalisation and Education Policy*, Paris and elsewhere: IAU and Elsevier Press.

Hinton, Christina D. (2005), *Report of the Third Meeting of the Lifelong Learning Network*, Saitama, Japan, 21–22 January, Paris: OECD, see http://www.oecd.org/ dataoecd /63/58/34900796.pdf, last access: August 2006.

Istance, D. (2003), 'Schooling and Lifelong Learning: Insights from OECD Analyses', *European Journal of Education*, **38** (1), 85–98.

Jakobi, Anja (2006), *A World-wide Norm of Lifelong Learning. A Study of Global Policy Development*, Dissertation, Faculty of Sociology, University of Bielefeld, Germany.

Jacobi, A. and K. Martens (2007), 'Diffusion und Konvergenz durch internationale Organisation: Der Einfluss der OECD in der Bildungspolitik', *Politische Vierteljahresschrift*, special issue: 'Transfer, Diffusion und Konvergenz von Politiken', K. Holzinger, H. Jörgens and C. Knill (eds), pp. 247–270.

Kennedy, Kerry J. (1995), 'An Analysis of the Policy Contexts of Recent Curriculum Reform Efforts in Australia, Great Britain and the United States', in David S.G. Carter and Marnie H. O'Neill (eds), *International Perspectives on Educational*

Reform and Policy Implementation, London and Washington, DC: Falmer Press, pp. 71–85.

Lechner, Frank J. and John Boli (2005), 'Constructing World Culture. UN Meetings as a Global Ritual', in Frank L. Lechner and John Boli (eds), *World Culture. Origins and Consequences*, Malden, Oxford and Victoria: Blackwell, pp. 81–108.

Marcussen, Martin (2004), 'OECD Governance Through Soft Law', in Ulrika Mörth (ed.), *Soft Law in Governance and Regulation. An Interdisciplinary Analysis*, Cheltenham, UK and Northampton, MA: Edward Elgar, pp. 103–128.

Martens, Kerstin (2005), *(Ab)using International Organisations? States, the OECD and Educational Policy*, paper presented to the Annual Meeting of the International Studies Association, Honolulu, USA, 2–6 March.

Meyer, J.W., J. Boli, G.M. Thomas and F.O. Ramirez (1997), 'World Society and the Nation-state', *American Journal of Sociology*, **103** (1), 144–181.

National Commission for Excellence in Education (1983), *A Nation at Risk,* see www.Goalline.Org/Goal%20line/Natatrisk.Html, last access: March 2005.

OECD (1963), *Chemistry today: A Guide for Teachers*, Paris: OECD.

OECD (1964), *Mathematics today: A Guide for Teachers*, Paris: OECD.

OECD (1973), *Recurrent Education: A Strategy for Lifelong Learning*, Paris: OECD.

OECD (1975), *Recurrent Education: Trends and Issues*, Paris: OECD.

OECD (1985), *Education in Modern Society*, Paris: OECD.

OECD (1986), *Recurrent Education Revisited*, Paris: OECD.

OECD (1989), *Education and the Economy in a Changing Society*, Paris: OECD.

OECD (1995), *The OECD Jobs Study: Implementing the Strategy*, Paris: OECD.

OECD (1996), *Lifelong Learning for All*, Paris: OECD.

OECD (1999), *Towards Lifelong Learning in Hungary*, Paris: OECD.

OECD (2000), *Motivating Students for Lifelong Learning*, Paris: OECD.

OECD (2001a), *Communiqué: Investing in Competencies for All. Meeting of the OECD Education Ministers*, Paris, 3–4 April 2001.

OECD (2001b), *Education Policy Analysis*, Paris: OECD.

OECD (2002a), *Completing the Foundations for Lifelong Learning – An OECD Survey of Upper Secondary Schools*, Paris: OECD.

OECD (2002b), *Lifelong Learning in Norway*, Paris: OECD.

OECD (2002c), *OECD Programme on Educational Building. International Seminar on Educational Infrastructure*, Guadelajara, Mexico, 24–27 February.

OECD (2004a), *Co-financing Lifelong Learning. Towards a Systemic Approach*, Paris: OECD.

OECD (2004b), *The Role of National Qualification Systems in Promoting Lifelong Learning. Report from Thematic Group 1: The Development and Use of 'Qualification Frameworks' as a Means of Reforming and Managing Qualification Systems*, Paris: OECD.

OECD (2005a), *OECD Work on Education 2005–2006*, Paris: OECD.

OECD (2005b), 'What Pisa Assesses', see http://www.Pisa.Oecd.Org/Pages/0,2966, En_32252351_32235918_1_1_1_1_1,00.Html, last access: September 2005.

Papadopoulos, George (1994), *Education 1960 – 1990. The OECD Perspective*, Paris: OECD.

Radaelli, C.M. (2000), 'Policy Transfer in the European Union: Institutional Isomorphism as a Source of Legitimacy', *Governance*, **13** (1), 25–43.

Rinne, R., J. Kallo and S. Hokka (2004), 'Too Eager to Comply? OECD Education Policies and the Finnish Response', *European Educational Research Journal*, **3** (2), 454–485.

Schäfer, Armin (2004), 'A New Form of Governance? Comparing the Open Method of Coordination to Multilateral Surveillance by the IMF and the OECD', *Max-Planck Working Paper*, **4** (5).

Schuller, T. (2005), 'Constructing International Policy Research: The Role of CERI/OECD', *European Educational Research Journal*, **4** (3), 170–180.

Schuller, Tom, Hans G. Schuetze, and David Istance (2002), 'From Recurrent Education to the Knowledge Society: An Introduction', in David Istance, Hans G. Schuetze and Tom Schuller (eds), *International Perspectives on Lifelong Learning. From Recurrent Education to the Knowledge Society*, Buckingham, UK: Open University Press, pp. 1 – 21.

Snow, D.A., E.B. Rocheford Jr., S.K. Worden and R.D. Benford (1986), 'Frame Alignment Processes, Micromobilization, and Movement Participation', *American Sociological Review*, **51** (4), 464–81.

Stone, Deborah A. (1989), 'Causal Stories and Formation of Policy Agendas', *Political Science Quarterly*, **104** (2), 281–300.

UK Education Policy Report (2004), *Education Strategies in the United Kingdom*, see http://www.Ibe.Unesco.Org/International/Ice47/English/Natreps/Nrep_Main.Htm, last access: July 2005.

Wurzburg, Gregor (2003), *Charts of the Lifelong Learning Workshop Sponsored by the World Bank and the Slovak Governance Institute: Lifelong Learning - What Lessons from Experience in the OECD?*, December 2003, see www.Worldbank. Org/Education/Lifelong_Learning, last access: July 2005.

6.   Are Welfare States Converging? Recent Social Policy Developments in Advanced OECD Countries

Peter Starke and Herbert Obinger

INTRODUCTION

This chapter is in search of the big picture. Its main objective is to map the broad trajectories of welfare state change in advanced OECD countries over recent decades. In particular, we are interested in examining whether or not there are signs of cross-national convergence of welfare states. It is widely acknowledged among scholars of the welfare state that an ever more competitive economic environment, changing demographics, new social risks connected to changing work and family patterns, increasing public debt, the end of full employment and declining economic growth have put the advanced welfare states under strain. There is, however, much dispute about the repercussions of these challenges for mature welfare states that are members of the OECD. Different scenarios are depicted in the theoretical literature and even the existing empirical evidence shows apparent inconsistencies with respect to the ways in which advanced welfare states have responded to these mounting pressures.

Following Knill, we define policy convergence 'as any increase in the similarity between one or more characteristics of a certain policy [...] across a given set of political jurisdictions [...] over a given period of time' (Knill 2005: 768). Thus we need to specify the policy, the set of political jurisdictions and the period of time under consideration.

Since the welfare state is an 'umbrella term covering a range of governmental activities that have distinctive characteristics' (Pierson 2001: 11), we focus on a broad set of output and outcome indicators of welfare state policies. In doing this, we also attempt to bring together several pieces of evidence that have so far been discussed separately. More specifically, we examine recent developments in (i) social spending, both in terms of total spending and disaggregated measures, (ii) welfare state funding, (iii) benefit generosity and (iv) decommodification. All these measures are quantifiable and thus allow a relatively straightforward empirical examination of the different concepts of convergence described further in this chapter. In addition to quantitative convergence, we are interested in whether or not there is an increasing *qualitative* similarity between welfare regimes. Such a homogenisation of institutional structures is often referred to as isomorphism (Knill 2005: 768). To capture some of those changes, we will look at major reform trajectories, new issues and common solutions in a number of policy sub-fields across welfare states.

Our set of political jurisdictions consists of about 18–21 advanced OECD democracies which are analysed over the period between 1980 and 2001. The reason why our analysis starts in 1980 is influenced not only by data availability, but also by the fact that the so-called 'golden age' of welfare capitalism is said to have peaked around that time. Since then, the international political economy has undergone major transformations which, arguably, have put mature welfare states under strain (Scharpf 2000). The resulting pressures are often regarded as factors driving convergence. In any case, studying convergence requires a comparative research design capable of analysing social policy changes over longer spans of time, since many attempts at welfare state reform only take effect in the long run and social policy changes typically occur in an incremental fashion, with welfare states behaving like 'elephants on the move' (Hinrichs 2001; Hinrichs and Kangas 2003). Our approach is an attempt to do exactly that.

The rest of the chapter is organized as follows: in the next section we start our analysis with a brief overview of different scenarios of cross-national convergence and non-convergence to be found in the literature on the adjustment pathways of welfare states. In addition, we provide an overview of the causes and causal mechanisms that underpin these accounts. The following section introduces different types of convergence and discusses ways to measure them empirically. In the section on empirical analysis we use these measures to examine convergence for a broad set of quantitative indicators. In addition, we highlight the kind of qualitative reforms that may have contributed to convergent trends in the social policy profiles of OECD countries. The final section offers some concluding observations.

CONVERGENCE, PERSISTENCE OR DIVERGENCE? SCENARIOS AND CAUSES

A variety of convergence scenarios can be found in the comparative welfare state literature. However, the relevant causes of convergence emphasised in the literature vary a great deal, as does the expected direction of change (up-wards versus downwards). Conversely, there are several theories emanating from the mainstream of comparative welfare state research that suggest that we should expect not convergence but rather persistent differences or even divergence of welfare states. Again, however, there is no clear consensus as to why this is the case. Different causal factors are suggested to explain non-convergence. Finally, there is no agreement in the literature about the direc-tion of welfare state change that can be theoretically expected. The different scenarios are depicted in Table 6.1.

Convergence

The classification of causal factors triggering convergence is inspired by Holzinger and Knill's taxonomy, which comprises five factors: independent problem-solving, transnational communication, international harmonisation, regulatory competition and imposition (Holzinger and Knill 2005).[1]

Table 6.1   Welfare state convergence and divergence: scenarios and causal factors

Result	Causes	Example	Direction of Change	Authors (for example)
Convergence	Similar problems and pressures	(De-) Industriali-sation, demo-graphic changes, new social risks	Upwards	Wilensky; Iversen and Cusack; Zöllner; Taylor-Gooby
	Imitation and policy learning	OMC, OECD and World Bank	Unclear	Mosher and Trubek; Orenstein
	Legal harmonisation	EU: positive and negative integra-tion	Unclear	Leibfried and Pierson; Scharpf
	Regulatory competi-tion	Race to the bottom	Downwards	Tanzi, Sinn
Persistence/ Divergence	Political-institutional factors	New politics	Status quo	Pierson
		Old politics	Unclear	Huber and Stephens; Korpi and Palme; Swank; Garrett

The study of convergence processes is by no means a new theme in wel-fare state research. The earliest analyses date back to the functionalist school of welfare state research of the 1950s and 1960s. Here, the main driving forces of convergence were similar shifts in the economic structure and the related social problems and needs which, nevertheless, had to be tackled independently by each country. Whereas early functionalists focused on the problems stemming from the transition from agrarian to industrial societies (for example Wilensky and Lebeaux 1958; Kerr et al. 1960; Zöllner 1963; Wilensky 1975), more recent functionalist studies focus on consequences such as deindustrialisation, the erosion of traditional family structures, the rise in atypical work and demographic shifts (Iversen and Cusack 2000; Taylor-Gooby 2004; Armingeon and Bonoli 2006). It is claimed that the associated 'new social risks' give rise in all advanced OECD countries to a similar set of problems that need to be addressed independently through social policy reforms. Both the old and new functionalism share the expectation of 'convergence towards the top'.

In contrast to functionalist convergence scenarios stressing independent problem-solving, a relatively recent approach highlights convergence in social policy as the result of policy learning and imitation fostered through transnational policy networks. Analyses focus on so-called 'soft' mecha-nisms, such as the European Union's open method of coordination (OMC) (Mosher and Trubek 2003), as well as policy promotion and benchmarking procedures developed by international organisations such as the OECD (for example OECD 1994; see Armingeon and Beyeler 2004) and the World Bank (for example World Bank 1994; see Orenstein 2005). The crucial causal mechanisms driving policy convergence are transnational communication and the exchange of policy ideas.

A third potential cause of convergence is legal harmonisation linked to the process of European integration and the resulting growth of European law in the realm of social policy. Two main channels are relevant for suprana-tional harmonisation: on the one hand, so-called positive integration in the form of an active social policy mediated by binding EU legislation and, on the other hand, negative integration through the judicial imposition of market compatibility requirements (Leibfried and Pierson 1995; Leibfried 2005). Despite the undeniable progress that has been made in the realm of positive integration during the last 20 years or so, most authors agree that there is still a significant asymmetry in favour of negative integration (Scharpf 1999, 2002). The net effect of both types of European integration on the direction of social policy harmonisation is, however, unclear.

The fourth convergence scenario foresees a decline in social standards paralleled by a convergence towards a residual or 'liberal' model of social provision as the result of international regulatory competition. Against the backdrop of economic globalisation and the European common market, gov-ernments are being caught in a downward spiral ('race to the bottom'), re-ducing tax burdens and levels of regulation to attract mobile capital or to counter mere threats of capital exit (Sinn 2002; Tanzi 2002; cf. Mosley

2003). In a nutshell, governments have to respond to the anonymous market forces unleashed by globalisation. As Margaret Thatcher put it: 'there is no alternative' (the TINA hypothesis).

Persistence and Divergence

However, the 'mainstream' in comparative welfare state research is far from convinced about claims that welfare states have a strong tendency to become more similar. Globalisation, European integration and policy learning often play only a minor role. Instead, path dependency, domestic politics and country-specific pressures are seen as crucial in explaining the persistence of the existing policy variation or even welfare state divergence. The two most influential schools of thought are the classic theories of welfare state research ('old politics') and a more recent strand, the 'new politics of the welfare state'.

According to the 'old politics' approach, socio-economic problems do not necessarily lead to convergence since pressures always needs to be politically mediated. Consequently, the distinctive national patterns of reaction depend on institutional configurations and the political balance of power. Hence, variables such as the partisan composition of government, institutional veto positions and the cooperation of state and interest groups play a crucial role (Garrett 1998; Huber and Stephens 2001; Swank 2002; Korpi and Palme 2003). In consequence, 'old politics' scholars do not anticipate a race to the bottom triggered by globalisation.

Paul Pierson (1994, 1996, 2001), the most important representative of the 'new politics' school, also argues that the welfare state is largely immune to radical retrenchment and a race to the bottom. However, this resilience cannot be attributed to political power resources and ideological orientations but rather to institutional rigidities and a new logic underlying policymaking. The options and strategies available to contemporary political elites differ fundamentally from those that characterised the 'golden age of the welfare state': This logic is driven by a politics of blame avoidance that has restrained politicians from trying to cut back the welfare state, given that such efforts invite electoral retribution. Furthermore, radical reforms frequently fail because of the 'stickiness' of existing welfare state institutions and/or the density of institutional veto points in the political system (Pierson 1998: 552–553). As a result of external pressures, authors inclined to the 'new politics' approach expect neither radical change nor convergence but rather incremental, path-dependent reforms that can be explained by domestic political and institutional factors (see Starke 2006).

To sum up, we find several convergence scenarios in the literature, but there are also at least two influential schools that foresee either the persistence of the existing cross-national variation or even divergent trajectories for welfare states. In the following section, we analyse to what extent the development of social policy in core OECD member states is consistent with some of these scenarios. Moreover, we are interested not only in the increase or decrease of similarities but also in the direction of change, whether towards an expansion or a retrenchment of the welfare state.

TYPES OF CONVERGENCE

In general, convergence denotes increasing similarity of policies over time. However, convergence is a multi-faceted concept and several types are identified in the literature (for an overview see Knill 2005: 768–69; Heichel et al. 2005: 831–34). The most common approach to gauging convergence is to compare the variation in policies at two points in time. A decline in statistical measures of dispersion such as the standard deviation over time is denoted by the term σ-convergence (*sigma*-convergence) (Barro and Sala-i-Martin 1992; Sala-i-Martin 1994). Whereas σ-convergence focuses on cross-sectional dispersion, β-convergence (*beta*-convergence) denotes an inverse relationship between the initial value of a particular policy indicator (for example social expenditure) and its subsequent growth rate.[2] The latter type is a necessary but not sufficient condition for the former to occur (see Barro and Sala-i-Martin 1995: 31–32). A simple test for β-convergence is to correlate the starting value of a particular policy indicator with its subsequent growth rate or change for the period of interest. If the coefficient of correlation is negative, then there is evidence of β-convergence. This concept of convergence is thus equivalent with catch-up on the part of policy laggards.

The concept of δ-convergence (*delta*-convergence) provides a useful starting point for examining the TINA hypothesis. This type of convergence refers to changes in a country's distance from an exemplary model (Knill 2005: 769). The reason for introducing this type of convergence is that 'policies may approach the model by parallel moves without becoming more similar' (Heichel et al. 2005: 833). In other words, δ-convergence does not necessarily coincide with σ-convergence. The concept of δ-convergence can be fruitfully applied to the welfare state. More specifically, we examine to what extent it is reasonable to speak of a convergence towards the liberal model of welfare provision. Since this scenario is often depicted in the public debate, we use the US as a reference point and investigate whether or not other nations have converged towards this welfare regime over time. In addition to this possible 'Americanisation', we conduct a cross-check by examining whether (or not) the advanced welfare states have approached the Swedish model over time.

EMPIRICAL ANALYSIS, 1980–2001

Social Expenditure

Total social expenditure

Table 6.2 *Public social expenditure as per cent of GDP and as per cent of total government outlays*

	Social expenditure as per cent of GDP				Social expenditure as per cent of total government outlays		
	1980	1990	2001	1980-01	1990	2001[†]	1990-01
Australia	11.3	14.2	18.0	6.7	41.9	53.4	11.5
Austria	22.5	24.1	26.0	3.5	49.4	54.2	4.8
Belgium	24.1	26.9	27.2	3.1	52.2	57.0	4.8
Canada	14.3	18.6	17.8	3.5	39.7	42.6	2.9
Denmark	29.1	29.3	29.2	0.1	54.7	57.7	3.0
Finland	18.5	24.8	24.8	6.3	55.8	56.1	0.3
France	21.1	26.6	28.5	7.4	56.0	58.3	2.3
Germany	23.0	22.8	27.4	4.4	50.7	63.3	12.6
Greece	11.5	20.9	24.3	12.8	42.8	46.4	3.6
Ireland	17.0	18.6	13.8	-3.2	46.6	47.1	0.5
Italy	18.4	23.3	24.4	6.0	43.9	54.7	10.8
Japan	10.2	11.2	16.9	6.7	36.7	45.9	9.2
Netherlands	26.9	27.6	21.8	-5.1	48.7	52.4	3.7
New Zealand	17.2	21.9	18.5	1.3	--	--	--
Norway	17.9	24.7	23.9	6.0	49.7	58.6	8.9
Portugal	10.9	13.9	21.1	10.2	34.2	53.1	18.9
Spain	15.9	19.5	19.6	3.7	46.4	52.0	5.6
Sweden	28.8	30.8	28.9	0.1	52.3	55.0	2.7
Switzerland	14.2	17.9	26.4	12.2	--	--	--
United Kingdom	17.9	19.5	21.8	3.9	48.6	52.1	3.5
USA	13.3	13.4	14.8	1.5	38.0	44.4	6.4
Mean	18.3	21.4	22.6	4.4	46.9	52.8	6.1
Range	18.9	19.6	15.4	-	24.6	20.7	
Standard Deviation	5.7	5.4	4.7	-	6.8	5.4	
Coefficient of Variation	0.31	0.25	0.21	-	0.14	0.10	
Catch-up				r= -.59*			r= -.57*

Note: † = Social expenditure 2001 as per cent of total outlays of government in 2000 (Canada = 1998, Switzerland = 1999, USA = 1997); * = p < .05.

Source: OECD (2001, 2004a)

The trajectory of social expenditure between 1980 and 2001 suggests that the welfare state is *not* on the retreat. On the contrary, social expenditure as a share of GDP increased in all but two countries, Ireland and the Netherlands. The decline in the social spending to GDP ratio in Ireland results mainly from that country's exceptional economic growth, which exceeded that of all OECD countries during this period. Overall, however, the contemporary social expenditure to GDP ratio is on average more than four percentage points higher than 21 years ago. Moreover, Castles (2001: 201, 2006) has shown that the reach of the welfare state has also increased relative to other public spending categories. This becomes evident when social expenditure is expressed relative to the total government spending. These figures are displayed on the right-hand side of Table 6.2. In 2001, the corresponding ratio was higher in all advanced OECD countries than eleven years ago. Hence, the welfare state has apparently crowded out public expenditure devoted to other public policies.[3]

The rise in social expenditure was paralleled by convergence. All statistical measures of dispersion displayed in the lower part of Table 6.2 are declining and therefore indicative of σ-convergence. This also holds for the relative weight of the welfare state as calculated by the share of social expenditure in total public spending. Convergence in social spending levels was only temporarily interrupted by the economic slump of the early 1990s (Bouget 2003). In addition, σ-convergence was accompanied by β-convergence. This is indicated by the negative sign of our catch-up measure – the correlation coefficient (Pearson's r) between the initial expenditure level and the subsequent change – in the last row of Table 6.2. This is graphically illustrated in Figure 6.1 which shows that spending growth was highest in countries which had been in the rearguard of the international spending league in 1980.

An alternative test for catch-up is to examine the relationship between the timing of the adoption of core social programmes and recent social expenditure growth. The underlying assumption is that contemporary social spending levels are, among other things, likely to be influenced by the cross-national variation in the timing of welfare state consolidation which, in turn, is a proxy for the degree of maturation of contemporary welfare states. Indeed, it turns out that the scatter plot displayed in Figure 6.2, which shows the growth rate of social expenditure over the last two decades and the date when four core social security programmes (old age pensions, health insurance, work injury and unemployment compensation) were introduced on average at the national level is highly consistent with this welfare state maturation hypothesis. As expected, social expenditure growth is higher in welfare state laggards with the notable exception of the welfare states in North America. Overall, these findings lend strong support to the notion of 'growth to limits' in advanced welfare states (Flora 1986). By analogy with neoclassical growth theory, it can be argued that mature welfare states are converging towards national steady states (Iversen 2001; Kittel and Obinger 2003; Castles 2004).

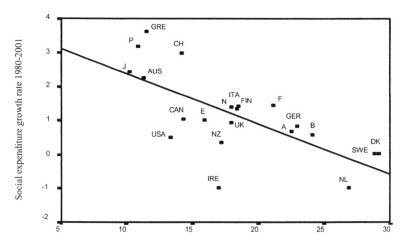

Social expenditure as % of GDP 1980

Source: OECD 2004a

Figure 6.1   Average annual social expenditure growth (in per cent), 1980–2001

We can conclude that aggregate social expenditure levels are converging. This is evident from a decline in the dispersion of spending levels over time, which in turn is driven by strong catch-up among the spending laggards. Hence we find evidence that σ-convergence and β-convergence coincide. With respect to the direction of change, social expenditure levels have increased, in both absolute and relative terms – which runs counter to expectations of a 'race to the bottom' (see Castles 2004).

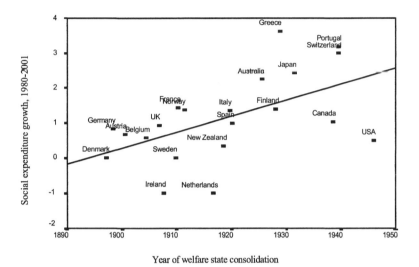

Year of welfare state consolidation

Source: OECD 2004a. Data on the timing of the introduction of the four programmes are
taken from Schmidt (2005)

*Figure 6.2   Social expenditure growth 1980–2001 and welfare state
consolidation*

Social expenditure in cash and in kind

Turning now to the pattern of expenditure convergence at a more disaggre-
gate level, we first test to what extent the relation between social expenditure
in cash and in kind has changed and whether convergence of some sort can
be observed during the 1980 to 2001 period. The question as to whether expenditure is provided in cash (i.e. via income transfers) or in kind (in the
form of social services, for example childcare services or elderly care) is not
a trivial one. Indeed, one of the central characteristics of national welfare
state regimes lies precisely in the roles of transfers and services in the particular 'welfare mix'. Usually, the main distinction is between transfer-heavy
continental European (as well as some of the English-speaking) welfare
states and the service-oriented Nordic countries. Recently, however, social
services have attracted a lot of attention from social policy researchers and
practitioners alike, due to their alleged problem-solving capacities when it
comes to finding answers to 'new' challenges such as declining birth-rates,
long-term unemployment and new employment and family structures.

Table 6.3 presents transfer and service expenditure data (as share of GDP) for 21 OECD countries for the years 1980 and 2001. A number of observations are relevant here. The first basic conclusion that can be drawn from the table is that – as for total public expenditure – there is no empirical evidence in favour of the 'race to the bottom' hypothesis. Granted, a number of countries – namely Denmark, Ireland, the Netherlands, New Zealand, Sweden and the USA – have lowered expenditure in cash, and Ireland has reduced social expenditure in kind relative to GDP, although once again the Irish case has to be seen against the backdrop of record growth in GDP. However, these are exceptions. Overall, there has been an increase of 2.2 percentage points in the mean expenditure devoted to both income transfers and social services in the core OECD. Moreover, the average cash/service ratio has tilted slightly towards services, from 0.56 to 0.63 (not shown in the table).

Have countries converged with respect to public social expenditure in cash and in kind? Yes, they have, in both cases. All the convergence indicators – the range, standard deviation and coefficient of variation – diminished between 1980 and 2001. As in the case of total public social expenditure, therefore, there is evidence of quite substantial σ-convergence. What is more, convergence was even slightly stronger for service expenditure (as can be seen from the reduction in the coefficient of variation). Moreover, the negative correlation coefficients in the last row of Table 6.3 suggest that there was a moderate level of β-convergence, or catch-up. Countries such as Belgium and the Netherlands with high initial cash spending froze or even reduced transfer expenditure, whereas 'cash transfer laggards' such as Australia, Canada and Japan experienced above-average growth in transfer expenditure as a share of GDP. The same is true of social services. In-kind expenditure growth in Sweden and other 'social service states' stagnated, whereas the laggards of Southern and Continental Europe substantially expanded their commitment in the area of social service provision.

Table 6.3 *Public social expenditure in cash and in kind, in percentage of GDP, 1980 and 2001*

	Public social expenditure in cash			Public social expenditure in kind		
	1980	2001	1980–2001	1980	2001	1980–2001
Australia	6.4	10.0	3.6	5.0	8.0	3.0
Austria	16.5	19.1	2.6	5.9	6.9	1.0
Belgium	18.5	18.5	0.0	5.7	8.7	3.0
Canada	5.9	8.4	2.5	8.4	9.8	1.4
Denmark	16.2	15.4	-0.8	12.8	13.8	1.0
Finland	11.2	15.6	4.4	7.3	9.1	1.8
France	14.4	18.3	3.9	6.7	10.2	3.5
Germany	15.2	15.9	0.7	7.8	11.5	3.7
Greece	7.7	16.5	8.8	3.8	7.8	4.0
Ireland	9.6	7.9	-1.7	7.4	5.8	-1.6
Italy	12.5	18.7	6.2	6.0	7.2	1.2
Japan	5.3	9.1	3.8	4.9	7.8	2.9
Netherlands	20.1	13.7	-6.4	6.8	8.0	1.2
New Zealand	11.9	11.6	-0.3	5.3	6.9	1.6
Norway	10.0	11.6	1.6	7.9	12.3	4.4
Portugal	7.2	13.3	6.1	3.7	7.8	4.1
Spain	11.4	13.2	1.8	4.5	6.4	1.9
Sweden	14.8	14.6	-0.2	14.1	14.3	0.2
Switzerland	9.9	18.3	8.4	4.2	8.1	3.9
United Kingdom	11.6	13.7	2.1	6.4	8.1	1.7
USA	8.5	8.0	-0.5	4.8	6.7	1.9
Mean	11.7	13.9	2.2	6.6	8.8	2.2
Range	14.8	11.2		10.4	8.5	
Standard deviation	4.2	3.7		2.7	2.4	
Coefficient of variation	0.36	0.27		0.41	0.27	
Catch-up			r = -.55*			r = -.46*

Note: Significance: * = p < 0.05.

Source: Data are based on OECD 2004a; data kindly provided by Francis G. Castles

Welfare State Funding

When the focus shifts from expenditures to revenues, the picture is roughly similar. Compared to social spending, however, the convergence is less pronounced and not consistent for different statistical measures of dispersion.

Table 6.4   *Welfare state funding, 1980 and 2001*

	Total taxation as per cent of GDP			Social security contributions as per cent of GDP			Social security contributions as per cent of total taxation		
	1980	2001	Change	1980	2001	Change	1980	2001	Change
Australia	27.2	30.4	3.2	0.0	0.0	0.0	0.0	0.0	0.0
Austria	39.8	45.2	5.4	12.3	14.8	2.5	30.9	32.7	1.8
Belgium	42.4	45.9	3.5	12.3	14.4	2.1	29.0	31.4	2.4
Canada	30.9	35.0	4.1	3.3	5.1	1.8	10.7	14.6	3.9
Denmark	43.9	49.9	6.0	0.8	2.2	1.4	1.8	4.4	2.6
Finland	36.2	46.0	9.8	8.4	12.4	4.0	23.2	27.0	3.8
France	40.6	44.9	4.3	8.4	16.2	7.8	42.9	36.1	-6.8
Germany	37.5	36.8	-0.7	12.9	14.6	1.7	34.4	39.7	5.3
Greece	24.2	36.6	12.4	7.9	11.7	3.8	32.6	32.0	-0.7
Ireland	31.4	30.1	-1.3	4.5	4.3	-0.2	14.3	14.3	0.0
Italy	30.4	43.0	12.6	11.6	12.3	0.7	38.2	28.6	-9.5
Japan	25.3	27.4	2.1	7.4	10.3	2.9	29.2	37.6	8.3
Netherlands	43.6	39.8	-3.8	16.6	14.4	-2.2	38.1	36.2	-1.9
New Zealand	30.6	33.3	2.7	0.0	0.0	0.0	0.0	0.0	0.0
Norway	42.5	43.3	0.8	9.0	9.2	0.2	21.2	21.2	0.0
Portugal	24.1	35.6	11.5	7.1	11.0	3.9	29.5	30.9	1.4
Spain	23.1	35.0	11.9	11.2	12.5	1.3	48.5	35.7	-12.8
Sweden	47.3	51.9	4.6	13.6	15.3	1.7	28.7	29.5	0.7
Switzerland	28.0	30.0	2.0	8.5	7.7	-0.8	30.4	25.7	-4.7
UK	35.2	37.2	2.0	5.9	6.3	0.4	16.8	16.9	0.2
USA	26.4	28.9	2.5	5.8	7.0	1.2	22.0	24.2	2.2
Mean	33.9	38.4	4.6	8.0	9.6	1.6	24.9	24.7	-0.2
Range	24.2	24.5	16.4	16.6	16.2	10.0	48.5	39.7	21.1
Standard deviation	7.7	7.2		4.6	5.1		13.6	12.1	
Coefficient of variation	0.23	0.19		0.57	0.53		0.55	0.49	
Catch-up			r = -.40			r =.02			r = -.47*

Note: Significance: * = p < 0.05.

Source: OECD (2004b).

Table 6.4 shows the evolution of total taxation, social security contributions (both expressed as a percentage of GDP) and the contribution/tax ratio over the last two decades. Note that, from the outset, the variation in the revenue mix of different welfare states has been substantial. Some countries finance a large part of social expenditure through earmarked social contributions whereas others, such as the Danish and the New Zealand welfare states, are based more or less exclusively on (direct and indirect) taxes. There are reasons to expect particularly strong pressure on social contributions, however. Since contributions make up the largest component of non-wage labour costs, globalists would expect a roll-back of this type of revenue and, in consequence, convergence in welfare state financing. Yet the figures presented in Table 6.4 tell a different story. Social security contributions in fact increased, while the cross-national dispersion decreased slightly. Similar developments can be seen for the total tax/GDP ratio as well as for the welfare state funding patterns reflected in the ratio of social security contributions to total tax revenue. In addition to σ-convergence, our indicator mapping the funding patterns shows signs of β-convergence, mainly caused by a considerable reduction in contribution funding in those countries with a high initial share of social security contributions (see last three columns of Table 6.4).

Replacement Rates

An analysis of social expenditure is certainly not sufficient to get a balanced picture of recent developments in the welfare state. Rising spending levels neither rule out a decline in welfare state generosity on the micro level nor do they provide compelling evidence that globalists are wrong in seeing globalisation as the great equalizer of welfare states.[4] In order to provide better insights into the black box of social spending, researchers affiliated to the Swedish Institute for Social Research developed the Social Citizenship Indicator Programme (SCIP), a data set providing information about benefit levels, coverage and the funding principles of social insurance programmes in 18 OECD countries since 1930. Unfortunately, we can report only the empirical results of this research programme because the data set is not publicly accessible. Though this data set does not capture the entire welfare state and is not free from difficulties,[5] the empirical findings are extremely intriguing and challenge the argument that welfare states are immune to cutbacks.

This group of researchers has also examined whether there is any evidence for convergence of net replacement rates, coverage and funding patterns. In their analysis of four social insurance schemes over the 1960–2000 period, Montanari (2001) and Montanari and Palme (2004) find that benefit levels declined in the 1990s, but they do not detect strong evidence of convergence in replacement rates in 18 OECD countries. This also holds when the analysis is restricted to 11 EU member states.

Unemployment insurance is the only scheme where the standard deviation in both samples declined after 1980. Montanari and Palme therefore conclude that cross-national differences in benefit levels remained largely intact during the period in question.

Table 6.5   Net replacement rates in 18 countries, 1980 and 2001

| | Social Insurance Programme | | | | | |
| | Sickness | | Unemployment | | Standard pension | |
	1980	2001	1980	2001	1980	2001
Australia	0.42	0.47	0.39	0.47	0.35	0.38
Austria	0.81	0.85	0.66	0.64	0.74	0.77
Belgium	0.86	0.87	0.67	0.60	0.82	0.76
Canada	0.62	0.67	0.62	0.67	0.49	0.61
Denmark	0.79	0.63	0.79	0.63	0.52	0.58
Finland	0.48	0.72	0.41	0.61	0.57	0.61
France	0.60	0.62	0.64	0.65	0.63	0.55
Germany	1.00	0.93	0.69	0.66	0.71	0.63
Ireland	0.72	0.41	0.72	0.41	0.43	0.45
Italy	0.70	0.79	0.08	0.45	0.58	0.88
Japan	0.50	0.59	0.67	0.61	0.61	0.61
Netherlands	0.87	0.76	0.87	0.76	0.61	0.55
New Zealand	0.49	0.42	0.46	0.42	0.49	0.48
Norway	1.00	1.00	0.73	0.68	0.55	0.63
Sweden	0.97	0.82	0.83	0.70	0.66	0.61
Switzerland	0.83	0.00	0.76	0.78	0.48	0.49
United Kingdom	0.55	0.24	0.55	0.36	0.43	0.56
USA	0.00	0.00	0.65	0.56	0.65	0.68
Mean	0.68	0.60	0.62	0.59	0.57	0.60
Range	1.0	1.0	0.79	0.42	0.47	0.49
Standard deviation	0.25	0.29	0.19	0.12	0.12	0.12
Coefficient of variation	0.37	0.49	0.30	0.21	0.21	0.20
Catch-up	$r = -0.27$		$r = -0.76$**		$r = -0.39$	

Note: Significance: ** = significant on 0.01 level.

Source: Scruggs (2004). For some countries missing data for 1980 and 2001 were substituted by figures for 1981 and 2000 respectively.

Lyle Scruggs (2004) recently compiled a data set on welfare state entitlements in 18 OECD countries. The data set is publicly available and provides information on the benefits offered by three social insurance schemes between 1971 and 2002. Replacement rates are calculated for different household types in relation to an average production worker's wage. In addition, the data collection contains information about qualifying conditions and coverage rates. We have utilized this data set to examine whether or not net replacement rates converged between 1980 and 2001. In line with Allan and Scruggs (2004) we used the average replacement rate for a single person and that for a family consisting of two adults and two children for each of the three schemes. Table 6.5 shows benefit levels for the years 1980 and 2001.

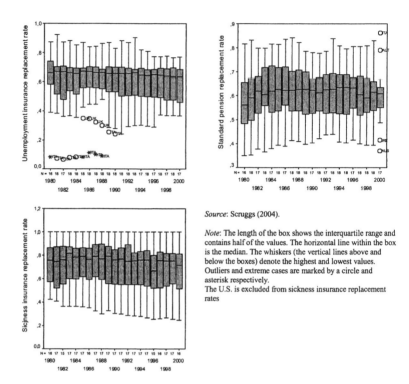

Figure 6.3   Cross-national variation in replacement rates, 1980–2000

First of all, these figures show that the average level of sickness and unemployment benefits declined. In terms of convergence, unemployment
benefits show signs not only of σ-convergence – as evident from the substantial decline in all measures of dispersion over time – but also of strong β-
convergence. The coincidence of a declining mean and shrinking variance
suggests a sort of 'race to the bottom'. In contrast, there is no evidence of
convergence of any kind in the replacement rates offered by pension and
sickness cash benefits.

This is also evident when we look at Figure 6.3. Since Table 6.5 is based
on only two points of observation, we have constructed box plots for each
year in order to map the fluctuations in the distribution of replacement rates
over the entire period (Figure 6.3). Judged by the length of the boxes and the
respective whiskers, the box plots strongly confirm the findings summarised
in Table 6.5. A decline in the cross-national dispersion can be observed only
for unemployment insurance replacement rates. Extreme laggards such as

Italy increased benefits, whereas the most generous countries reduced their level of unemployment compensation.

Decommodification

In this section we examine whether social policy outcomes are subject to convergence. More specifically, we are interested in changes in the extent of and cross-national variation in decommodification. Decommodification refers to the degree to which individuals can maintain a decent standard of living independently of (labour) market participation (Esping-Andersen 1990). It is highest if benefits are based on social rights, i.e. not granted on the basis of means tests and without barriers to entitlement barriers such as qualifying periods. Decommodification is one of the crucial distinguishing features underpinning Esping-Andersen's classification of welfare regimes.

Following the methodology used by Esping-Andersen (1990), Scruggs (2004) has calculated annual cross-national decommodification scores based on qualifying conditions, generosity of replacement rates and coverage. Table 6.6 reports these scores, which are the sum of the decommodification scores for each of the three schemes already discussed. The summary statistics reported in the lower rows point to a remarkable stability in the degree of decommodification. There is neither a decline nor any evidence of σ- or β-convergence.

Given the prominent role given to decommodification in Esping-Andersen's regime typology, the presence of δ-convergence would suggest that welfare regimes are crumbling and possibly that welfare states are becoming increasingly isomorphic. In general, this type of convergence reflects convergence towards a particular reference model. On the one hand, as we have seen in the section following on from the introduction, one prominent theory suggests that welfare states will converge towards the bottom of the distribution. In terms of decommodification, this bottom position was held by the United States, with an overall score of 18.6 in 1980. The concept of δ-convergence can be used to test empirically the extent to which countries have approached the US decommodification level or, in other words, to what extent 'Americanization' – which is also one of the buzzwords of the public debate on the future of the welfare state – has indeed taken place.

As can easily be seen from Table 6.6, such a shift has clearly *not* taken place. In only 5 of 17 logically possible cases did countries reduce their distance from the US level of decommodification between 1980 and 2001. These cases are shown in bold.

Table 6.6   *Decommodification scores and country-specific distances relative to the US and Sweden, 1980 and 2001*

	DECOM 1980	DECOM 2001	Distance from USA 1980	Distance from USA 2001	Distance from Sweden 1980	Distance from Sweden[6] 2001
Australia	20.1	18.3	1.4	**0.0**	16.3	**14.3**
Austria	27.8	28.7	9.2	10.4	8.6	**3.9**
Belgium	30.5	30.9	11.9	12.7	5.9	**1.6**
Canada	25.0	25.1	6.3	6.8	11.4	**7.5**
Denmark	33.0	34.8	14.3	16.6	3.4	**-2.3**
Finland	27.9	30.1	9.3	11.9	8.5	**2.4**
France	27.8	27.1	9.1	**8.8**	8.7	**5.5**
Germany	29.6	30.5	11.0	12.3	6.8	**2.0**
Ireland	21.8	26.7	3.2	8.4	14.6	**5.9**
Italy	20.6	26.5	1.9	8.3	15.8	**6.0**
Japan	20.0	21.4	1.4	3.1	16.4	**11.2**
Netherlands	31.8	34.4	13.2	16.2	4.6	**-1.9**
New Zealand	23.8	23.0	5.2	**4.7**	12.6	**9.6**
Norway	33.5	37.2	14.9	19.0	2.9	**-4.7**
Sweden	36.4	32.6	17.8	**14.3**	0.0	**0.0**
Switzerland	32.2	21.8	13.6	**3.5**	4.2	**10.8**
United Kingdom	22.9	24.8	4.2	6.5	13.5	**7.7**
USA	18.6	18.3	0.0	0.0	17.8	**14.3**
Mean	26.9	27.3				
Range	17.8	19.0				
Standard deviation	5.4	5.6				
Coefficient of variation	0.20	0.20				
Catch-up	r = -0.30					

Note: The catch-up indicator denotes the correlation coefficient (Pearson's r) between the initial decommodification scores (DECOM) and the change between 1980 and 2001.

Source: Scruggs (2004), own calculations

Moreover, we cross-checked this result with an empirical analysis of the counter-scenario, which might be called 'Swedenisation'. 'Swedenisation' is defined as any reduction in the distance between a country's decommodification score and that of Sweden – the welfare state with the highest score at the beginning of the period. There are also substantive reasons for using Sweden as a benchmark. Particularly in Europe, welfare state advocates frequently argue that countries should strive to emulate the Nordic or social democratic welfare state model, most closely associated with Sweden, as it may be a viable way to combine a high level of social security with favourable macro-economic and labour-market performance. The result of our analysis of δ-convergence is striking. Except for Switzerland, all countries moved closer to the Swedish level of decommodification between 1980 and 2001! Of course, this is in part due to the fact that even Sweden reduced its high decommodification score somewhat, but nonetheless this is a remarkable demonstration of the fact that, if anything, the US is by no means the 'vanishing point' for the recent reform trajectories of advanced OECD welfare states.

Qualitative Policy Convergence

Analysis of aggregate levels of social expenditure and replacement rates may well leave undetected social policy developments that may be indicative of a creeping convergence in the configuration of welfare states (Gilbert 2002). Social protection in OECD member states relies on a vast diversity of policy instruments, ranging from mandated provision, wage regulation and tax expenditure to publicly provided social services and transfer payments. Some of these instruments are not easily captured by analyses of social expenditure. Consequently, a finding of spending stability does not preclude major policy changes. In short, an analysis of expenditure itself is not enough to deliver a balanced judgment (Castles 1994: 350). The question here, therefore, is whether or not isomorphism, i.e. a clear trend towards similar policy instruments and welfare state institutions across countries, can be observed. This question is investigated with reference to four welfare state areas (pensions, labour market policy, health care and family policy) that have undergone quite extensive reforms in the last 20 years or so. However, we can provide only a broad-brush overview of recent reform activities, a more nuanced in-depth study being beyond the scope of this chapter.

1. *Pensions.* An often cited example in this respect is the emergence of multi-pillar pension systems (Orenstein 2005), with state pensions being increasingly supplemented by occupational and private pensions. Recent pension reforms have strengthened the importance of private, defined contribution components in the retirement income mix (Hinrichs 2006). Thus new, funded instruments with defined contribution schemes are being added to the existing pay-as-you-go systems offering defined benefits. Only a few countries, for instance New Zealand, have so far largely resisted such changes. Upon closer inspection, however, the concept of a 'multi-pillar pension system' appears quite diverse. What pension reforms virtually everywhere have in common is that the income package of future beneficiaries will rely on a mix of state and occupational pensions as well as individual saving accounts (Hinrichs 2006). However, the precise mix of the various 'pillars', average benefit

levels, the redistributive aspect and the state's role in all this still varies a great deal. Moreover, the options for reform are constrained to some extent by the institutional make-up of existing pension arrangements. Countries already operating a multi-pillar system have been more active in introducing reforms than countries where benefit provision has traditionally been more or less monopolised by the state. These latter have begun to put in place multi-pillar systems while at the same time reforming state pensions in such a way as to tighten the links between contributions and benefits, raise the retirement age or modify indexing formulas (Hinrichs 2006).

2. *Labour market policy.* In a similar vein, it has been argued that OECD countries have shifted the emphasis from passive labour market policy to activation. Activation comprises not only 'active labour market policies' in a narrow sense – for example training schemes or direct work creation programmes which, in many countries, have been in place for decades – but, more generally, policies that make assistance dependent, if at all possible, on reciprocal activity of some sort. In this sense, activation is also increasingly becoming part of previously 'passive' assistance schemes, through the addition of compulsory work requirements and the imposition of stricter sanctions. This also applies in some cases to social assistance schemes targeted at groups other than the unemployed. Moreover, the type of activity beneficiaries take up ranges from strict 'workfare', where benefit receipt is tied to compulsory work of some sort, to 'softer' schemes that offer beneficiaries individual assistance and a variety of options to choose from, including job-creation programmes, retraining and intensive case management. Put simply, the individual mix of 'carrot' and 'stick' varies substantially across welfare states. In general, it is fair to say that in all countries cuts in unemployment benefits (as shown earlier) combined with activation policies have raised expectations of work and strengthened individual obligations (see Clasen et al. 2001; Lødemel and Trickey 2001 for comparative studies). It would probably be premature to talk of clear convergence in this field, since these new obligations are only one part of more general labour market reforms in virtually all countries and they could well lead to greater divergence. In Denmark, for instance, 'activation' is but one element of the generous but market-friendly 'flexicurity' approach, whereas in English-speaking countries there is a trend towards workfare combined with in-work benefits – for example tax credits – to prop up low wages in less regulated markets in order to 'make work pay'. The spread of negative income taxes and in-work-benefits across the English-speaking world (Nolan 2006) is, in our view, an important example of conditional convergence, in the sense that the adoption of similar policies is restricted

to families of nations sharing similar welfare state architectures and belief systems. It is not yet clear to what extent recent policy changes in Continental European countries – namely Germany, Italy and perhaps France – may eventually converge on one or the other options – or even constitute a third path of labour market adjustment conditioned by a different policy legacy.

3. *Health care* is characterised by increased private co-funding. User charges and co-payments for consultations, hospital treatments and prescription drugs are now well established in many countries. As a result, the share of private health care funding has increased in the entire OECD area. This recalibration of the public-private mix is also evident in the fact that some countries with universal health systems have tried to introduce quasi-markets and so-called purchaser/provider splits into their systems. Examples include the UK, the Netherlands and New Zealand. Continental countries like Germany, whose health care systems have traditionally been characterized by corporatist self-governance, have strengthened competition among providers, while liberal health care systems increasingly rely on hierarchical modes of governance such as 'managed care' in the US. Thus the various types of health care systems have adopted modes of governance hitherto unfamiliar to that type, which has led to a blurring of health care regulatory regimes (Rothgang et al. 2005: 207). In contrast, convergence is discernible neither in service provision nor in benefit packages.

4. *Family policy* seems to be a top priority in contemporary social policy. Parental leave schemes (including childcare leave for fathers) have spread across countries and although the precise entitlements still vary significantly between welfare states (Tanaka 2005; Henderson and White 2004), there is now only one country among the core OECD members without any form of paid parental leave: the United States. Transfer payments and the number of childcare facilities have also increased despite (or because of?) a declining number of children. In addition, unpaid family work is now taken into account in the calculation of individual pension entitlements in many countries. Despite this change of emphasis in all countries, there are good reasons to doubt that convergence will be as marked as some expect. While Nordic nations have strengthened 'defamilialisation' by transferring many family tasks and responsibilities to social services, most Continental European and English-speaking countries have opted to support family incomes, either through transfer payments or tax benefits. Micro-level studies of entitlements show that the pioneers in this field – mainly to be found in Northern Europe – have continued to expand their commitment to families, whereas the English-speaking or 'liberal' welfare states have not

kept pace with this expansion, particularly in the area of state support for working parents. The result has been divergence, not convergence (Gauthier 2002).

In sum, closer examination of recent policy reforms reveals an interesting picture. While many countries have taken fairly similar paths in attempting to deal with a fairly similar set of priorities, there are few signs of direct policy convergence. Even in fields such as labour market policies, where 'activation' is the buzzword throughout the OECD, there are persistent differences and distinct combinations of instruments and approaches across welfare states. With respect to policy reforms, our conclusion, albeit a tentative one, is that goals are converging while the means used to achieve them are diverging (or at least remaining different). Seeleib-Kaiser (2001) coined the term 'divergent convergence' to describe this phenomenon. Of course, welfare policies always have a wide range of objectives to be achieved simultaneously. However, some of these objectives have been placed high on the agenda virtually everywhere. Family policy, for instance, has been acknowledged as one of the crucial fields of state intervention, regarded as essential in order to alleviate child poverty and achieve a suitable work/life balance and other overarching objectives. Similarly, multi-pillar pension schemes have been promoted in several countries in order to respond to demographic developments and to allow for some diversification of risk. More generally, and in line with the dual transformation of the welfare state as exemplified by the German case (Bleses and Seeleib-Kaiser 2004), increasing state intervention in family policy, combined with partial privatisation of pensions, can be observed across the OECD area.

Nevertheless, different countries are using different means to achieve these goals and, although they often borrow heavily from each other, there is little evidence of a common reform trajectory towards a uniform model – be it at the 'bottom' or the 'top' of the league. What can be observed, however, is a good deal of experimentation with models of provision and structures of entitlements imported from other regime types. As a result, we have what might be called a 'blurring of regimes' (Goodin and Rein 2001) or regime 'trespassing' (Esping-Andersen 2005: 929). This is a necessary but insufficient condition for structural convergence. Even though the demarcation lines between different welfare regimes have not disappeared, they are now less polarised than they were in the 'golden age' of capitalism.

CONCLUSION

In this chapter we have used a broad range of social policy indicators to examine whether or not welfare states have converged over the two decades between 1980 and 2001. This period was characterised by fundamental changes in the international political economy that were paralleled by mounting domestic challenges resulting from population ageing, the emergence of new social risks, deindustrialisation and an unfavourable economic performance. Many social policy scholars have argued that these challenges are likely to trigger a convergence of welfare states, although there are conflicting views about the direction in which the mean of the distribution will move.

Table 6.7   Overview of results

Indicator	Change of mean (direction)	Convergence?	Type of convergence
Social expenditure			
Total	upwards	yes	sigma, beta
In cash	upwards	yes	sigma, beta
In kind	upwards	yes	sigma, beta
Funding			
Taxes	upwards	(yes)	sigma
Contributions	upwards	(yes)	sigma
Financing structure	stability	yes	sigma, beta
Replacement rates			
Sickness	downwards	no	---
Unemployment	downwards	yes	sigma, beta
Pensions	upwards	no	---
Decommodification			
level	stability	no	---
delta (US)	---	no	---
delta (Sweden)	---	yes	delta

Our findings are heterogeneous and thus coincide fully with a recent article reviewing convergence research in public policy (Heichel et al. 2005: 820). Heichel et al. speculate that the conflicting findings in the empirical literature might originate from differences in the sample, time period and the dependent variable under investigation. In this chapter we have compared the development of a broad set of welfare state indicators for a coherent sample and time period. Our main finding is that convergence critically hinges on the dependent variable under review. The same holds for the trend change in the mean distribution (see Table 6.7).

Nonetheless, the majority of indicators analysed point to convergence. However, the degree of convergence is generally rather moderate. In addition, the direction of change varies, as does the type of convergence. More specifically, we found convergence in social spending which was paralleled by rising spending levels. On the funding side, the increase in revenue was to a very limited extent accompanied by convergence. In terms of benefit levels, our analysis uncovered a decline in benefit generosity, with strong convergent trends restricted to unemployment insurance. No changes whatsoever were found in cross-national levels of decommodification. Interestingly, rather than following the liberal path towards the American welfare model, countries appear to be moving towards the Swedish level of decommodification.

Our brief overview of recent reform trends in four programme areas suggests increasing similarities in policy goals but persisting cross-national variations in the instruments used to achieve these goals. When the mosaic is assembled, it depicts limited convergence at best. What can definitely be ruled out is the 'race to the bottom scenario' hypothesised by globalists. In contrast, the findings lend more support to neo-functionalists predicting upwards convergence. Moreover, the existence of convergence and the similarity of the objectives being pursued are also consistent with theories of policy learning and harmonisation. And yet the degree of convergence is limited and the implementation of common goals varies across countries. This is where mainstream comparative welfare state research, with its emphasis on the role of domestic politics and institutional inertia arising from path dependency, comes into play. Politics still seems to be playing an important role in shaping national adjustment pathways during the 'silver age of the welfare state' (Taylor-Gooby 2002). Perhaps, however, this is all just a matter of time – after all, the literature on path dependency has taught us that welfare states tend to react like supertankers. Current changes, even small ones, can lead to large departures from an earlier course in the long run.

NOTES

1. In the case of the core OECD welfare states at least, we are not aware of any convergence studies that focus on *imposition* by other countries or international organisations. Imposition is therefore not included in Table 6.1.
2. However, a lack of *absolute* convergence does not mean that convergence does not exist at all because convergence may depend upon a broad set of contextual parameters. This type of convergence is referred to as *conditional* β-convergence, which is based on the assumption that catch-up of laggards is conditioned by a broad set of political, economic and institutional factors beyond the initial value of the dependent variable. Hence, catch-up of laggards only

occurs once the effects of a set of other variables are controlled for. Technically speaking, the baseline model is augmented by additional right-hand side variables to hold the effects of other variables affecting the position of the steady-state constant.

3. For an early account of this crowding-out argument see Cerny (1995).
4. For instance, rising spending levels may be driven by increased case loads connected to unemployment caused by globalisation (Cerny 1995; Clayton and Pontusson 1998).
5. The main problem is to make benefit levels comparable across different and often occupationally fragmented social insurance schemes. In addition, benefits stemming from other social transfer payments, tax breaks for social purposes and social services are not captured.
6. Negative signs reflect the fact that Norway, Denmark and the Netherlands have overtaken Sweden as the top decommodifiers in 2001.

REFERENCES

Allan, J. and L. Scruggs (2004), 'Political Partisanship and Welfare State Reform in Advanced Industrial Societies', *American Journal of Political Science*, **48** (3), 496–512.

Armingeon, Klaus and Michelle Beyeler (eds) (2004), *The OECD and European Welfare States*, Cheltenham, UK and Northampton, MA: Edward Elgar.

Armingeon, Klaus and Giuliano Bonoli (eds) (2006), *The Politics of Post-industrial Welfare States. Adopting Post-war Social Policies to New Social Risks*, London and New York: Routledge.

Barro, R.J. and X. Sala-i-Martin (1992), 'Convergence', *Journal of Political Economy*, **100** (2), 223–51.

Barro, Robert J. and Xavier Sala-i-Martin (1995), *Economic Growth*, New York: McGraw-Hill.

Bleses, Peter and Martin Seeleib-Kaiser (2004), *Dual Transformation of the German Welfare State*, Basingstoke, UK: Palgrave Macmillan.

Bouget, D. (2003), 'Convergence in the Social Welfare Systems in Europe: From Goal to Reality', *Social Policy & Administration*, **37** (6), 674–93.

Castles, F.G. (1994), 'Is Expenditure Enough? On the Nature of the Dependent Variable in Comparative Public Policy Analysis', *Journal of Commonwealth & Comparative Politics*, **32** (3), 349–63.

Castles, F.G. (2001), 'On the Political Economy of Recent Public Sector Development', *Journal of European Social Policy*, **11** (3), 195–211.

Castles, Francis G. (2004), *The Future of The Welfare State*, Oxford: Oxford University Press.

Castles, Francis G. (2006), *The Growth of the Post-war Public Expenditure State: Long-term Trajectories and Recent Trends*, TranState Working Paper No. 35, Bremen: TranState Research Centre.

Cerny, P.G. (1995), 'Globalization and the Changing Logic of Collective Action', *International Organization*, **49** (4), 595–625.

Clasen, Jochen, Jon Kvist and Wim van Oorschot (2001), 'On Condition of Work: Increasing Work Requirements in Unemployment Compensation Schemes', in Mikko Kautto, Johan Fritzell, Bjørn Hvinden, Jon Kvist and Hannu Uusitalo (eds), *Nordic Welfare States in the European Context*, London and New York: Routledge, pp. 198–231.

Clayton, R. and J. Pontusson (1998), 'Welfare State Retrenchment Revisted. Entitlement Cuts, Public Sector Restructuring, and Inegalitarian Trends in Advanced Capitalist Societies', *World Politics*, **51** (1), 67–98.

Esping-Andersen, Gøsta (1990), *The Three Worlds of Welfare Capitalism*, Cambridge: Polity Press.

Esping-Andersen, G. (2005), 'New Risks, New Welfare, Book Review of Peter Taylor-Gooby (ed.)', *Perspectives on Politics*, **3**, 929–30.

Flora, Peter (ed.) (1986), *Growth to Limits*, Berlin: de Gruyter.

Garrett, Geoffrey (1998), *Partisan Politics in the Global Economy*, Cambridge: Cambridge University Press.

Gauthier, A.H. (2002), 'Family Policies in Industrialized Countries: Is There Convergence?', *Population*, **57** (3), 447–74.

Gilbert, Neil (2002), *Transformation of the Welfare State: The Silent Surrender of Public Responsibility*, Oxford: Oxford University Press.

Goodin, R.E. and M. Rein (2001), 'Regime on Pillars: Alternative Welfare State Logics and Dynamics', *Public Administration*, **79** (4), 769–801.

Heichel, S., J. Pape and T. Sommerer (2005), 'Is There Convergence in Convergence Research? An Overview of Empirical Studies on Policy Convergence', *Journal of European Public Policy*, **12** (5), 817–40.

Henderson, A. and L.A. White (2004), 'Shrinking Welfare States? Comparing Maternity Leave Benefits and Child Care Programs in European Union and North American Welfare states, 1985–2000', *Journal of European Public Policy*, **11** (3), 497–519.

Hinrichs, Karl (2001), 'Elephants on the Move. Patterns of Public Pension Reform in OECD Countries', in Stephan Leibfried (ed.), *Welfare State Futures*, Cambridge: Cambridge University Press, pp. 77–102.

Hinrichs, Karl (2006), 'Pension Reforms in Europe: Convergence of Old-age Security Systems?', in Per Kristen Mydske and Ingo Peters (eds), *The Transformation of the European Nation-state*, Berlin: Berliner Wissenschafts-Verlag, pp. 71–92.

Hinrichs, K. and O. Kangas (2003), 'When Is a Change Big Enough To Be a System Shift? Small System-shifting Changes in German and Finnish Pension Policies', *Social Policy & Administration*, **37** (6), 573–91.

Holzinger, K. and C. Knill (2005), 'Causes and Conditions of Cross-national Policy Convergence', *Journal of European Public Policy*, **12** (5), 775–96.

Huber, Evelyne and John D. Stephens (2001), *Development and Crisis of the Welfare State: Parties and Policies in Global Markets*, Chicago: University of Chicago Press.

Iversen, Torben (2001), 'The Dynamics of Welfare State Expansion: Trade Openness, De-industrialization, and Partisan Politics', in Paul Pierson (ed.), *The New Politics of the Welfare State*, Oxford: Oxford University Press, pp. 45–79.

Iversen, T. and T.R. Cusack (2000), 'The Causes of Welfare State Expansion: Deindustrialization or Globalization?', *World Politics*, **52** (3), 313–49.

Kerr, Clark, John T. Dunlap, Frederick H. Harbison and Charles A. Myers (1960), *Industrialism and Industrial Man*, Cambridge: Harvard University Press.

Kittel, B. and H. Obinger (2003), 'Political Parties, Institutions, and the Dynamics of Social Expenditure in Times of Austerity', *Journal of European Public Policy*, **10** (1), 20–45.

Knill, C. (2005), 'Introduction: Cross-national Public Policy Convergence: Concepts, Approaches and Explanatory Factors', *Journal of European Public Policy*, **12** (5), 764–74.

Korpi, W. and J. Palme (2003), 'New Politics and Class Politics in the Context of Austerity and Globalization: Welfare States Regress in 18 Countries, 1975–95', *American Political Science Review*, **97** (3), 425–46.

Leibfried, Stephan and Paul Pierson (eds) (1995), *European Social Policy. Between Fragmentation and Integration*, Washington, DC: Brookings Institution.

Leibfried, Stephan (2005), 'Social Policy. Left To Courts and Markets?', in Helen Wallace, William Wallace and Mark A. Pollack (eds), *Policy-making in the European Union*, Oxford: Oxford University Press.

Lødemel, Ivar and Heather Trickey (eds) (2001), *An Offer You Can't Refuse – Workfare in International Perspective*, Bristol: The Policy Press.

Montanari, I. (2001), 'Modernization, Globalization and the Welfare State: A Comparative Analysis of Old and New Convergence of Social Insurance Since 1930', *British Journal of Sociology*, **52** (3), 469–94.

Montanari, Ingalill and Joakim Palme (2004), *Convergence Pressures and Responses: Recent Social Insurance Developments in Modern Welfare States*, paper presented at the ESPAnet Conference in Oxford, September 9–11.

Mosher, J.S. and D.M. Trubek (2003), 'Alternative Approaches to Governance in the EU: EU Social Policy and the European Employment Strategy', *Journal of Common Market Studies*, **41** (1), 63–88.

Mosley, Layna (2003), *Global Capital and National Governments*, Cambridge, UK: Cambridge University Press.

Nolan, P. (2006), 'Tax Relief for Breadwinners or Caregivers? The Designs of Earned and Child Tax Cedits in Five Anglo-American Countries', *Journal of Comparative Policy Analysis: Research and Practice*, **8** (2), 167–83.

OECD (1994), *The OECD Jobs Study: Facts, Analysis, Strategies*, Paris: OECD.

OECD (2001), *Social Expenditure Data Base*, Paris: OECD.

OECD (2004a), *Social Expenditure Data Base*, Paris: OECD.

OECD (2004b), *Revenue Statistics 1965–2003*, Paris: OECD.

Orenstein, M. A. (2005), 'The New Pension Reform as Global Policy', *Global Social Policy*, **5** (2), 175–202.

Pierson, Paul (1994), *Dismantling the Welfare State? Reagan, Thatcher, and the Politics of Retrenchment*, Cambridge: Cambridge University Press.

Pierson, P. (1996), 'The New Politics of the Welfare State', *World Politics*, **48** (2), 143–79.

Pierson, P. (1998), 'Irresistible Forces, Immovable Objects: Post-industrial Welfare States Confront Permanent Austerity', *Journal of European Public Policy*, **5**, 539–60.

Pierson, Paul (ed.) (2001), *The New Politics of the Welfare State*, Oxford, UK: Oxford University Press.

Rothgang, Heinz, Mirella Cacace, Simone Grimmeisen and Claus Wendt (2005), 'The Changing Role of the State in Healthcare Systems', in Stephan Leibfried and Michael Zürn (eds), *Transformations of the State?*, Cambridge: Cambridge University Press, pp. 187–212.

Sala-i-Martin, X. (1994), 'Cross-sectional Regressions and the Empirics of Economic Growth', *European Economic Review*, **38**, 739–47.

Scharpf, Fritz W. (1999), *Governing in Europe. Effective and Democratic?*, Oxford, UK: Oxford University Press.

Scharpf, F.W. (2000), 'The Viability of Advanced Welfare States in the International Economy: Vulnerabilities and Options', *Journal of European Public Policy*, **7** (2), 190–228.

Scharpf, F.W. (2002), 'The European Social Model: Coping With the Challenges of Diversity', *Journal of Common Market Studies*, **40** (4), 645–70.

Schmidt, Manfred G. (2005), *Sozialpolitik in Deutschland. Historische Entwicklung und internationaler Vergleich*, Wiesbaden: Verlag für Sozialwissenschaften.

Scruggs, Lyle (2004), *Welfare State Entitlements Data Set: A Comparative Institutional Analysis of Eighteen Welfare States*, Version 1.1, Storrs: University of Connecticut.

Seeleib-Kaiser, Martin (2001), *Globalisierung und Sozialpolitik. Ein Vergleich der Diskurse und Wohlfahrtssysteme in Deutschland, Japan und den USA*, Frankfurt and New York: Campus.

Sinn, H.-W. (2002), 'EU Enlargement and the Future of the Welfare State', *Scottish Journal of Political Economy*, **49**, 104–15.

Starke, P. (2006), 'The Politics of Welfare State Retrenchment: A Literature Review', *Social Policy & Administration*, **40** (1), 104–20.

Swank, Duane H. (2002), *Global Capital, Political Institutions, and Policy Change in Developed Welfare States*, Cambridge, UK: Cambridge University Press.

Tanaka, S. (2005), 'Parental Leave and Child Health Across OECD Countries', *The Economic Journal*, **115** (501), F7–F28.

Tanzi, V. (2002), 'Globalization and the Future of Social Protection', *Scottish Journal of Political Economy*, **49** (1), 116–27.

Taylor-Gooby, P. (2002), 'The Silver Age of the Welfare State: Perspectives on Resilience', *Journal of Social Policy*, **31** (4), 597–621.

Taylor-Gooby, Peter (ed.) (2004), *New Risks, New Welfare. The Transformation of the European Welfare State*, Oxford, UK: Oxford University Press.

Wilensky, Harold (1975), *The Welfare State and Equality*, Berkeley, CA: University of California Press.

Wilensky, Harold and Charles Lebeaux (1958), *Industrial Society and Social Welfare*, New York: The Free Press.

World Bank (1994), *Averting the Old Age Crisis. Policies to Protect the Old and Promote Growth*, Oxford, UK: Oxford University Press.

Zöllner, Detlev (1963), *Öffentliche Sozialleistungen und wirtschaftliche Entwicklung. Ein zeitlicher und internationaler Vergleich*, Berlin: Duncker and Humblot.

Part II
The Politics of Welfare State Reform

7. Competitive Transformation and the State Regulation of Health Insurance Systems: Germany, Switzerland and the Netherlands Compared[1]

Thomas Gerlinger

INTRODUCTION

Health care systems in OECD countries are currently going through a period of profound change. The primary objective of this process is to reduce public expenditure on health as well as the financial burden on companies (whether in the form of taxation or contributions), in order to improve their competitiveness in an increasingly globalised economy. True, the first attempts to damp down costs date from the mid-1970s, when the Fordist growth regime came to an end, but they were mostly restricted to cautious changes to the existing structures (Alber and Bernardi-Schenkluhn 1992; Oliver et al. 2005). The focus of these efforts was on the containment of administrative costs, a moderate shifting of treatment costs on to patients and limited adjustments to existing regulatory systems. No attempt was made in those years to implement structural reforms to health care systems, that is to introduce measures likely to give rise to a 'redistribution of competences and responsibilities with regard to the financing, provision and regulation of medical services' (Webber 1988: 157). It was only in the course of the 1990s that health policy in most OECD countries acquired the dynamic that has persisted until the present time (for example Wendt 2003; Blank and Burau 2007). The intensification of international locational competition, the rise in unemployment and the increasingly evident limitations of earlier cost-reduction strategies led to a change of direction in health policy. Against this background, the problem-solving strategies that had been pursued to date were increasingly perceived as inadequate and there was growing determination to implement structural changes in health care systems.

This dynamic is characterised, firstly, by a rapid succession of attempts at reform and, secondly, by the use of new instruments of governance, the aim of which is to change the behavioural incentives for financing bodies, service providers, insured individuals and patients. The most important of these instruments are the introduction of global or sectoral budgets, the introduction or extension of competition between insurance funds, the creation of opportunities for concluding selective agreements, the privatisation to a significant degree of treatment costs and the increased use of prospective forms of payment, such as fixed budgets and flat-rate payment arrangements (Freeman and Moran 2000).

These new forms of payment are of far-reaching importance, because they shift the morbidity risk in part or even in whole on to service providers (for example Herder-Dorneich 1994). At the same time, their use means that service providers' profits will increase to the extent that they are successful in reducing the cost of care provided under these prospective forms of payment. There are two possible strategies that service providers can adopt in responding to the new incentive structures. Firstly, they can rationalise their care processes in business management terms, thereby fulfilling the legislature's intention of making service provision more efficient. In many cases, however, such rationalisation is accompanied by downward pressure on wages and salaries and increased demands on medical personnel. Secondly, service providers can cut back on patient benefits. The intention here is to stop providing services and treatments that are not clinically indicated; however, there is also a risk with such a strategy that the quality of care will suffer. This can happen, for example, if service providers fail to offer necessary treatments or if patients are induced to pay the full cost of certain services or treatments themselves.

The reasons for this change lie primarily in factors outside the policy area, that is changes in the societal environment of healthcare systems. Of particular importance in this regard is the perceived pressure to reduce the financial burdens on companies. Pursuit of this objective has led to the diffusion of the methods of new public management, already implemented in other areas of public policy, into the sphere of health policy. Although the implementation of such methods varies from country to country, both in significance and in the form it takes, a common trend towards a 'regulated market' or 'regulated competition' can be identified in all health care systems, whether state or corporatist (for example Freeman 2000; Saltman 2002).

The aim of the present chapter is to investigate whether and in what way the state's role in this transformation process is changing. We will be examining those health insurance systems that aim to channel competition primarily through rival (public or private) health insurance schemes. In other words, we are focusing on those systems characterised by a plurality of health insurance providers that has developed over time. The countries in question are Germany, Switzerland and the Netherlands. This way of organising competition through rival insurance funds sets these countries apart from those with state health care systems, with their regional monopolies (Saltman et al. 2004). However, they also differ from those health insurance systems that until now have largely maintained a state or corporatist mode of regulation for their health care systems, such as those in France (Hassenteufel 2001) or Austria (Wendt 2003).

The chapter begins with a report on the stage the reform process had reached in the three countries on the eve of the structural reforms, that is at the end of the 1980s or the beginning of the 1990s. This is followed by a description of the current state of the health care systems. In the next section, individual areas of state action will be singled out and investigated in order to ascertain how state activity in these areas has changed. Finally, our findings will be briefly summarised and the prospects for the future outlined.

THE HEALTH CARE SYSTEMS ON THE EVE OF THE STRUCTURAL REFORMS

Our aim in this section is briefly to outline the structural characteristics of the three health care systems under investigation at the end of the 1980s or the beginning of the 1990s. The financing, health care and regulatory systems will be described separately.

Germany

The German health care system is characterised by a division between social and private insurance (Rosenbrock and Gerlinger 2006). The statutory health insurance system (SHI) catered for employees up to a certain income threshold, for whom membership was compulsory. Access to the private health insurance (PHI) was confined to civil servants, the self-employed and higher-earning employees. However, these groups could also opt into the statutory health insurance system or forego insurance cover completely. At the beginning of the 1990s, around 90 per cent of the population were members of a statutory health insurance fund – the vast majority of them as employees or their family members. For the remaining 10 per cent covered by private health insurance, the principles of the insurance market applied; for those covered by the statutory health insurance funds, however, the state offered virtually universal access to health care services. The statutory health insurance funds were financed solely by means of contributions based on gross pay which, in accordance with the individual insurance principle, were deducted until a specified upper limit had been reached and paid in equal shares by employers and employees. At the beginning of the 1990s, there were around 1100 health insurance funds providing statutory health insurance; the majority of employees for whom membership was compulsory were permanently assigned to one or other of these funds, usually on the basis of occupational status (Enquete-Kommission 1990: 358–465). The main player in the provision of health care was the office-based physician. As far as ambulant health care was concerned, insured patients had the right to choose their own doctor; this applied not only to general practitioners but also to specialists. On the other hand, hospitals provided ambulant treatment only in a small number of exceptional cases (Simon 2008).

The regulatory system at the beginning of the 1990s was characterised by a complex mix of governance forms (Alber 1992). The individual health care sectors were governed by separate regulatory systems, each with a different mix of state, corporatist and market elements. The hospital sector was dominated by state-hierarchical forms of governance, while the ambulant sector was characterised by corporatism. The provision of medicines, for its part, was driven largely by the competitive principle (Rosenbrock and Gerlinger 2006).

Another characteristic feature of the German health care system was the existence of state framework legislation. The state delegated far-reaching governance competences to corporatist bodies on which the health insurance funds and doctors or hospitals were equally represented ('joint self-governance'). These bodies gave substance to the state's general requirements through negotiations and specified the price, volume and quality of services for their members in binding collective agreements (Gerlinger 2002). The state had oversight of these associations and institutions, allowing them a certain degree of freedom to act that was not insignificant but reduced compared with the 1970s. In the ambulant sector, the associations representing the health insurance funds had to negotiate agreements with the panel doctors' associations, which had regional monopolies on the representation of SHI physicians.

In contrast, the associations representing the health insurance funds in the hospital sector negotiated contracts with individual hospitals. Here, too, they were under a compulsion to conclude contracts with all hospitals included by the *Länder* in their state hospital services plan. By virtue of their right to draw up a hospital services plan and their involvement in shaping hospital legislation, the *Länder* were the most important players in the regulation of hospital-based services (Simon 2000).

For their part, the health insurance funds, operating in accordance with the general requirements laid down by central government and under central government supervision, managed their affairs through a system of self-governance involving both employers and the insured. One of their most important tasks was to set the contribution rate.

From 1977 onwards, a number of items of legislation had been enacted with a view to cutting costs. However, this legislation left the financing, care and regulatory structures largely untouched. The measures introduced during this period included attempts to induce service providers to contain spending by changing the payment systems and deliberately strengthening the financing organisations. In those years, characteristically, corporatist regulatory competences were expanded in order to put the associations representing the health insurance funds and service providers in a position to urge their members to cut costs (Döhler and Manow-Borgwardt 1992). Overall, this structurally conservative health policy proved unable to contain costs effectively (Rosenbrock and Gerlinger 2006: 113–117).

Shielded by a revenue-oriented expenditure policy, the incentive structures remained unchanged for the actors. On the one hand, the maintenance of the system of payment for individual services in the ambulant sector and of the prime cost principle in the hospital sector continued to provide incentives to increase the volume of services provided. On the other hand, the extremely rigid system of member allocation meant that the health insurance funds enjoyed a de facto right of continuance. Competition for members was confined to that segment of the statutory health insurance system in which members enjoyed freedom of choice, primarily white-collar employees and those insuring themselves voluntarily (Enquete-Kommission 1990: 358–465). True, the financing organisations were anxious, even under these conditions, to avoid increasing the contributions rate; nevertheless, the negative effects that the insurance funds might suffer as a result of any conceivable increases were limited and manageable. To that extent, the traditional cost-reduction policy was characterised by the contradiction between the overall goal of keeping the contributions rate stable and the financial incentives for the individual actors.

At the beginning of the 1990s, the German health care system was regarded as incapable of reform. A number of different reasons were adduced in explanation: the power of organised interest groups within the health system, the need to form coalition governments, which meant that the FDP in particular was in a position to water down or even defeat structural reforms that would have damaged the interests of service providers, and the major role played by the *Länder* in the reform process, the main result of which was a block on any reorganisation of the hospital sector (for example Rosewitz and Webber 1990; Simon 2000).

Switzerland

The health care system in Switzerland had traditionally been based on private medical insurance. Consequently, at the beginning of the 1990s, it was the most market-oriented of the three health care systems under investigation (Bernardi-Schenkluhn 1992; Hitz and Ulrich 2003).

Since there was no national obligation to take out insurance until the first half of the 1990s, the management of compulsory insurance was devolved to the cantons. They used this right in different ways and usually restricted the obligation to take out insurance to the socially less advantaged groups. Thus at the beginning of the 1990s, only about one quarter of the Swiss population was compulsorily insured, although more than 99 per cent had health insurance with an approved insurer (Bernardi-Schenkluhn 1992). The reason for this was that medical treatment was not provided at the lower social insurance rates of payment unless patients had opted to take out health insurance with an approved insurer. The list of services covered was strongly regulated at federal level and very extensive. However, it did not include dental services. Furthermore, there was a time restriction on the payment of hospital costs, and until 1996 health insurance funds could place a restriction on new members for a period of five years, whereby they exempted themselves from meeting the costs of treating pre-existing chronic conditions (Bernardi-Schenkluhn 1992: 196–198). As far as per diem indemnities for sickness were concerned, central government laid down only minimum requirements, which could be developed further by the cantons.

Financing was based on per capita premiums, the level of which depended on age at entry and gender. However, premiums for women could not exceed those for men by more than 10 per cent. Employers were not involved in the collection of health insurance contributions (Frei and Hill 1990). The health insurance funds' revenues were supplemented by subsidies from federal government and the cantons. The cantons' objective in providing the subsidies was to lower the per capita premium for socially disadvantaged groups. Patients had to make a greater contribution to the costs of treatments than their counterparts in Germany or the Netherlands, with the level of co-payments set at 10 per cent. As a result, lengthy hospital stays placed a considerable financial burden on patients, while older people were burdened by high premiums and gaps in coverage (Bernardi-Schenkluhn 1992: 213–216).

As far as ambulant health services were concerned, office-based physicians were the main providers. However, hospitals also offered out-patient services. Office-based physicians were reimbursed for each individual service or treatment they provided. There was no demand planning for office-based physicians: the prevailing principle was that of unrestricted freedom of establishment. Hospitals were approved on the basis of the cantons' hospital services plans. Half of the cost of hospital treatment – whether in-patient or out-patient – was borne by the cantons.

As far as the regulatory system was concerned, the pronounced federalist structure was (and remains) probably the most distinctive feature of the Swiss health care system (Minder et al. 2000; Kocher 2007). The division of labour between central government and the cantons did not follow any clear principle but had emerged gradually out of a lengthy process shaped by many ad hoc compromises. In many cases, the division of competences was neither plausible nor functional, while in others it was actually unclear and contradictory. Overall, the regulatory system was confusing and attracted very considerable criticism as a result. On occasions, it was even said – not entirely without justification – that there were 26 different health care systems in Switzerland (for example Hoffmeyer 1993: 17). The cantons enjoyed very far-reaching regulatory competences, such as the planning of hospital services, the approval and control of medicines, the authorisation of supply contracts, definition of the groups covered by insurance and the fixing of subsidies for health insurers (Minder et al. 2000; Vatter 2003). Thus the cantons' competences in the area of health policy went far beyond those of the German *Länder*. The federal government's most important competence was the enactment of framework legislation governing health insurance.

As in Germany, the associations representing service providers and financing bodies had traditionally played an important role in the governance of the health care system, alongside the state actors. At canton level, they concluded agreements on the prices of medical services. In contrast to Germany, however, these associations are not corporate bodies under public law but associations under private law.

Until the first half of the 1990s, the legal basis for the health care system was the Illness and Accident Insurance Act, as amended in 1964. This legislation and the reform efforts that accompanied it began to attract criticism very soon after the legislation had come into force. The criticism pertained to the sharp increases in expenditure, the gaps in the list of services covered, the absence of a national obligation to take out health insurance, the confusing system for fixing premiums, the high financial burdens on the elderly and the socially disadvantaged and the inadequate cooperation between the cantons. However, three decades passed before extensive reforms were introduced. True, attempts had been made to reform the system, but they had come to nothing because of the influence of the associations, obstruction at federal level or failure in the necessary referendums (Immergut 1992). In contrast to Germany and the Netherlands, the legislation governing the health service in Switzerland remained unamended between 1975 and the early 1990s, apart from minor changes that could be made by regulation or decree.

The Netherlands

The Dutch health care system at the beginning of the 1990s was characterised by a complicated mix of social and private health insurance, as well as separate systems for civil servants (Minder et al. 2000). In the decades following the end of the Second World War, virtually the entire population was integrated into the fragmented insurance system and the list of approved services was comprehensively extended. As far as long-term nursing and psychiatric care were concerned, a single insurance scheme (Algemene Wet Bijzondere Ziektekoste – AWBZ) had existed since 1968 for the whole population. However, insurance cover for acute medical conditions was divided into a statutory scheme (Ziekenfondswet – ZFW) and a private scheme. Access to the private scheme was restricted to individuals with an income above a certain threshold; in 1990, around 40 per cent of the population qualified. Prior to the reforms that introduced greater competition into the system, the rigid allocation system and the existence of regional monopolies meant that members of the statutory insurance system had virtually no opportunities to switch to another insurance fund. Those in the private scheme, on the other hand, had a free choice of insurance provider; unlike their counterparts in Germany, however, they were not entitled to opt into the statutory scheme, in order to take advantage of free insurance for family members, for example.

The ZFW was financed by a hybrid system based on income-related contributions paid by both employers and employees. These contributions were supplemented by tax-funded subsidies from the state amounting to around 10 per cent of total expenditure. In contrast to the fully-funded PKV scheme in Germany, private health insurance in the Netherlands was based on an age cohort-dependent pay-as-you-go system.

The main actors in the provision of medical care were the family doctors (general practitioners), who acted as gate-keepers. Specialist treatment was largely provided in hospitals and could usually be accessed only after referral by a GP. Apart from the state-funded university teaching hospitals, the vast majority of hospitals were owned by religious denominations. The health insurance funds were obliged to enter into contracts with office-based physicians and hospitals.

The regulatory system was characterised by wide-ranging state competences. It was the state that fixed the contribution rates for both the AWBZ and the ZFW, drew up the hospital services plans and set hospital budgets, as well as accrediting doctors to provide ambulant services. Hospital services planning was centrally regulated. New hospitals could not be built, existing ones extended or service provision changed without obtaining the government's prior approval. However, the twelve provinces played an important role in hospital services planning, since they had to implement the plans in accordance with the government's substantive and procedural requirements and in cooperation with other actors, such as local authorities, service providers, etc. (den Exter et al. 2004). Thus the state in the Netherlands had far greater opportunities to involve itself in regulating the health care system than existed in either Germany or Switzerland.

Although the Dutch government did indeed have very wide-ranging governance and planning competences in respect of the health care system, it was not regarded as having any great ability to push through fundamental reforms (Schut 1995). One key reason for this was the highly consensual corporatism that characterised the Dutch political system as a consequence of the strong 'pillarisation' of Dutch society. This manifested itself in the health care system in the strong links between political parties, trade unions and church and other interest groups, with each actor able to slow down or even halt any change processes (Björkman and Okma 1997). The Dutch habit of forming coalition governments also helped these interests to find a way into government policy. In the 1970s and 1980s, a number of cost-cutting pieces of legislation were enacted, as they had been in Germany (Hartmann 2002: 133–146). They usually introduced changes into the payment systems for doctors and hospitals, but their overall impact was very limited and they were unable effectively to contain the rise in expenditure in the health care system.

REFORMS OF THE REGULATORY SYSTEMS, 1990–2007

In what respects have the characteristics of the three national health care services changed since the introduction of structural reforms?

Germany

The change of direction towards regulated competition in the German health care system occurred in 1993, when the Health Care Reform Act (Gesundheitsstrukturgesetz) came into force. This change in health care policy and strategy was initiated in response to an accumulation of problems in the health system's societal environment as well as in the social health insurance system.

The Reform Act introduced a number of instruments of governance that were either new to the statutory health insurance system or revised in such a way that they made lasting changes to the incentive structures for the actors involved in the provision of medical care. Two instruments took centre stage. Firstly, individuals were given the right to choose their own health insurance provider (open enrolment). This amounted to the introduction of competition between the health insurance funds, which as a result lost the implicit guarantee of continued existence they had hitherto enjoyed. A low contribution rate now became the decisive parameter in the competition to attract members. Secondly, the introduction of all-inclusive prices and/or individual budgets for the payment of medical services shifted the financial risk of treating patients on to individual service providers. To put it simply, the new payment forms reduced the incentive for service providers to expand their service provision and to some extent even encouraged them to reduce the amount of treatment provided in individual cases (Gerlinger 1998).

The key objective of this change was to put in place a competitive regime in the health care system, in short to establish a regulated market that would form the basis for a system of managed care. To this day, the main element in this competitive regime has been the struggle between health insurance funds to attract members. Even after the introduction of open enrolment, relations with service providers were managed primarily by means of collective contracts. In most cases, it was not the individual health insurance funds but their representative associations that were the parties to negotiations, with the contracts frequently being concluded 'uniformly and jointly' for all types of health insurer, as stipulated in the relevant clauses of the Reform Act (Rosenbrock and Gerlinger 2006). Similarly, individual doctors were not directly involved in negotiations with the panel doctors' associations, which had a monopoly on representation and contracting in the ambulant sector. It was only in the hospital sector that negotiations took place with each individual hospital that had a supply contract; again, such contracts could only be concluded 'uniformly and jointly' with the health insurers' associations (Simon 2000). It was in the light of these circumstances that the health insurers called for the liberalisation of contracting policy, in order to enable them to enter into and, when necessary, terminate specific contracts with individual service providers or groups of providers. In short, the competitive regime was to be extended to relations between service providers and health insurers.

This liberalisation of the law of contract did indeed take place subsequently and proceeded by way of a series of incremental changes. It particularly affected the core area of the corporatist regime, namely the ambulant sector (Gerlinger 2002). The state increased the room for manoeuvre available to individual actors at the micro level in health care and payment policy. As the possible courses of action open to individual actors were increased, so collective contracts began to diminish importance. Health insurance funds now no longer need the agreement of the panel doctors' associations in order to enter into specific contracts with doctors or groups of doctors pertaining to the provision of integrated care, GP-based care and ambulant GP and specialist care or to participation in disease management programmes and pilot projects. Considerable use is being made of these opportunities (Kassenärztliche Bundesvereinigung 2008), even though the overwhelming majority of services continue to be managed by means of collective contracts with the panel doctors' associations. The trend towards a further reduction in the importance of such arrangements, which have to be made 'uniformly and jointly', is evident (for example Kania and Blanke 2000; Noweski 2008). It is anticipated that, from 2009 onwards, health insurers' freedom to enter into selective contracts will be extended to the hospital sector (Gerlinger 2008).

The introduction of open enrolment was accompanied by the introduction of a risk structure compensation scheme between the health insurers. The following criteria were taken into account in the first instance: income, age, gender, number of jointly insured family members exempt from contributions and receipt of benefits for reduced earning capacity. Since it did not take account of disease characteristics, it fulfilled its intended function of preventing risk selection by the health insurers, but did so only very inadequately. Moreover, it created negative incentives to improve the care of expensive, chronically ill insurees (Jacobs et al. 2002). Consequently, the risk structure compensation scheme was reformed in stages. Since 2002, health insurers have been receiving additional funds for certain groups of chronically ill patients who enrol in disease management programmes. In accordance with the Health Reform Act of 2007, 50 to 80 particularly costly illnesses will be included in the risk structure compensation scheme from 2009 onwards.

Switzerland

After years of debate, the Swiss health care system underwent wide-ranging reforms from 1996 onwards, when the Health Insurance Act of 1994 came into force (for example Baur et al. 2000: 97–110; Minder et al. 2000). The declared objectives of the reform included a strengthening of solidarity in health care financing, cost reductions in social health insurance and the guaranteeing of higher care quality.

The 1994 Health Insurance Act makes a distinction between compulsory basic insurance and voluntary supplementary insurance. The legislation introduced a nationwide obligation to take out basic insurance. There are some 100 health insurers offering this basic insurance; they may be corporate bodies under private or public law. Insurees continue to have the right to choose their health insurer; for their part, however, health insurers are under an obligation to contract.

The list of basic benefits is common to all insurees. It contains a very comprehensive set of medical treatments and nursing care. Dental treatment (including dentures) and compensation for lost earnings in the event of illness are not included in the list of benefits but can be covered by taking out supplementary health insurance assessed on the basis of individual risk status. Furthermore, the Health Insurance Act plugged existing gaps in long-term nursing care and abolished exclusions, such as the five-year restriction on the treatment of pre-existing conditions in the case of new members. The Act further stipulated that per capita premiums could no longer be calculated on the basis of insurees' gender and age on entry into the scheme. Under these circumstances, it is hardly surprising that the reform of health insurance in Switzerland was widely interpreted as a step towards greater social justice.

Nevertheless, premiums continue to be set independently of insurees' financial capacity. Consequently, there is a redistribution of resources between the well and the sick, between young and old and between men and women but not between the well-off and the less well-off. Unlike their counterparts in Germany and the Netherlands, employers still make no contribution to health insurance funds. In order to reduce the high financial burden that would otherwise fall on the less well-off, those on low incomes are paid a subsidy, funded jointly by the federal government and the cantons. Reductions in premiums are subject to a nationwide regulatory framework. These regulations stipulate, for example, that children and young adults have to pay only a reduced per capita premium. Furthermore, the regulations give the cantons greater freedom to introduce further measures to reduce premiums (Rosenbrock and Gerlinger 2006).

In addition to the per capita premium, adult insurees have to pay in full the costs of treatment up to a ceiling of 300 Swiss francs per year (annual excess). They must also pay 10 per cent of the costs of treatment above this level up to a limit of 7,000 Swiss francs (retained amount), i.e. a maximum of 700 Swiss francs per year (Rosenbrock and Gerlinger 2006). The only exceptions to this are certain medical preventive and maternity services. The maximum amount any adult with the basic insurance can be required to pay is 1,000 Swiss francs per year. The level of both the annual excess and the threshold for the 10 per cent retention are set by the Swiss Federal Council.

In principle, there are three possible ways in which insurees can reduce the per capita premiums they have to pay (Klingenberger 2002; Wirthner and Ulrich 2003):

1. They can opt to pay a higher excess than 300 Swiss francs and receive a discount on their premium in exchange. The regulations governing increases in the excess and discounts on premiums are laid down by the Federal Government.
2. Insurees can take out an insurance policy with a no-claims bonus, which is similar in operation to a motor insurance policy. The longer an insuree goes without incurring any costs, the greater the reduction in the insur-

ance premium. After five years, the discount reaches the statutory maximum value of 45 per cent.

3. Insurees can take out policies with a restricted choice of service providers. This has encouraged the development of various forms of managed care (health maintenance organisations, doctors' networks, GP/gatekeeper model), as a result of which Switzerland is now a pioneer in the development of new forms of health care and insurance in Europe.

Open enrolment has been accompanied by the introduction of a risk structure compensation scheme. As in Germany and the Netherlands, the aim here is to restrict the incentives created for health insurers to engage in risk selection and to establish a 'level playing field' for competing insurance providers. However, the risk structure compensation scheme takes account only of two demographic factors, namely age and gender, and thus does not adequately equalise the differences in the financial risks faced by health insurers compared with morbidity-based approaches (van de Ven et al. 2003; Behrend et al. 2007). Furthermore, this equalising takes place at cantonal rather then national level. As a result, health insurers in Switzerland are able to take advantage of a range of opportunities to engage in risk selection (Leu and Beck 2007).

The Netherlands

The starting point for the change in the Dutch health care system was the 1987 report by the Dekker Commission (named after its chairman), which delivered a wide-ranging critique of the existing system. The main targets of criticism were the large increases in expenditure, the lack of efficiency in patient care and the inadequate incentives for health insurers to operate economically.

In essence, the Dekker Report envisaged a transition to regulated competition. Insurees were to be given greater freedom of choice, health insurers' obligation to contract with the service providers was to be abolished, the health insurance system was to be converted into a uniform basic insurance scheme and the detailed state planning of health services was to be reduced to framework planning (Hartmann 2002). Despite the initial euphoria that greeted the report, individual interest groups adopted an obstructive attitude as the reforms were introduced step-by-step (Schut 1995). When the 'purple coalition' government, made up of the Social Democratic Labour Party, the free market liberal party VVD and the moderate liberal party D66, came to power in 1994, the process came to a complete standstill because the various elements in the coalition were unable to reach a consensus on the reforms (Okma 1997).

Among the important changes that occurred in this first phase of reform from the mid-1980s to the mid-1990s was the introduction of open enrolment and of a basic price list in the private health insurance system (Wet op de Toegang tot Ziektekostenverzekeringen – WTZ) and the abolition of the health insurers' obligation to contract with the office-based physicians (Lieverdink 2001). The introduction of open enrolment in the statutory health insurance system (Ziekenfondswet – ZFW) was accompanied by the intro-duction of a small per capita premium, the aim being to introducing competi-tion into the system, since contribution rates are set centrally, in contrast to the German health insurance system. Introduced in 1989, this additional financial burden on employees overturned the joint funding principle. In 1995, the employers' share of the income-related contributions to the statu-tory health insurance fund was 7.25 per cent, while employers had to pay 1.1 per cent plus the per capita premium, which varied depending on the type of insurance. In addition, the state subsided the statutory health insurance scheme and even the private insurance funds paid a contribution to the statu-tory system, as compensation for the lower share of pensioners among their insurees.

Since 1994, the health insurers have been able to conclude contracts with doctors and hospitals. This contractual freedom was intended to encourage competition between doctors and hospitals. However, the incentives for com-petition remained weak. Since contributions were set at a uniform rate across the country and the level of the per capita premium was low, insurees had virtually no incentive to change health insurer (Greß 2002). Nor did the in-centives bring about the expected changes in behaviour in the relations be-tween financing bodies and service providers. The health insurers made vir-tually no use of selective contracts in their dealings with GPs, because they feared they would lose patients, particularly in view of the low GP density (Groenewegen and Greß 2000).

After 19 years of gradual changes, the most comprehensive structural re-form of the Dutch health care system since 1941 came into force in 2006 (for example van Ginneken 2006). The division that had hitherto existed in acute medicine between the social and private insurance systems was abolished by the introduction of a uniform obligation on all citizens to take out insurance. The financing of the so-called basic package is based on two pillars. The first is an earnings-related contribution of 6.5 per cent, which is paid in full by employers for all employees earning up to around €30,000; however, employees have to pay tax on it. Together with a considerably reduced state subsidy, this money is paid into the health fund, from which risk-adjusted payments are made to the individual health insurers. Exactly as in Switzer-land, this mechanism is intended to guarantee a 'level playing field' and prevent risk selection. However, the Dutch morbidity-based risk structure compensation scheme is considerably more effective than its Swiss counterpart, which takes account solely demographic factors (Greß 2006; Behrend et al. 2007). However, since the allocations from the central fund are not sufficient to cover the costs incurred, the health insurers have to levy income-related per capita premiums as a second source of funds; these premiums constitute the main parameter in the competition between health insurers. Individuals whose incomes fall below a certain threshold are eligible for a state subsidy of up to €432, while dual-earner households can receive up to €864 (Daley and Gubb 2007).

THE CHANGE IN STATE REGULATION

Our aim in this section is to identify the characteristic features of state regulatory activity in the transformation processes outlined above. Our main concern is to ascertain whether common trends are emerging in the three health care systems under investigation with regard to the changes in the functions of the state and in the way it exercises those functions.

Introduction of Compulsory Insurance and Standardisation of Insurance Conditions

Until the 1990s, none of the countries under investigation had a general obligation to take out insurance in a unitary health insurance system. In Switzerland, there was an obligation to take out insurance, which differed from canton to canton, only for the lower income groups. In Germany and the Netherlands, compulsory insurance existed only for those with earnings below a certain level. In both the German and Dutch health care systems, there was a division between statutory and private health insurance; in Germany, it applied to all medical services, including care, whereas in the Netherlands it applied only to acute medical care.

Since the mid-1990s, a general obligation to take out insurance has been introduced in all three systems; this has been accompanied by tendential weakening of the division between social and private full coverage insurance. This trend is particularly evident in Switzerland and the Netherlands, whereas it is much less evident in Germany, where its emergence was also delayed. In Switzerland and the Netherlands, an obligation to take out insurance in a single system covering the entire population was introduced. In implementing this measure, these two countries have taken on certain characteristics of the state health care systems in other European countries. Germany is the only one of these health care systems that has maintained a distinction between statutory and private full coverage insurance and also makes no provision for financial transfers between the two systems.

However, the health reform that came into force in 2007 contains a number of provisions that in effect bring the statutory and private health insurance systems in Germany closer together (Gerlinger et al. 2007). Thus the health insurers have been given wide-ranging opportunities to introduce so-called alternative insurance rates, which offer reductions on the standard rates if insurees undertake to pay part of the costs of treatment themselves or do not claim any benefits. From 1 January 2009, private insurers will be obliged to provide insurance at a so-called 'basic rate' to all those requesting it; the range of benefits is comparable with that provided by the public (statutory) insurance systems and those laid down for non-risk dependent premiums. Furthermore, the maximum premium may not exceed the maximum amount paid under the statutory insurance scheme. In all probability, it will be mainly older people and the chronically sick who will take advantage of this opportunity. Since their basic rate contributions will probably not cover their treatment costs, there will be a need within the private insurance system for cross-subsidies and thus a higher level of internal solidarity among private insurers.

Thus tentative steps are being made in Germany towards narrowing the gap between the two systems. Whether this will lead to the establishment of a unitary insurance system, as in Switzerland and the Netherlands, will depend above all on how the balance of power in the German Parliament evolves. The SPD, Greens and the Left are basically in favour of such a system, while the CDU/CSU and FDP are opposed.

Privatisatising Costs and Guaranteeing General Access to Medical Care

In all three health care systems, the costs of medical treatment have to a significant degree been privatised since the beginning of the 1990s. Two instruments in particular have been used by the three governments: increased co-payments and the introduction of a range of options for insurees. These options offer insurees financial incentives to pay an annual amount towards the cost of any treatment or to pay reduced premiums if they do not claim any benefits or agree to join managed care schemes. Thus the unification of insurance systems that had previously been partially divided (already noted in the first part of this section) has been accompanied by an individualisation of costs depending on the risk of illness; the greater the individual need for treatment, the higher the financial burden on those concerned. This process is most advanced by far in Switzerland, where insurees have to pay not only the full cost of treatment up to 300 Swiss francs in any one year but also 10 per cent of all costs up to a maximum of 7,000 Swiss francs.

On the other hand, the segmentation of benefits plays different roles in the various health care systems. In Switzerland, the wide-ranging reform of health insurance was actually accompanied by a moderate extension – and standardisation – of the list of benefits. Prior to the reform, however, the Swiss system was also the most highly privatised of the three under consideration here. Criticism of benefit exclusions and the level of the annual excess and of unjustifiable differences between the cantons in the benefits they granted was one of the most important factors that triggered the reform. It is noteworthy that, in implementing the Health Insurance Act, Switzerland extended the range of health insurance benefits in the 1990s, contrary to the international trend (Kocher et al. 2002).

In the Netherlands, the exclusion of dental treatment and physiotherapy constituted a serious curtailment of the list of benefits. On the other hand, the various coalition governments have made efforts to avoid exclusions from medical treatment. Exclusions have for the most part been confined to payments unrelated to insurance, such as death or funeral benefits and maternity allowances, or professional treatment for trivial illnesses. In addition, certain groups are exempted from co-payments and the sum individuals spend on co-payments each year is limited (Maarse and Okma 2004).

Another aspect of the reorganisation of financing structures also contributes to the privatisation of costs, namely the exempting of employers from health insurance contributions and the general trend towards decoupling employers' contributions from the cost of health insurance. Switzerland is an exception in this regard, in the sense that employers there have never had to contribute to the financing of health insurance. However, in the Netherlands in particular and, to a lesser extent, in Germany as well, the reform measures have partially decoupled employers' contributions from the evolution of health insurance expenditure. The two countries have taken different routes in this regard. In the Netherlands, the decoupling took place through the introduction of partial financing based on per capita premiums unrelated to income. In Germany, it was a result of the departure from joint financing. Since 2005, premiums covering dental prostheses and sickness pay – around 7 per cent of total expenditure on health insurance premiums – have had to be paid solely by the insured population and no longer by employers. Secondly, the 2007 Health Act stipulates that, from 2009 onwards, any possible future deficits in the statutory health insurance system will have to be covered initially solely by additional contributions paid by insurees. Only when the total amount of these additional contributions has reached 5 per cent of total expenditure on statutory health insurance will the federal government have to raise the national contribution rate, thereby forcing employers as well to help make good the deficit.

In all three countries, furthermore, the share of expenditure on health insurance funded out of taxation has increased considerably. In Switzerland, there were state subsidies prior to the 1994 reform, and thus the increase since then has been only moderate; in the Netherlands, however, funding through taxation traditionally played only a small role, while in Germany it had no part at all. In the Netherlands, it has increased considerably in significance with the introduction and uprating of per capita premiums, which has made it necessary to provide subsidies for the less well-off. In Germany, it was introduced explicitly with a view to effecting a necessary reduction in labour costs and is planned to rise to at least €14 billion by 2014, around 10 per cent of expenditure on statutory health insurance in 2007.

There are no reliable data on whether the privatisation of costs has forced dependent family members in lower income groups to forego medically necessary treatment, thereby also increasing health inequalities. However, if due account is taken of the established link between social status and the incidence of disease, then it must be assumed that this change has further increased *social* inequality in Germany.

In all three countries, however, it would seem that more extensive plans for the privatisation of health insurance costs have not to date been put into practice. The Dekker Plan in the Netherlands, the positions adopted in the 1990s' Swiss debate on health reform and the German debate of the same period on the introduction of optional benefits all went considerably beyond the privatisation measures introduced recently. In the Netherlands, the introduction of a basic health insurance plan, proposed by the Dekker Commission and initially taken up, had to be watered down before it could be implemented, primarily because of the serious financial burden it would place on those on low incomes (Maarse and Okma 2004). In Germany, the serious exclusions from benefits introduced in 1997 by the CDU-CSU/FDP coalition were only a brief episode. They were largely reversed when the SDP-Green coalition came to power the following year; according to many observers, one of the factors to which they owed their election victory was the benefit reductions introduced by the Christian Democrats and Liberals.

Looking back over the last two decades, it is clear that privatisation has also made considerable inroads in the area of health insurance coverage. Nevertheless, in all the countries under investigation here, considerably fewer cuts have been made in health insurance than in other parts of the social security system. However, it would be premature to conclude, as is sometimes the case, that social protection in the event of sickness has been decoupled from the protection against other risks (unemployment, pensions, social welfare) (for example Okma 2002), particularly if such a conclusion is to be used as a basis for predicting future developments. One important reason for the *relative* restraint in the privatisation of risk very probably lies in the political elites' fear of a further loss of legitimacy among sections of the electorate it is attempting to woo. However, the dynamic of market-driven governance points to the widespread integration of patients and insurees into a system of financial incentives. The less they feel at risk of a loss of legitimacy in the course of such a process, the more the political elites will be inclined to force the pace of privatisation in the area of health insurance coverage as well.

The State as Architect of Political Order in the Health Care Systems

At the end of the 1980s and beginning of the 1990s, the state in Germany, Switzerland and the Netherlands was regarded as ineffectual with regard to health care policy. The results of attempts to reform health care policy over the previous 15 years were evidence enough of the state's lack of assertiveness. In Germany and the Netherlands, the reforms were far from producing the expected effects, because the plans had been watered down during the process of policy formulation or subsequently in the course of implementation. In Switzerland, health reforms had not been implemented at all because of the veto wielded by a disparate set of interest groups.

At the end of the 1980s, the health care systems in all three countries under consideration were regarded as highly resistant to reform and governments were credited with very little capacity to act in health care policy. In all three countries, responsibility for this situation was attributed to the large number and diversity of well-organised interest groups, as well as to the need to form coalition governments, which also restricted the ability of those governments to shape health care policy. In Germany and Switzerland, a further constraining factor was the markedly federalist structure of the political systems; additionally, in Switzerland, health policy reforms were subject to a referendum (Rosewitz and Webber 1990; Immergut 1992).

In all three health care systems, nevertheless, the state, acting as the 'architect of political order' (Döhler 1995), did manage to bring order into the systems and to launch the processes of transformation already outlined above (see above: Okma 2008). As already noted, one of the main focuses of this change in health care policy lay in the accelerated privatisation of costs and risks. However, it would be mistaken to reduce health care policy to this aspect alone. Despite their closeness in many cases to the interests of service providers, the political decision-makers in all three systems (least of all probably in Switzerland) displayed a certain degree of readiness to take on doctors, hospital services providers and pharmaceutical companies. Where this occurred, the resultant change was, in part at least, enforced, since there are certain limits on the extent to which the financial burden can be shifted on to insurees and patients if the risks of a loss of legitimacy are not to become too great for the governing parties. In structuring a health care system as one part of a comprehensive social security system, it is not simply a question, as it might be for example in pension insurance schemes and in broad sections of unemployment insurance schemes, of 'simply' redistributing money or cushioning certain life risks; what is at stake also is the management of personal services within an important economic sector. To a greater extent than in other areas of social security, this opens up opportunities to pursue the goal of reducing expenditure not simply by cutting benefits but also by rationalising service production, that is by including service providers in the reform process. It can reasonably be assumed that this 'material' peculiarity has helped to ensure that health policy has to date been less affected than other areas by the ubiquitous trend towards the privatisation of social security.

The 'big bang', that is the *one* masterstroke that would have resolved a large number of governance problems for a lengthy period, has not occurred in any of the three countries. Rather, the transformation processes since the 1990s have also been shaped by numerous and various compromises, which have toned down, delayed and softened many of the proposals for reform. It is true that individual items of legislation can be identified that are of particular significance in that they represent a change of direction (see the section on reforming the regulatory system above), but they were followed almost at once by a number of further regulatory measures that sought to amend or fine-tune them. One fundamental characteristic of reform policy in these health care systems was the attempt not to resolve everything at once but to put in place (temporary) solutions in individual areas. One inevitable result of this approach was to make the political governance of health care systems more complex. The decision to opt for incremental change was due not only to the complexity of the object of regulation but also to the need to keep the number of opponents of reform within limits. To that extent, health policy in these countries certainly had elements of 'muddling through', but it would be a misrepresentation of the political elites' strategic objectives to reduce it solely to such ad hocery.

However, can the state's reclaiming of its ability to act in reforming the governance of these health care systems really be characterised as a return to the primacy of politics? Such an interpretation would suggest that the political elites have in fact displayed a greater readiness to take on powerful interest groups in the reorganisation of their health services, even when those groups are part of the state's own clientele. In both Germany and Switzerland, as well as in the Netherlands, service providers, particularly the associations representing doctors and the pharmaceutical industry, have been some of the most vociferous opponents of the health care reforms (for example Bandelow 1998; Hartmann 2002; Rosenbrock and Gerlinger 2006), since state regulation particularly strengthens those actors from whom the political elites expect effective expenditure restriction and increases in efficiency. Under these circumstances, clientelist relations are not irrelevant, it is true, but the sectional interests in the health system can no longer rely so strongly on political decision-makers taking their interests into account. Nevertheless, the notion of the primacy of politics seems to me to be misleading, for two reasons. Firstly, it conceals the fact that clientelist interests, particularly on the service providers' side, continue to play a significant role in shaping health care systems and constitute a barrier to the rationalisation of system structures. Secondly, it ignores the fact that this transformation process is driven largely by economic motives and objectives. The most important reason for the transformation processes is to reduce the financial burden on employers, and the restructuring of the health systems is intended to make the supply of and demand for goods and services in the health care sector subject to stronger economic incentives.

Increase in Regulatory Density and Extension of State Intervention

The decline in state intervention in health care systems, which observers regard as expected or desirable (for example Oberender et al. 2006), has not transpired either in Germany or in Switzerland.

True, the state has increased the freedom of action individual actors enjoy at the micro level, particularly by abolishing the funding bodies' obligations to contract with service providers and allowing health insurers and insurees to individualise financing conditions. In this regard, therefore, it is possible to speak of the state's withdrawal from health care policy. However, the health care markets that have emerged in all three systems are politically constituted markets.

One characteristic of political governance in these health care systems is that the state has retained a large part of its previous regulatory competences. In all three systems, the state is still responsible for drawing up the list of benefits, for paying benefits and for capacity planning. However, the liberalisation at the micro level has meant that these responsibilities have gradually been reduced to a framework planning competence. The Swiss state even extended its capacity planning, hitherto confined to the hospital sector, to office-based physicians, by introducing a moratorium on new licences in 2003 because of the continuously high increases in expenditure. And in all three countries, the introduction of market-type incentives has been accompanied by the introduction or continuation of implicit or explicit budgets.

On the other hand, the establishment of competition with the health care systems has opened up many new spheres of competence for state governance. Firstly, differential governance of the financial incentives offered to the individual actors is required in order to ensure that their behaviour in the new competitive regime is compatible with the political objectives that the newly created markets are expected to achieve. The focus here is primarily on the provisions governing the ways in which the markets themselves are constituted, that is on the rules that specify the actors' rights and responsibilities in an action system increasingly shaped by financial incentives and define the boundaries of their behaviour: contributions should be increased only when absolutely necessary, insurees should receive all the necessary medical treatments and the efficiency and quality of care should be increased as far as possible. In this way, perceived faulty incentives (for example cream skimming or benefits rationing) are to be corrected and anticipated faulty incentives avoided. Thus the establishment of markets must be supported by comprehensive state re-regulation (for example Vogel 1996; Majone 1997; Lütz and Czada 2000). The upshot is that that the legislature in all three countries is encasing the health care system in an increasingly dense web of statutory regulations.

This has led to an increasing emphasis in health insurance legislation on quality assurance, in order to prevent service providers following the incentive to reduce costs even if it means accepting quality deficiencies and rationing. Until well into the 1990s, there were virtually no concrete regulations on quality insurance in health insurance legislation. Since then, however, the picture has changed dramatically. Since the 1990s, numerous provisions on quality assurance have been added to health insurance legislation in Germany and Switzerland and they are frequently further reinforced by sub-legal regulations. In the Netherlands, which was one of the pioneers of quality assurance in Europe, a separate quality assurance act was passed in 1996; it brought together activities that had previously been separate and laid down new requirements (Hartmann 2002; den Exter et al. 2004). It assigns responsibility for quality assurance to service providers and lays down the corresponding general standards. Thus establishments have to report regularly on quality assurance and regular recertification is stipulated for hospitals and doctors.

Secondly, spheres of competence have been extended not only for the legislature but also for the executive. The implementation of market mechanisms has created a need for more intensive state supervision in order to avoid and/or prevent undesirable opportunistic reactions to financial incentives on the part of the actors. By assuming these responsibilities, certain existing institutions have gained considerably in importance (for example the *Bundesamt für Gesundheit* (Federal Health Office) in Switzerland or the *Bundesversicherungsamt* (Federal Insurance Office) in Germany). At the same time, there is growing pressure to assess medical procedures on the basis of their efficacy and cost effectiveness in order to ensure that increasingly scarce financial resources are used as efficiently as possible. As the evaluation of diagnostic and therapeutic procedures proceeds apace, so science is becoming increasingly important as a level of governance. This competence has been assigned in part to already existing institutions, such as the *Gemeinsame Bundesausschuss* (Federal Joint Committee) in Germany and the *Bundesamt für Gesundheit* (Federal Health Office) in Switzerland, but new institutions have also been established, such as the *Institut für Qualität und Wirtschaftlichkeit im Gesundheitswesen* (Institute for Quality and Efficiency in Health Care) in Germany and the drug licensing body *Swissmedic* in Switzerland.

The Centralisation of Regulatory Competences

In all three countries, the transformation processes have resulted in the centralisation of regulatory competences and a trend towards the standardisation of the legal framework within which the health care systems evolve. Regional differences are becoming less pronounced. These processes are most evident in Germany and Switzerland. As ever, it is in Switzerland that federal structures in health policy are most pronounced. The trend towards standardisation is much weaker in the Netherlands, where central government assumed responsibility for planning in the immediate post-war years. Even here, however, it can be observed to some extent: in the 1990s, the Dutch Parliament abolished the regional restrictions on the activities of health insurers. This particularly affects hospital capacity planning and licences for ambulant medical services.

In Germany, this centralisation of regulatory competences is taking place by stealth. In part it is being deliberately driven by the legislature, but it is also in part an unintended consequence of the policy of incremental reform (Gerlinger 2008). The centralisation is manifested in the establishment and enhanced status of the Federal Joint Committee. This is the most important executive committee in the system of joint self-governance. The health insurance funds and doctors' associations have equal representation on it; there are also three independent members and non-voting patient representatives. The Federal Joint Committee now has a wide-ranging remit to issue binding guidelines for virtually all areas of medical care. In addition, it also has a duty to evaluate the benefits and cost-efficiency of all treatments and other services that are prescribed or are to be prescribed at the health insurers' expense (Urban 2001). This gives the Federal Joint Committee considerable power to influence the composition of the list of benefits provided under statutory health insurance. At the beginning of the present decade, the Committee's sphere of competence, which had hitherto been confined to the ambulant sector, was extended to include all medical care, thereby transforming it into a 'cross-sectoral negotiating mechanism' (Döhler 2002: 33).

However, the extension of regulatory competences at federal level goes far beyond the enhanced status and importance of the Federal Joint Committee. Since the year 2000, the regulations governing the payment of benefits for both hospital and ambulant care have been standardised at federal level (Gerlinger 2008). Thus, for example, the Deutsche Krankenhausgesellschaft (the German Hospital Organisation, the umbrella organisation of hospital operators in Germany) has been given the task, jointly with the umbrella organisations of the statutory health insurance funds, of establishing national cost weights for hospital treatments (DRGs) and adapting them to current developments. This exercise is of fundamental importance for the development of an appropriate payment system, which is currently being placed on a completely new footing. The scope for health insurance funds and service providers at *Land* level to deviate from these national standards has been severely reduced. However, probably the most important step towards the centralisation of regulatory competences was the passing into law of the 2007 Health Reform Act. With effect from 1 January 2009, the new legislation removes the power of the approximately 230 health insurance funds to set their contribution rates independently and gives the federal government the right to set what will henceforth be a single national contribution rate. Thus in recent years, the federal level has also become considerably more important in the supervision of joint self-governance, to the detriment of the *Land* level.

In Switzerland as well, regulatory competences have also shifted in the last few years from the cantons to the federal level. The most significant manifestation of these unitarising tendencies was the passing of the Health Insurance Act, already mentioned above. The introduction of a national obligation to take out insurance, the drawing up of a standardised national list of benefits, the introduction of uniform regulations governing the premium subsidies paid to the socially disadvantaged and the creation of a new national drug licensing institution (Swissmedic) are all important centralising innovations.

However, the cantons continue to be the most decisive actors in health policy. The federal framework legislation gives them considerable latitude in policy making. In view of the relatively small populations concerned, the location of hospital services planning or of risk structure compensation at cantonal level is regarded as less efficient and has consequently attracted considerable criticism (Achtermann and Berset 2006). In 2003, the federal government and the cantons launched the Nationale Gesundheitspolitik Schweiz, National Health Policy for Switzerland. Federal and cantonal authorities are seeking to strengthen their cooperation. In particular, they wish to establish a consensus between policy makers and the actors in the health care system. In view of the strongly federalist culture of the national health care system, the current stage of development can be regarded at least as an intermediate stage on the road towards greater centralisation.

Thus as a result of putting in place a regulated health care market, a clear trend has emerged towards the unitarisation of capacities and conditions for acting. The main intention behind this trend is to create a 'level playing field', since the competitive regime is intended to be national in scope and consequently requires rules that are nationally applicable. Thus the retention of particular regulatory competences at a level below that of the central state – the *Länder* in Germany and the cantons in Switzerland, seems to be dysfunctional.

CONCLUSION

In recent decades, the health care systems under consideration here have been through a process of change which has taken them in essentially the same direction, although the core of their institutional regimes has remained intact. The individual health care systems have reached different points along this path, their progress determined by their historical legacies and starting points.

In all three health care systems, risks and costs have been privatised to varying degrees and employers have seen their financial burdens reduced. At the same time, a trend has emerged towards the establishment of a unitary health insurance scheme (Netherlands and Switzerland) or a cautious narrowing of existing differences between social and private health insurance (Germany).

In all three health care systems, the state plays a prominent role as the architect of political order. It constitutes the institutional fulcrum of the transformation process. It has put in place a differentiated system of financial incentives, which it is constantly modifying in the light of experience of the reactions of the actors in the health care systems. This competitive transformation of health care systems requires governments to display greater assertiveness than in the past vis-à-vis service providers. A further shared characteristic is the incremental nature of the transformation. Proceeding in this stepwise manner makes it possible both to take full account of the complexity of the governance problems and to limit the number of opponents of reform.

The expectation that the shift towards a health care governance regime in which competition plays a much greater role would lead to the state's withdrawal from health care policy has to date remained unfulfilled. In fact, the opposite is the case. It is true that, in abolishing the obligation to contract, the state has given individual actors' greater freedom of action. To that extent, it is possible to speak of a partial withdrawal. At the same time, however, new tasks have emerged. Since the logics underpinning economics, on the one hand, and medical practice, on the other, are fundamentally incompatible with each other, the introduction of financial incentives brings with it a need for strong regulation. New regulatory spheres continue to emerge (for example quality assurance) and there is an increased need for state supervision in order to identify and penalise undesirable reactions on the actors' part. As a result, there continues to be a high level of state intervention in all three systems, and indeed an increase in regulatory density can be observed. However, the linkage between the establishment of a market and state regulation is highly variable. If a high level of state intervention can still be observed, this suggests that the political elites regard such intervention to be desirable or necessary. Whether this perception lasts will depend largely on the social conflicts surrounding health care policy.

NOTE

1. I am grateful to Ralf Götze for his valuable advice. The author is of course solely responsible for any remaining deficiencies and errors.

REFERENCES

Achtermann, Wally and Christel Berset (eds) (2006), *Gesundheitspolitiken in der Schweiz – Potential für eine nationale Gesundheitspolitik, Bd. 1: Analyse und Perspektiven,* Bern: Bundesamt für Gesundheit.

Alber, Jens (ed.) (1992), *Das Gesundheitswesen der Bundesrepublik Deutschland. Entwicklung, Struktur und Funktionsweise,* Frankfurt am Main, New York: Campus.

Alber, Jens and Brigitte Bernardi-Schenkluhn (eds) (1992), *Westeuropäische Gesundheitssysteme im Vergleich. Bundesrepublik Deutschland, Schweiz, Frankreich, Italien, Großbritannien,* Frankfurt am Main, New York: Campus.

Bandelow, Nils C. (ed.) (1998), *Gesundheitspolitik. Der Staat in der Hand einzelner Interessengruppen?,* Opladen: Leske & Budrich.

Baur, Rita, Andrea Heimer and Silvia Wieseler (2000), 'Gesundheitssysteme und Reformansätze im internationalen Vergleich', in Jan Böcken, Martin Butzlaff and Andreas Esche (eds), *Reformen im Gesundheitswesen. Ergebnisse der internationalen Recherche,* Gütersloh: Verlag Bertelsmann Stiftung, pp. 23–149.

Behrend, C., F. Buchnerand, M. Happich et al. (2007), 'Risk-adjusted Capitation Payments: How Well Do Prinicipal Inpatient Diagnosis-based Models Work in the German Situation? Results from a Large Data set', *European Journal of Health Economics,* **8** (1), 31–39.

Bernardi-Schenkluhn, Brigitte (1992), 'Schweiz', in Jens Alber and Brigitte Bernardi-Schenkluhn (eds), *Westeuropäische Gesundheitssysteme im Vergleich. Bundesrepublik Deutschland, Schweiz, Frankreich, Italien, Großbritannien*, Frankfurt am Main, New York: Campus, pp. 177–321.

Björkman, James W. and Kieke G.H. Okma (1997), 'Restructuring Health Care Systems in The Netherlands: The Institutional Heritage of Dutch Health Policy Reforms', in James W. Björkman and Christa Altenstetter (eds), *Health Policy Reform, National Variations and Globalization*, London: Macmillan, pp. 79–108.

Blank, Robert H. and Viola Burau (eds) (2007), *Comparative Health Policy*, 2nd ed, London: Palgrave.

Daley, C. and J. Gubb (2007), 'Health Reform in the Netherlands', *Civitas*, **11**, 1–14, www.civitas.org.uk/nhs/netherlands.pdf, last access 14 March 2008.

den Exter, André et al. (2004), *Health Care Systems in Transition: Netherlands*, Copenhagen: WHO Regional Office for Europe on Behalf of the European Observatory on Health Systems and Policies.

Döhler, M. (1995), 'The State as Architect of Political Order: Policy Dynamics in German Health Care', *Governance*, **8**, 380–404.

Döhler, Marian (2002), 'Gesundheitspolitik in der Verhandlungsdemokratie', in Winand Gellner and Markus Schön (eds), *Paradigmenwechsel in der Gesundheitspolitik?*, Baden-Baden: Nomos, pp. 25–40.

Döhler, M. and P. Manow-Borgwardt (1992), 'Korporatisierung als gesundheitspolitische Strategie', *Staatswissenschaften und Staatspraxis*, **3**, 64–106.

Douven, Rudy (2007), 'Morbidity-based Risk Adjustment in the Netherlands', in Eberhard Wille, Volker Ulrich and Udo Schneider (eds), *Wettbewerb und Risikostrukturausgleich im internationalen Vergleich. Erfahrungen aus den USA, der Schweiz, den Niederlanden und Deutschland*, Baden-Baden: Nomos, pp. 161–202.

Enquete-Kommission (1990), *Strukturreform der gesetzlichen Krankenversicherung. Endbericht der Enquete-Kommission des 11. Deutschen Bundestages*, 'Strukturreform der gesetzlichen Krankenversicherung', Bd. 1, Bonn: Deutscher Bundestag.

Freeman, Richard (ed.) (2000), *The Politics of Health in Europe*, Manchester: Manchester University Press.

Freeman, R. and M. Moran (2000), 'Reforming Health Care in Europe', *West European Politics*, **23**, 35–58.

Frei, Andreas and Stephan Hill (eds) (1990), *Das schweizerische Gesundheitswesen*, Basel: Verlag G. Krebs.

Gerlinger, T. (1998), 'Punktlandungsübungen im Hamsterrad. Über Handlungsanreize und Steuerungswirkungen der kassenärztlichen Vergütungsreform', *Jahrbuch für Kritische Medizin*, **28**, 99–124.

Gerlinger, T. (2002), *Zwischen Korporatismus und Wettbewerb: Gesundheitspolitische Steuerung im Wandel*, Wissenschaftszentrum Berlin für Sozialforschung, Arbeitsgruppe Public Health, Discussion Paper P02–204, Berlin: WZB.

Gerlinger, Thomas (2008), 'Wettbewerbsinduzierte Unitarisierung. Der Wandel der Bund-Länder-Beziehungen in der Gesundheitspolitik', in Europäisches Zentrum für Föderalismus-Forschung Tübingen (ed.), *Jahrbuch des Föderalismus 2008*, Baden-Baden: Nomos (im Erscheinen).

Gerlinger, Thomas, Kai Mosebach and Rolf Schmucker (2007), *Wettbewerbssteuerung in der Gesundheitspolitik. Die Auswirkungen des GKV-WSG auf das Akteurshandeln im Gesundheitswesen*, Johann Wolfgang Goethe-Universität Frankfurt, Institut für Medizinische Soziologie, Diskussionspapier 2007-1, Frankfurt am Main: Johann Wolfgang Goethe-Universität Frankfurt am Main.

Greß, Stefan (ed) (2002), *Krankenversicherung und Wettbewerb. Das Beispiel Niederlande*, Frankfurt am Main and New York: Campus.

Greß, S. (2006), 'Regulated Competition in Social Health Insurance: A Three-country Comparison', *International Social Security Review*, **59**, 27–47.

Groenewegen, P.P. and S. Greß (2000), 'Die Auswirkungen der wettbewerbsorientierten Reformen im niederländischen Gesundheitssystem auf die Beziehungen zwischen Hausärzten, Krankenkassen und Versicherten', *Das Gesundheitswesen*, **62**, 568–576.

Hartmann, Anja K. (ed.) (2002), *Zwischen Differenzierung und Integration. Die Entwicklung des Gesundheitssystems in den Niederlanden und der Bundesrepublik*, Opladen: Leske & Budrich.

Hassenteufel, P. (2001), 'Liberalisation Through the State. Why is the French Health Insurance System Becoming So British?', *Public Policy and Administration*, **16**, 84–95.

Herder-Dorneich, Philipp (ed.) (1994), *Ökonomische Theorie des Gesundheitswesens. Problemgeschichte, Problembereiche, Theoretische Grundlagen*, Baden-Baden: Nomos.

Hitz, Patrik and Volker Ulrich (2003), 'Steuerung von Gesundheitssystemen – Kriterien, Ansätze und offene Fragen', in Christoph A. Zenger and Tarzis Jung (eds), *Management im Gesundheitswesen und in der Gesundheitspolitik. Kontext – Normen – Perspektiven*, Bern et al.: Verlag Hans Huber, pp. 197–210.

Hoffmeyer, Ullrich (ed.) (1993), *Gesundheitsreform in der Schweiz. Auszug aus einem internationalen Vergleich*, Zürich: Verlag Neue Zürcher Zeitung.

Immergut, Ellen (ed.) (1992), *Health Politics: Interests and Institutions in Western Europe*, Cambridge: Cambridge University Press.

Jacobs, Klaus, Peter Reschke, Dieter Cassel et al. (eds) (2002), *Zur Wirkung des Risikostrukturausgleichs in der gesetzlichen Krankenversicherung*, Baden-Baden: Nomos.

Kania, Helga and Bernhard Blanke (2000), 'Von der "Korporatisierung" zum Wettbewerb. Gesundheitspolitische Kurswechsel in den Neunzigerjahren', in Roland Czada and Hellmut Wollmann (eds), *Von der Bonner zur Berliner Republik. 10 Jahre Deutsche Einheit*, Wiesbaden: Westdeutscher Verlag, pp. 567–591.

Kassenärztliche Bundesvereinigung (2008), *Ärztliche Kooperationsformen*, http://www.kbv.de/publikationen/10686.html, last access 6 March 2008.

Klingenberger, David (2002), *Health Maintenance Organizations in der Schweiz – Darstellung und Kritik*, IDZ-Information Nr. 1/2002, Köln: Institut der Deutschen Zahnärzte.

Kocher, Gerhard (2007), 'Kompetenz- und Aufgabenteilung Bund – Kantone – Gemeinden', in Gerhard Kocher and Willy Oggier (eds), *Gesundheitswesen Schweiz 2007–2009. Eine aktuelle Übersicht*, 3. Aufl., Bern: Verlag Hans Huber, pp. 109–118.

Kocher, R., S. Greß and J. Wasem (2002), 'Vorbild für einen regulierten Wettbewerb in der deutschen Krankenversicherung?', *Soziale Sicherheit* (Switzerland), 299–307.

Leu, Robert E. and Konstantin Beck (2007), 'Risikoselektion und Risikostrukturausgleich in der Schweiz', in Eberhard Wille, Volker Ulrich and Udo Schneider (eds), *Wettbewerb und Risikostrukturausgleich im internationalen Vergleich. Erfahrungen aus den USA, der Schweiz, den Niederlanden und Deutschland*, Baden-Baden: Nomos, pp. 115–159.

Lieverdink, H. (2001), 'The Marginal Success of Regulated Competition Policy in the Netherlands', *Social Science & Medicine*, **52**, 1183–1194.

Lütz, Susanne and Roland Czada (2000), 'Marktkonstitution als politische Aufgabe: Problemskizze und Theorieüberblick', in Roland Czada and Susanne Lütz (eds), *Die politische Konstitution von Märkten*, Wiesbaden: Westdeutscher Verlag, pp. 9–35.

Maarse, Hans and Kieke H.G. Okma (2004), 'The Privatisation Paradox in Dutch Health Care', in Hans Maarse (ed.), *Privatisation in European Health Care: A Comparative Analysis of Eight Countries*, Maarssen: Elsevier, pp. 97–116.

Majone, G. (1997), 'From the Positive to the Regulatory State: Causes and Consequences to Changes in the Mode of Governance', *Journal of Public Policy*, **2**, 139–167.

Minder, Andreas, Hans Schönholzer and Marianne Amiet (2000), *Health Care Systems in Transition: Switzerland*, Copenhagen: WHO Regional Office for Europe on behalf of the European Observatory on Health Systems and Policies.

Noweski, Michael (2008), *Der Gesundheitsmarkt. Liberalisierung und Reregulierung als Resultat politischer Koalitionen*, Berlin: Verlag Dr. Köster.

Oberender, Peter, Ansgar Hebborn and Jürgen Zerth (eds) (2006), *Wachstumsmarkt Gesundheit*, 2., überarb. u. aktualis. Aufl., Stuttgart: Lucius & Lucius.

Okma, Kieke G.H. (1997), *Studies in Dutch Health Politics, Policies and Law*, Utrecht; University of Utrecht.

Okma, Kieke G.H. (2002), 'Health Care and the Welfare States: Two Worlds of Welfare Drifting Apart?', in Jos Berghman, Herbert Feigl and Ad Nagelkerke (eds), *Social Security in Transition*, Leiden: Kluwer Law International, pp. 229–238.

Okma, Kieke G.H. (2008), *Recent Changes in Dutch Health Insurance: Individual Mandate or Social Insurance?*, paper presented at the Annual Meeting of the National Academy of Social Insurance, Washington, DC, 30 and 31 January.

Oliver, A., E. Mossialos and D. Wilsford (eds) (2005), 'Legacies and Latitude in European Health Policy', *Journal of Health Politics, Policy and Law*, **30** (Special Issue, No. 1–2), 1–314.

Rosenbrock, Rolf and Thomas Gerlinger (2006), *Gesundheitspolitik. Eine systematische Einführung*, 2., vollst. überarb. u. erw. Aufl., Bern: Verlag Hans Huber.

Rosewitz, Bernd and Douglas Webber (1990), *Reformversuche und Reformblockaden im deutschen Gesundheitswesen*, Frankfurt am Main and New York: Campus.

Saltman, R.B. (2002), 'Regulating incentives: The Past and Present Role of the State in Health Care Systems', *Social Science & Medicine*, **54**, 1677–1684.

Saltman, Richard B., Reinhard Busse and Josep Figueras (eds) (2004), *Social Health Insurance Systems in Western Europe. European Observatory on Health Care Systems Series*, Buckingham, UK: Open University Press.

Schut, F.T. (1995), 'Health Care Reform in the Netherlands: Balancing Corporatism, Etatism, and Market Mechanisms', *Journal of Health Politics, Policy and Law*, **20**, 615–652.

Simon, Michael (2000), *Krankenhauspolitik in der Bundesrepublik Deutschland. Historische Entwicklung und Probleme der politischen Steuerung stationärer Krankenversorgung*, Opladen and Wiesbaden: Westdeutscher Verlag.

Simon, Michael (2008), *Das Gesundheitssystem. Eine Einführung in Struktur und Funktionsweise*, 2., vollst. überarb. Aufl., Bern: Verlag Hans Huber.

Urban, Hans-Jürgen (2001), *Wettbewerbskorporatistische Regulierung im Politikfeld Gesundheit. Der Bundesausschuss der Ärzte und Krankenkassen und die gesundheitspolitische Wende*, Wissenschaftszentrum Berlin für Sozialforschung, Arbeitsgruppe Public Health, Discussion Paper P01–206, Berlin: WZB.

van de Ven, W.P.M., K. Beck, F. Buchner et al. (2003), 'Risk Adjustment and Risk Selection on the Sickness Fund Insurance Market in Five European Countries', *Health Policy*, **77**, 75–98.

van Ginneken, E., R. Busse and C. Gericke (2006), 'Das neue Krankenversicherungssystem in den Niederlanden: Erste Erfahrungen mit der Mischung aus Kopfpauschalen, Bürgerversicherung und einem zentralen Fonds', *Gesundheits- und Sozialpolitik*, **60**, 10–18.

Vatter, Adrian (2003), 'Strukturen, Prozesse und Inhalte der schweizerischen Gesundheitspolitik', in Christoph A. Zenger and Tarzis Jung (eds), *Management im Gesundheitswesen und in der Gesundheitspolitik. Kontext – Normen – Perspektiven*, Bern et al.: Verlag Hans Huber, pp. 155–165.

Vogel, Steven K. (1996), *Freer Markets, More Rules. Regulatory Reform in Advanced Industrial Countries*, Ithaca and London: Cornell University Press.

Webber, D. (1988), 'Krankheit, Geld und Politik. Zur Geschichte der Gesundheitsreformen in Deutschland', *Leviathan*, **16**, 156–203.

Wendt, Claus (2003), *Krankenversicherung oder Gesundheitsversorgung? Gesundheitssysteme im Vergleich*, Wiesbaden: Westdeutscher Verlag.

Wirthner, A and V. Ulrich (2003), 'Managed Care', in Christoph A. Zenger and Tarzis Jung (eds), *Management im Gesundheitswesen und in der Gesundheitspolitik. Kontext – Normen – Perspektiven*, Bern et al.: Verlag Hans Huber, pp. 255–267.

8. Pension Politics in the 21st Century: From Class Conflict to Modernising Compromise?

Giuliano Bonoli

INTRODUCTION

Current debates on pension policy are overwhelmingly focused on the expected impact of population ageing on the financial viability of current arrangements. However, demographic pressures are not the only problem pension policy-makers have to face. Changes in labour markets that have taken place over the last two to three decades have brought into the labour force of Western countries a whole new range of career profiles, which are usually not well provided for by the pension systems inherited from the post-war years. Above all, this is a result of the large-scale entry into employment of women, and particularly of mothers, whose careers tend to be punctuated by interruptions and/or long spells of part-time employment: two situations that tend to result in more or less serious pension penalties at retirement age. However, the labour market has also undergone other important changes from this perspective. New risks such as long-term or cyclical unemployment have become more widespread since the 1970s, and changes in the organisation of work and in technology mean that the risk of possessing obsolete skills is also on the increase and may result in more frequent job changes or time spent out of the labour market in order to acquire new skills. All these labour market situations tend to generate lower pension entitlements than those obtained by standard workers who spend their entire working life in full-time employment. Yet it is generally on this ever rarer career profile that our pension systems are modelled.

Workers who are not well provided for by existing arrangements are increasing in number and constitute, at least potentially, an electorally significant constituency. As a result, we can expect political entrepreneurs to be responsive to their needs and to bring them into the pension policy arena, where they will compete for attention with other pension issues, such as adapting to population ageing. The joint presence of these two pressures on pension policy may provide a much appreciated opportunity for political exchange between political actors concerned about the long-term financial sustainability of pension arrangement and those concerned about the inclusion of atypical workers in a decent pension settlement.

In this chapter, it is argued that the governance of pension system reform processes will be increasingly based on compromise. Countries will tend to combine different interests into instances of political exchange which we denote here by the term 'modernising compromises'. These compromises modernise pension systems in so far as they include elements of adaptation to new social demands. They are compromises, because the inclusion of such measures broadens the support base of a reform, and makes the adoption of unpopular retrenchment measures more likely.

Modernising compromises look like the way forward in pension reform, capable of producing politically acceptable policy change. Nonetheless, they are rare, though not non-existent. The objective of this chapter is to identify the conditions under which such compromises are possible and even likely, and those under which they are not. It starts with an explanation of why we can expect modernising compromises to occur, and under what conditions these are most likely from a theoretical point of view. Then the chapter moves on to the discussion of pension reform trajectories in Sweden, France, Switzerland, Italy and Germany, five countries that all successfully adapted their pension systems in the 1990s. In the final part, the various pension reforms are compared in order to test empirically the validity of the hypotheses considered.

MODERNISING COMPROMISES IN PENSION REFORM: THE ARGUMENT

The 1990s and early 2000s demonstrated that pension reforms are extremely difficult political exercises. The ability to retire from work at the age of 60 or 65 and enjoy a standard of living close to the one experienced while in employment is a feature of industrial societies to which citizens are extremely attached. The political science literature has long recognised this essential feature of pension policy in the current context of austerity, and has emphasised the fact that welfare reforms in general, but in particular the retrenchment of pension arrangements, is a politically treacherous exercise that has pushed governments to develop skilful, if intransparent, policy making strategies such as obfuscation or the inclusion of side payments in reform (Pierson 1994; Pierson and Weaver 1993).

Political actors defending the status quo against retrenchment have several advantages in the political confrontation on pension reform. First, they can rely on the overall popularity of pension arrangements to find supporters and even to enlarge their social basis. Second, the opposite camp, supporting retrenchment, faces a stronger risk of defection. In fact, political actors (parties, and especially unions) belonging to the pro-retrenchment coalition may be tempted to reap the popularity dividend of opposing reform and either abandon the pro-retrenchment camp or adopt an ambiguous position on reform (Bonoli 2000). Opponents of reform can often count on easy-to-mobilise constituencies, consisting of older workers, who are obviously looking forward to their retirement and, having been socialised in the world of work in the 1960s and 1970s, are likely to have a strong class identity and inclination to resort to informal protest. In many countries, it is these workers who make up the bulk of union members.

This feature of pension reform is confirmed by the failures of governments that have attempted to impose cuts unilaterally. The clearest examples are the failed reform initiatives undertaken by the Berlusconi government in 1994 in Italy and the Juppé government in 1995 in France. On both occasions, governments prepared their reform plans without any significant negotiation with the unions and attempted to impose them unilaterally. The result was massive and sustained informal protest which led first to the abandonment of the reform plans, and subsequently to the fall of the governments (Bonoli 2000; Natali 2002).

Faced with immense problems of political feasibility and under the pressure of actual or predicted financial imbalances due to population ageing, governments have, with the few exceptions mentioned above, been inclined to search for compromises with the relevant political actors, in particular the unions (Bonoli 2000; Myles and Pierson, 2001; Natali 2002). Compromises have often simply taken the shape of moderation in the extent of cuts, often below what pension experts regard as essential to restore the financial soundness of schemes, or have taken the shape of 'quid pro quos'. These can be described as real instances of political exchange between a reform-oriented government and a coalition, usually structured around the labour movement, defending the status quo. Quid pro quos are likely to be more effective factors of political feasibility than moderation, as they require the inclusion of new elements in the reform that constitute an advantage for political actors representing those who are otherwise losing in the reform.

Such quid pro quos can take several different forms. In Italy, for example, the unions obtained a very long phasing-in period for the reform, so that most of their current members (retired people and older workers) would not be affected by the changes. In Sweden, an overall reduction of pension entitlements was accompanied by a change in the formula that, in comparison to the pre-reform system, is more favourable to blue-collar workers. These elements, and those which are reviewed in the case studies presented below, are not simply instances of moderation in pension reform but are real concessions targeted at key actors whose, by virtue of their mobilising capacity, can conceivably disrupt the policy-making process and prevent the successful adoption of the reform. From the point of view of the actor concerned, these quid pro quos represent an improvement of the policy, and in this respect they are much more effective in ensuring the acceptance of a reform than compromises based on moderation. The actors who benefit from these deals are not simply going to reluctantly accept the reform; they will have a stake in it.

Policy-makers wishing to contain the future growth of pension expenditure are likely to be on the look-out for quid pro quos that can ensure the adoption of at least partially retrenchment-oriented reforms. In this respect, the existence in pension policy of issues other than population ageing may constitute a serious opportunity for them. The adaptation of pension systems to changing labour market and family structures is certainly one of these issues. Generally speaking, the pension systems inherited from the post-war years are based on the assumption that full-time uninterrupted work is the norm. What's more, during the three decades of prosperity following the Second World War, work was generally characterised by high wage increases which were possible thanks to rising productivity in manufacturing. Today's labour markets, however, are very different. As large numbers of women have gained access to employment, the sort of career profiles that one finds in the workforce have become much more heterogeneous. Since women tend to be the main carers even in contemporary families, their working lives are typically characterised by interruptions and by long spells of part-time employment. In addition, post-industrial employment is characterised by higher levels of both cyclical and long-term unemployment than during the full-employment years after World War II.

The career profiles that result from these labour market changes are generally not particularly well catered for by existing pension systems, which were mostly constructed during the early post-war years. Of course, a majority of labour market participants continue to conform to the standard pattern of full-time uninterrupted work, but the size of the minority that does not fit into this group has increased dramatically over the last couple of decades (Bonoli and Gay-des-Combes 2003). Since the time they spend out of the labour market does not generate pension entitlements, they risk reaching retirement age without adequate pension coverage. This group is slowly gaining awareness of its situation, and it is beginning to represent an electorally significant constituency. Improving the pension coverage of these groups of marginal workers can be seen as an additional demand on pension systems.

Policy-makers can be seen as caught between two contrasting pressures. On the one hand, they need to keep pension schemes financially viable, especially in the context of a worsening population age structure. On the other hand, they must improve marginal and atypical workers' access to a decent pension income. Contrasting pressures, however, may turn out to be an opportunity for pension reform. In fact, we can expect that the presence of two sorts of demands on policy-makers will create scope for quid pro quos that combine cuts in the overall generosity of pension schemes with selective improvements in coverage targeted at disadvantaged workers. As generalised cuts concern a much larger number of persons than targeted improvements, it is possible to implement these quid pro quos in a way that generates substantial savings, and is therefore consistent with the overall aim of preserving the financial sustainability of pension systems. At the same time, relatively inexpensive improvements may help the reform to attract the support it needs to be adopted. The combination of retrenchment and selective expansion within a single pension reform can be described as a modernising compromise. It constitutes an instance of 'modernisation' of the pension system, in the sense that pensions are adapted to socio-economic changes that create new needs.

Modernising compromises are based on the quid pro quo logic described above and can combine, for example, changes in the pension formula that result in lower benefits or increases in retirement age with generous contribution credits for carers, or measures that strengthen the inclusion of part-time workers in pension schemes. In spite of their political robustness, modernising compromises have been rare in recent pension reforms, though not non-existent. Theoretically we can expect modernising compromises to be particularly likely under specific institutional and socio-economic conditions. These are explored by the following four hypotheses. For each of them, some evidence concerning the independent variable is also provided.

*Hypothesis 1: Modernising compromises are more likely in countries which –
initially – do not provide measures designed to improve the pension coverage
of non-standard workers*

Modernising compromises are likely to be one-off events. Once the deal has been made, i.e. once the position of non-standard workers has been improved through the adoption of dedicated policy measures, the pressure to solve this problem, and as a result the 'value' of this sort of measure as a token of political exchange, is reduced. It is of course also possible that the inclusion of non-standard employment in pension coverage could take place incrementally; under these circumstances, modernising compromises could occur more than once. However, it seems reasonable to expect this kind of policy package to be more attractive in countries where such provision is non-existent.

Among the five countries investigated in this paper, two – France and Germany – had introduced these sorts of adjustments before the 1990s. Switzerland and Italy, in contrast, do not make provision for atypical employment. The situation in Sweden is somewhat more complicated, because even though the pre-reform system did not include contribution credits, the generous rules applied de facto disregarded even fairly long periods out of employment or in part-time employment. However, the new system adopted in the 1990s removed these generous elements. At the beginning of the reform process, the situation in Sweden is thus comparable to that in Switzerland or Italy: i.e. there is no provision for non-standard workers.

Hypothesis 2: Veto points are conducive to (modernising) compromises

Veto points are a powerful incentive for policy-makers to seek negotiated policy solutions (Lehmbruch 1993; Neidhart 1970; Schmidt 1996; Tsebelis 1995, 2002). In political systems where interests that are not represented in government have effective opportunities to challenge the adoption of legislation, governments are often inclined to take account of their priorities and demands and develop policies that are in effect compromises. In the field of pension reform, countries with political systems characterised by a high density of veto points have tended to adopt less unilateral and more consensual policy solutions (Bonoli 2000, 2001). Veto points are thus associated with compromises, and can as a result be expected, all other things being equal, to favour the adoption of the sort of policy packages described as modernising compromises in this article.

Of our five countries, Switzerland's political system has the most veto points, followed by Germany. In contrast, France, Italy and Sweden are generally considered as countries where political power is relatively strongly concentrated in the executive branch of government (depending on electoral results).

Hypothesis 3: Modernising compromises are likely in countries where older employees and non-standard workers are represented by the same political actor

From a theoretical point of view, we can expect modernising compromises to take place when those who lose as a result of retrenchment and those who gain as a result of selective improvements are represented by the same political actor (for example a trade union confederation or a social democratic party). Under such conditions, a single political actor is both a winner and a loser in the reform, and may find the overall result satisfactory. A crucial variable in this respect is the membership composition of the unions. Where these are mostly made up of older workers, modernising compromises are unlikely. Why would a political actor representing people who are about to retire trade cuts in their pension entitlement for improvements in the position of non-unionised atypical workers? In contrast, in countries where union members include women and younger workers in non-standard employment, we can expect modernising compromises to be an acceptable deal for the labour movement. Modernising compromises are thus more likely in countries in which the unions and, in the case of a divided labour movement, those whose assent is essential to the adoption of a reform, have memberships that contain a substantial proportion people with a marginal labour market situation. Here we can expect the political gains to some of the organisation's members to outweigh or at least to compensate for the losses experienced by other members.

Table 8.1   *Trade union membership: non-active membership as a proportion of total membership, female density and per cent of female members, selected countries, 1998 or most recent available*

	Non-active members	Female union density	Proportion of female members, main union confederation
Austria	17.5	32.6	31.7
Denmark	14.0	59.2	48.4
Germany	19.0	16.7	30.4
Ireland	-	45.0	38.3
Italy	49.5	-	-
Netherlands	19.0	17.0	26.0
Sweden	-	89.5	48.4
Switzerland	13.3	14.0	22.1*
United Kingdom	-	-	38.5

Sources: Ebbinghaus and Visser 2000; * *Source:* USS, personal communication

Unfortunately, accurate comparative data on the age and gender composition of trade union membership for each of the five countries covered in this paper is apparently not available. Table 8.1, however, provides some information on this independent variable. The proportion of non-active members in a union, most of whom are retired persons, provides a rough indication of the age structure of the membership.

This argument can also be extended to countries where the most important political actor opposing reform is not the labour movement but a single-issue interest group. Under such circumstances, modernising compromises are most unlikely. It is in fact difficult to picture the US AARP acquiescing to pension cuts in return for measures that are likely to benefit not its members, but working mothers and marginal employees.

Hypothesis 4: Modernising compromises are likely in countries where there are ties between a social democratic party and the unions

Modernising compromises can also be expected in countries where losers and winners are represented by different political actors, but where these political actors are relatively strongly connected. Generally speaking, the link between social democratic parties and trade unions is strongest in countries with reformist labour movements and where social democratic parties and unions have tended to have either a balanced relationship or one dominated by the party. In our five country sample, strong connections between unions and social democrats exist in Sweden (party lead) and in Switzerland (balanced). Links are considerably less important or non-existent in Germany, France and Italy (Ebbinghaus 1995: 82–84).

An example of a country in which modernising compromises are particularly likely would be one with a trade union movement representing mostly core middle-aged industrial workers, likely to lose out in the reform, but with strong organisational and political ties with a social democratic party with a left-libertarian orientation (Kitschelt 1994) and a stronger inclination to take into account the problems of non-standard workers. This situation may even be more conducive to modernising compromises than the one in which both groups are presented by the same actor. Under such circumstances, the union leadership may give the impression of being ineffective in protecting the interests of some of its members. However, when the two groups are represented by different but connected political actors, the one representing the losers can openly defend the status quo against the reform, while the one representing the winners can support the reform, but because the two actors belong to the same political camp, one can expect the opposition to the reform to be somewhat moderated.

THE CASE STUDIES: PENSION REFORM IN FIVE COUNTRIES

The hypotheses presented in the previous section are tested against developments in pension policy in five Western European countries: Sweden, France, Switzerland, Italy and Germany. These countries all successfully introduced pension reforms in the 1990s, usually after negotiations with the unions or after the inclusion in the new pension legislation of substantial concessions to the unions. It is under these circumstances that modernising compromises can be adopted. The discussion of each national case includes a presentation of the main elements of the pension reform and of the policy-making process and a description of the provisions for atypical career profiles, essentially contribution credits for non-employed people.

The Swedish Reforms of the 1990s

In the 1990s, Sweden changed its pension system dramatically. The most notable new feature was arguably the shift from a defined benefit to a defined contribution system. The change did not affect the funding system, which remains largely based on the pay-as-you-go principle, but did affect the method of benefit calculation. In the new system, benefits are based on career earnings, whereas before the reform only the best 15 years would be considered. This means that, all other things being equal, the pensions calculated on the basis of the new formula will be lower than in the old system, especially for workers with career interruptions or for those experiencing big wage increases towards the end of their careers. In addition, the new formula is demographically weighted on the basis of the life expectancy of each cohort reaching retirement. If life expectancy increases, pensions are automatically adjusted downwards. Finally, the reform also includes provision for making funded individual retirement accounts compulsory. These accounts are known in Sweden as 'premium reserve' pensions. They are financed by a 2.5 per cent contribution and can be chosen by each insured person among some 500 competing providers, which include commercial companies, trade union funds, and a default fund run by the government.

The Swedish reform, in spite of the fact that it introduced some retrenchment elements especially for people with specific career profiles, was accepted in a consensual manner. The main losers in the reform were white-collar employees and managers, or those who start working relatively late after a long period spent in education. Losses are however more widespread, as about 80 per cent of the population is likely to lose between 7 and 8 per cent of their pension as a result of the reform (Anderson 2003: 24). This loss should, however, be offset by the income stream resulting from the new premium reserve pensions, which will depend to a significant extent on the returns on the invested capital and is, as a result, unpredictable.

The political success of a reform that created so many losers can be explained with reference to a number of quid pro quos that were negotiated between different actors. First, the blue collar union, LO,[1] obtained a new pension formula that is comparatively more advantageous to its members than the previous one. The system that existed prior to the 1990s was introduced in the late 1950s, after difficult and contentious negotiations among all relevant actors. At the time, the issue was to generalise second pillar pension coverage that was available only to some, mostly white-collar workers and managers, who were covered by company pension funds. The blue-collar union LO was behind that move, and in order to make the change acceptable to the middle classes, it accepted a pension formula which based the final benefit on earnings during the best 15 years. This formula was particularly advantageous for managers and white-collar workers, who start working later and tend to see their earnings increase faster towards the end of their careers. The formula that was in force prior to the 1990s reforms turned out to be well suited for women as well. In fact, career interruptions and periods on low earnings due, for example, to part-time work did not impact on pensions because of the 15 years rule in the formula.

In order not to penalise women but also to compensate white-collar workers who had lost out because of the change in the pension formula, the reform introduced generous contribution credits for several categories of non-employed people. These are granted for career interruptions due to child rearing, periods of unemployment, study, military service and sickness. With regard to child rearing, if a parent reduces working hours in the four years following the birth of a child, contributions are credited to his/her pension account on the basis of previous earnings. If he or she stops working completely, then the contribution credit will be based on 75 per cent of the average wage. If parents continue working as before having a child, their credited contributions will be based on their earning plus one base amount. Parents can claim only one child credit at any one time, but they remain entitled to it as long as they have children younger than four. People serving in the army receive a contribution credit based on 50 per cent of the average wage. Individuals who are not working because of unemployment or sickness receive contribution credits based on their insured earnings (Riksförsäkringsverket 2001). Contribution credits apply to both the pay-as-you-go scheme and the premium reserve pension, to which actual contributions are paid in by the government.

The Swedish reform combined overall retrenchment in pensions with the introduction of one of the most generous systems of contribution credits.

These credits, unlike those in most other countries, apply not only to the state pension, but also to private individual retirement accounts. Of course, to a large extent these contribution credits can be seen as a way to offset the losses that the lifetime earnings formula engenders for some disadvantaged workers. Many of those who are now entitled to contribution credits would probably have fared just as well (or even better) under the old system. However, the fact that their needs were taken into account when drafting the reform suggests that the political actors behind the compromise were sensitive to them.

France: the 1993 Pension Reform

The pension reform issue has been almost permanently on the agenda over the last decade in France. The popularity of the pension system, the divisions within the labour[2] movement and the fact that some of its most radical sections are not inclined to collaborate with government-sponsored retrenchment initiatives have made the reform of pensions a particularly thorny issue. Governments of different political persuasions have been equally fearful of the potential political consequences of pension reform and have tended to procrastinate policy change. On only two occasions have there been serious attempts at reforming the pension system. The first one was successfully carried through by the right-wing Balladur government in 1993, and is reviewed below. The second attempt, by the Juppé government made in 1995, failed after some three weeks of sustained union protest and public sector strikes.[3]

The French pension system contains several provisions related to family events. These, however, are meant not so much to compensate for contribution gaps due to child rearing but rather to encourage couples to have children. This is perfectly in line with France's natalist family policy. Mothers are entitled to two additional years of contributions for each child they have taken care of. Fathers can also receive extra contribution years if they take parental leave. In addition, parents who reduce their working hours or stop working altogether in order to take care of a child are entitled to a cash benefit, known as the *'allocation parentale d'éducation'*. The benefit is available to parents with at least two children and can last up to three years. Recipients of this benefit are credited with pension contributions equal to those due on a salary of €1,127 per month (in 2002). Finally, parents who have had at least three children are entitled to a pension bonus equal to 10 per cent of the benefit. These measures, however, have been in force since the 1970s or before. They are not related to the current drive to adapt pension systems to women's career profiles (France Pratique 2003; CNAV, personal communication).

Soon after the 1993 general election, the newly elected right-wing government started working on the pension reform issue. The trade unions, particularly the Communist CGT and the radical FO were rather reluctant to accept cutbacks, as they had been before. Ministry officials were certainly aware of the fact that a fully consensual solution was not possible. Nevertheless, what could be achieved was a situation in which at least the most radical sections of the labour movement would have refrained from staging an informal protest.

The government's position was to favour the adoption of the measures suggested in an earlier white paper published by their Socialist predecessors in 1991. The number of contribution years needed to be granted a full pension of 50 per cent of the reference salary was to be increased from 37.5 to 40. At the same time, the reference salary was to be calculated as the average of the best 25 years' earnings (instead of 10 years). Third, the indexation of benefits currently being paid was to be shifted from gross wages to prices. The overall impact of this series of measures, which were eventually adopted, would have been to reduce benefits and possibly to raise the retirement age, since employees would qualify for a full pension two and a half years later than under previous legislation.

These proposals, which were clearly unacceptable to the trade unions, were accompanied by plans to set up an 'old age solidarity fund' (*Fonds de Solidarité Vieillesse*), financed through general taxation (as opposed to contributions), which was to finance the non-contributory elements of the insurance-based pension schemes. The new fund is used to pay for minimum pensions, which are means-tested and paid regardless of contribution record, and the contribution credits given to unemployed people, to those serving in the army and to parents. Before the 1993 reform, these non-contributory benefits were partially financed by employment-related contributions. In fact, the shift in the funding of non-contributory elements from contributions to taxation was a key demand of the labour movement.

The French trade unions view the social security system as some sort of collective insurance plan covering all salaried employees and not as part of the state apparatus. From their perspective, the inclusion of non-contributory elements constitutes an infringement of the insurance principle according to which there must be a strict link between payments and benefits. This understanding of the role of social security was the basis upon which the whole system was built in 1945. As a matter of fact, the management of social security was placed in the hands not of civil servants but of joint committees on which both employers and employees were represented. This perception, however, is not shared by state actors. For them, the social security system is primarily a social policy instrument, which must intervene where social needs are identified. As a result, throughout the post-war period governments of different political persuasions have adopted measures to extend adequate coverage on a non-contributory basis to those who have been unable to build up a sufficient contribution record.

This diversity of views means that efforts to define the objectives of social security are a constant source of conflict between governments and the trade unions (Bonoli and Palier 1997). The state has been trying to expand its control over the system, while the trade unions have resisted such moves. For the latter, in fact, the managerial role they play is of crucial importance. First it gives them some sort of legitimacy in the eyes of public opinion, which somewhat compensates for their small membership. Second, it provides a substantial source of employment for union members (Rosanvallon 1995). For the trade unions, therefore, it is extremely important that the social security system remains under their control and that its financing is guaranteed.

The creation of a new 'old age solidarity fund' must be understood as a move towards meeting some of the unions' demands. The acceptance by the government of the separation between insurance-based and non-contributory provision was a de facto recognition that the main scheme was insurance-based and, by the same token, that the unions had a role to play in managing it. Moreover, the fund brought additional finance to pensions and as a result a balance between cutbacks in provision and increases in financial means was achieved. Thus the reform package included an element that was certainly going to be palatable to the trade unions, and that could be seen as a quid pro quo for their acceptance of retrenchment measures. This helps to explain why even the most radical sections of the labour movement refrained from attacking the new legislation through informal protest.

In France, there was a clear quid pro quo between the unions and the government.[4] However, political exchange here did not result in an improvement of pension coverage for people with atypical career patterns, in particular parents who reduce their working hours or stop working altogether in order to take care of their children. This may be due to the fact that such provision existed before and, unlike in Sweden, it was not affected by the reform. The French system is rather generous for mothers, as women with two children can obtain four extra contribution years and as a result take retirement earlier. Even though the credit is not meant to compensate for gaps in the contribution record (it is available also to mothers who stay in employment), periods spent out of the labour market for child rearing are probably well covered in France. However, other forms of non-employment and reduced hours employment do not benefit from the same treatment. Longer spells of part-time employment, whether in conjunction with child rearing or not, may result in substantial pension losses (proportional to the reduction in earnings).

Switzerland: Adapting Pensions to Women's Career Profiles (1995 Reform)

The origins of the 1995 pension reform go back to 1979, when, as a result of the adoption of a constitutional article on gender equality, it was decided that gender-based provision in the basic pension, for example the method of calculating couples' pensions, needed to be abolished (Bonoli 2000). Progress with this reform, however, was slow, and it was not until 1990 that a bill was produced by the government. The key element of the bill was the introduction of gender equality, but without abandoning couples' pensions. The bill made provision for the removal of any reference to gender in the pension formula, but did not take any proactive action in favour of women (such as contribution credits or sharing between spouses) as had been advocated by various actors.

Because it maintained couples' pensions, the 1990 pension reform bill was regarded by many, especially women's organisations and women MPs in the Social Democratic and Free Democratic parties, as a disappointment. Within the social security commission of the lower house of parliament, a consensus emerged on a radical modification of the bill that would take account of women's labour market position. By 1993 the bill had been significantly modified by parliament. It now envisaged the introduction of a contribution-sharing system between spouses and contribution credits for informal carers. Together with these measures, on which there was a relatively strong consensus, the new draft of the bill also included a more controversial proposal to raise the retirement age for women from 62 to 64 (the age for men is 65). This was imposed by the right-of-centre parliamentary majority, against the Social Democrats, allegedly in order to comply with the constitutional requirement of gender equality but also to achieve some savings in view of the predicted worsening of the ratio between pension scheme contributors and beneficiaries over the next few decades.

The increase in women's retirement age from 62 to 64 can be regarded as an instance of retrenchment rather than as a measure taken to comply with the constitutional article on gender equality. In fact, even though Switzerland does have a written constitution, there is no constitutional court entrusted with the task of interpreting or enforcing it. In practice, the constitution is interpreted by the government's own legal services, and on the issue of women's retirement age, the government's view was that the constitutional gender equality requirement was not to be applied until better labour market equality, in terms of wages, career patterns, had been achieved.

The introduction of the higher retirement age for women was fiercely attacked by the main union federations, USS and CSC.[5] Together they took advantage of the constitutional provision that allows any groups of citizens to challenge legislation passed by parliament in a referendum as long as they are able to produce 50,000 valid signatures demanding a vote. Both unions claimed to support contribution sharing and contribution credits for carers. However, they regarded the increase in women's retirement age as unacceptable, and were prepared to sacrifice the improvements in women's coverage if the increase in retirement age could be avoided. The referendum took place in June 1995, but the bill was accepted by 60.7 per cent of voters and as a result it became law.

Survey data suggest that the success of the bill at the polls was to a large extent due to the fact that it combined expansion measures (contribution credits) with an element of retrenchment (the increase in retirement age for women). Each measure was able to attract the support of different political camps, which dramatically increased the proportion of the electorate likely to vote in favour of the bill. It is fair to say that each one of the two measures, if adopted independently from the other one, would have been at a considerably higher risk of defeat at the polls. On this occasion, the improved coverage against a new social risk, that of being insufficiently covered by post-war welfare arrangements, was made possible but at the expense of an important concession: the acceptance of the increase in retirement age for women. Seemingly, the parliamentary coalition that supported the move, and in particular the Social Democratic party, cared more about younger women, who are the winners of the reform and are typical victims of the new social risks, than about older women in employment (who now have to wait two extra years before reaching retirement age). The trade unions, in contrast, assessed the same situation in opposite terms.

Italy: The 1995 Dini Reform

Until the early 1990s, Italy had one of the most generous and costly pension systems in Europe. The state scheme provided pensions equal to 70 per cent of average salary over the past five years from the age of 55 or 60 for women and men respectively. Financial pressures on the scheme intensified in the late 1980s, when the government budget deficit reached worrying proportions. A first attempt at containing pension expenditure was made in 1992. On that occasion, the statutory age of retirement was increased to 60 for women and 65 for men and the reference salary was changed from the average of the last 5 years to that of the last 10 years. Considering the unusual generosity of previous legislation and the fact that the changes adopted in 1992 were not enforced immediately but were meant to be phased in over a fairly long period, the 1992 reform constituted only a very limited attempt to deal with a very serious problem in financing pensions (Ferrera 1997; Natali 2002).

That is why towards the mid-1990s pension reform came back on the political agenda. First, in 1994 a right-of-centre government headed by Silvio Berlusconi tried to make a series of cuts in pensions without seeking external support. The response of the trade unions was to call a general strike, which persuaded the government to abandon its plans. In contrast, in 1995, a 'technical' government, which had the support of the left in parliament, managed to push through a more fundamental reform. The key modification was a shift from a defined-benefit system, where benefits are expressed as a proportion of earnings over a given number of years, to a defined-contribution system. Benefits now depend on the total amount of contributions paid by workers, which upon retirement is converted into an annuity whose value depends on the age of the person, on how the country's economy is performing and on the number of pensioners. The last two parameters are meant to allow the government to keep pension expenditure under control. The reform will most likely result in lower benefits (Artoni and Zanardi 1997; Ferrera 1997).

From the first stages of the preparatory work for the 1995 reform, it was clear that for the government it was essential to obtain the support, or at least the acquiescence, of the labour movement. Berlusconi's failure to retrench pensions unilaterally and the weakness of the 'technical' government, which did not have a majority in parliament (but was supported externally by a small number of centre-left parties), provided powerful incentives to seek consensus. As a matter of fact, the starting point for the negotiations was a document drafted by trade union experts.

The 1995 reform was adopted with the support of the trade unions who, in return for their approval, obtained a fairly long phasing-in period for the new system, which will become fully effective for people retiring from 2013 onwards. The key constituencies of the Italian trade union movement, current pensioners and older workers, were not affected by the reform (Regini and Regalia 1997: 215–217). The unions also managed to obtain equality of treatment for different occupational groups. Under the previous legislation, some groups (civil servants, but also some self-employed) were entitled to more generous treatment. More specifically, contribution rates for public-sector workers were increased to the same level as those paid by private sector employees (20 per cent of earnings), as were those paid by the self-employed, though to the lower rate of 15 per cent of earnings.

However, of greater importance for the introduction of equal treatment between employees and the self-employed was the impact of the shift to a defined contribution system on contribution evasion. Under the previous system, contribution evasion did not necessarily result in lower benefits, as the amount of the pension was based on the earnings declared during the last year prior to retirement. This meant that the self-employed, among whom contribution evasion is notoriously widespread, could take advantage of the system by getting high pensions in spite of having paid low contributions for most of their working life. With the new defined contribution system, evasion automatically results in lower benefits. The reform eliminated this opportunity for free riding for the self-employed and constituted a significant measure in favour of salaried employees. This helped considerably to make the reform acceptable to organised labour (Natali 2002: 102–111).

The reform also introduced measures that improve coverage for non-standard workers. For instance, pension contributions are credited for periods of inactivity due to maternity (five months) or parental leave (10 months), sickness or accident (twelve months), unemployment, and military service. Parents can also claim contribution credits for short periods of time spent caring for sick children (five days per year). The amounts credited are based on the average salary of the recipient. Contributions are neither credited for years spent as a student nor for longer periods of non-employment spent caring for children. These career interruptions can be compensated, but the missing contribution years must be bought back by the insured person. Nonworking partners of employed persons, essentially housewives, can obtain pension coverage, but need to pay for it (INPS 2001; Leonardi and Peruzzi 1995). According to the vast literature on the 1995 pension reform, these measures did not play any significant role in making the reform more acceptable to the unions or the electorate in general. In fact, they are rarely mentioned, which suggests that their role in the politics of the reform was rather limited. It should also be noted that the contribution credits introduced by the Italian reform are rather meagre in comparison with what carers can obtain in countries like Sweden or France.

Germany: The 2002 Pension Reform

As in other Western European countries, the pension reform issue was high on the agenda throughout the 1990s in Germany. First, in 1992, the indexation of pensions was shifted from gross to net wages (Schmähl 1993). Subsequently, the Kohl government introduced a more radical reform which, through a demographic weighting of benefits, would have reduced pension levels and contained costs in the medium to long term. The Kohl reform was, nonetheless, repealed by the social democratic government that came to power in 1998. Under pressure to deliver an alternative policy, the Social Democrats adopted a reform that modified the pension formula so as to gradually reduce the replacement rate from the current 70 per cent for a full contribution record to around 64 per cent by 2030.[6] Together with these cost containment measures, Germany has also introduced provision for a fully funded private pension, to which private-sector employees can voluntarily contribute tax free (with a ceiling) up to 4 per cent of their earnings. The reform also includes a commitment to reduce expenditure if a contribution rate (joint employer and employee) higher than 20 per cent of gross wages in 2020 and 22 per cent in 2030 is required (Hering, 2004; Hinrichs 2003; Nöcker 2001).

The adoption of the German reform proved extremely difficult for the government. Quid pro quos like the ones seen in other European countries are less clearly evident in this case. Substantial opposition from the left wing of the SPD could only be overcome through skilful policy-making by Schröder himself, based on isolating opponents rather than including them in the policy-making process (Hering, 2004). The German reform did, nonetheless, contain some expansion measures. Most notably, it introduced a means-tested benefit of last resort for older people who have not managed to build up a contribution credit sufficient to generate an adequate pension. Germany was in fact an exception in Western Europe in not having this kind of provision within the pension system. Older people with insufficient income were forced to rely on their adult children or, if this was not possible, general social assistance (Hinrichs 2003).

The introduction of a safety net in the pension system reflects many of the features of a modernising compromise, as it may constitute an additional protection for atypical workers (even though those who are out of the labour market for child rearing receive rather generous credits). This may have played a role in making the reform more acceptable to opponents of pension retrenchment, perhaps not so much the unions, but certainly sections of the SPD. The unions, in fact, obtained surprisingly little in the 2002 German reform. However, it is possible that the main deal between Schröder and organised labour took place outside pension policy. The unions acquiesced to pension reform and in return obtained a favourable revision of the industrial relations act, as a result of which works councils are now compulsory in smaller firms and the number of labour representatives in larger firms has been increased (Hinrichs 2003).

With regard to the introduction of contribution credits, the pre-reform structure of the German pension system left little room for modernising compromises. Since the mid-1980s, German pensions have taken into account periods of time spent out of the labour market for child rearing through the awarding contribution credits. These were increased in the 1990s, as a result of decisions of the Federal Constitutional Court, based on the view that the fact of having children should not result in lower pension entitlements (Langen 1998). Today, parents in Germany are entitled to contribution credits equal to those payable on an average wage (in 2002 €2,376.50) for each child under the age of three living in the same household. The contributions are credited to the mother, unless the parents request a different arrangement, regardless of employment status. However, if the parent is working, the total contribution is subject to a ceiling. Contributions are credited also to individuals who spend at least 14 hours per week engaged in caring tasks, provided they are not working more than 30 hours per week. Recipients of unemployment benefit maintain pension coverage (BMA 2001). These credits were reduced in the more recent round of reforms.

Contribution credits did become an issue in the 2002 reform, but in relation to the new funded individual retirement accounts. The funds invested in the new pension are exempt from taxation (up to a ceiling); however, in order not to disadvantage people who do not pay or pay very low rates of income tax, tax exemptions can be converted into subsidies if this is more advantageous for the insured person. In addition, parents get extra subsidies proportional to the number of children they have. When the reform is fully implemented (from 2008 onwards), parents will receive €185 for each child (Anderson and Meyer 2004). The combination of tax exemptions with subsidies in a private pension regime can be seen as a progressive move, capable of attracting the support of part of the anti-retrenchment camp. However, as in the case of the means-tested pension, these concessions may have bought the approval of SPD modernisers rather than union members. In addition, these subsidies simply reflect established practice in the fields of social insurance pensions and family policy. As a consequence, their introduction did not require a proactive stance on the part of the government, but simply resulted from the application of standard practice.

The German reform contains some elements of a modernising compromise, albeit in an attenuated form. Retrenchment was adopted together with some expansionary provisions that are likely to benefit individuals with interrupted or part-time careers. Given the fact that these are of little benefit to union members, it is difficult to see them as an essential element in the pension deal, though they may have been useful in obtaining SPD support in parliament. The overarching deal between the government and the unions, which made the reform possible, may well have taken place outside pension policy in the field of industrial relations.

Discussion

The presentation of the case studies above confirms the already anticipated view that modernising compromises in pension reform are rare, but not non-existent. Of the five cases reviewed, Sweden and Switzerland are the clearest examples of modernising compromises, where political deals are made that include the adoption of provisions designed to benefit non-standard employees, above all women who interrupt or reduce their labour market involvement when raising children. The German reform contains an important modernising element in the shape of a guaranteed minimum pension. This may turn out to be an important safety net for current atypical workers, but most likely it will concern only those at the very bottom of the earnings distribution and/or those with very long periods spent out of the labour market.

Table 8.2   *Determinants of modernising compromises (MC) in pension reform and outcomes*

	Sweden	France	Switzerland	Italy	Germany
Absence of provision for non-standard workers	X		X	X	
Political system with high veto point density			X		X
Feminised /young labour movement	X				
Strong connection between social democratic party and trade unions	X		X		
Outcome	*MC*		*MC*		*(MC)*

Table 8.2 summarises the existence or otherwise of the conditions identified above as likely to favour the emergence of modernising compromises in pension reform. On this basis, Switzerland and Sweden appear the countries most likely to have followed this path. Germany and Italy are somewhat less likely and, France is the least likely of the cases reviewed in this chapter. The empirical evidence tends to confirm this theory-driven expectation, as modernising compromises have clearly taken place in Sweden and Switzerland, and in a somewhat muted form, in Germany.

Unfortunately the limited number of cases combined with the large number of possible combinations of the various independent variables makes it impossible to assess the relative importance of each of factor considered. Taken together, however, they seem to be fairly successful in accounting for the observed pattern. It is interesting to note that the presence of generous provision for non-standard workers prior to the reform (Germany) does not entirely rule out the adoption of modernising compromise elements. This suggests that, contrary to the hypothesis advanced above, modernising compromises may not be one-off opportunities but may rather be repeated a number of times, with provision for non-standard workers being improved incrementally.

CONCLUSION

The comparative analysis of pension reform presented in this chapter both confirms findings of previous research and opens up new avenues for future analysis. As already argued in the literature (Bonoli 2000; Hinrichs 2001; Myles and Quadagno 1997; Myles and Pierson 2001; Schludi 2002), policymakers engaging in pension reform have a strong incentive to act in a consensual manner, or at least to take into account the interests of external influential actors, chiefly the labour movement. All the cases reviewed above are instances of successful policy-making based on the inclusion in reform packages of important concessions to the trade unions. The discussion of the German and the French cases suggests that the concession may not always be so easy to identify.

In the French case, the fact that the government gave in to a long standing demand by some sections of the labour movement was not sufficient to generate open support for the reform. Yet it was clear from interviews with trade unions and ministry officials that the setting-up of an 'old age solidarity fund' at the same time as the adoption of pension retrenchment measures made it easier for the unions to accept the reform (Bonoli 1997, 2000). Quid pro quos are not always self-evident and may require detailed actor-focused research to be uncovered.

The German case suggests a further complication. Quid pro quos may include decisions taken outside the field of pensions. When government and the unions are conducting negotiations in different policy areas, there is no reason why the latter may not accept losses in one area in exchange for gains elsewhere. This seems to be at least part of the German story and should be taken into account when analysing pension policy-making in general.

Compromises and quid pro quos seem to be frequent occurrences in pension reform, but those described here as 'modernising compromises' seem to be less common. The reason for this must be sought in the relative rarity of the conditions that have been identified as conducive to modernising compromises. The representation of winners and losers in pension reform varies in structure across countries and it is only under certain specific circumstances that a modernising compromise can be expected. Both groups of people need to be represented in the political arena and they must be represented by the same actor or by connected actors. The other conditions identified above (veto points in the political system and the absence of provision prior to the reform) may constitute an additional hurdle to the adoption of a modernising compromise, hence their relative rarity.

NOTES

1. The Swedish labour movement is divided by occupation. Blue-collar workers are represented by LO, the largest and most politically influential union federation in the country. White-collar employees are represented by TCO and people with tertiary education by SACO.
2. There are five major national trade union federations in France, which operate independently from each other. The divisions reflect the political spectrum. Starting from the left, the *Confédération Générale du Travail* (CGT) is of communist inspiration. *Force Ouvrière* (FO) originated from a division within the CGT in 1947 and constitutes its non-communist component (it is sometimes referred to as CGT-FO). The *Confédération Française Démocratique des Travailleurs* (CFDT) is a moderate union which in recent years has been much more co-operative with the government than its counterparts. Finally the *Confédération Française des Travailleurs Chrétiens* (CFTC) is a federation of Catholic unions. In addition, there is also a federation representing managers (CFE-CGC: *Confédération Française de l'Encadrement – Confédération Générale des Cadres*).
3. See Bonoli 1997, 2000 and Natali 2002 for explanations of the different outcomes of these two reform initiatives.
4. The quid pro quo did not result from formal negotiations, but the government included some concessions that were clearly intended to fulfil certain trade union expectations (Bonoli 2000).
5. Switzerland has two main union federations. The larger one is the USS, which is close to the Socialist Party, and the other is the Catholic CSC, which is close to the Christian Democrats. The CSC has recently merged with the country's white-collar union.
6. The government claimed that the replacement rate would decline to 67 per cent only, but this figure is based on earnings net of the non-compulsory contribution paid to a private pension. The figure of 64 per cent is based on net earnings according to the pre-reform definition and thus is comparable with the current replacement rate of 70 per cent (Nöcker 2001).

REFERENCES

Anderson, Karen (2003), *Pension Reform in Sweden: Radical Reform in a Mature Pension System*, paper presented at the workshop 'Social Policy Responses to Population Ageing in the Globalisation Era', University of Hokkaido, Sapporo (Japan) 27 February – 1st March.

Anderson, Karen and Traute Meyer (2004), 'Social Democratic Pension Politics in Germany and Sweden', in Giuliano Bonoli and Martin Powell (eds), *Social Democratic Party Policy in Contemporary Europe*, London: Routledge.

Artoni, Roberto and Alberto Zanardi (1997), 'The Evolution of the Italian Pension System', in MIRE (ed.), *Comparing Welfare States in Southern Europe*, Paris, pp. 243–266.

BMA (Bundesministerium für Arbeit) (2001), *Rentenversicherung*, http://www.bma. de/frame.asp?u=/de/sicherung/rente/rente.htm (visited 23/07/2001).

Bonoli, Giuliano and Bruno Palier (1997), 'Reclaiming Welfare. The Politics of Social Protection Reform in France', in Martin Rhodes (ed.), Southern European
Welfare States. Between Crisis and Reform, London: Francis Cass, pp. 240–259.

Bonoli, Giuliano and Benoît Gay-des-Combes (2003), 'Adapting Pension Systems to
Labour Market Changes in Western Europe', in Catherine Bochel and Martin
Powell (eds), Social Policy Review 15, Bristol, UK: The Policy Press.

Bonoli, G. (1997), 'Pension Politics in France: Patterns of Co-operation and Conflict
in Two Recent Reforms', West European Politics, 20 (4, October), 111–124.

Bonoli, Giuliano (ed.) (2000), *The Politics of Pension Reform. Institutions and Policy
Change in Western Europe*, Cambridge, UK: Cambridge University Press.

Bonoli, Giuliano (2001), 'Political Institutions, Veto Points, and the Process of Welfare State Adaptation', in Paul Pierson (ed.), The New Politics of the Welfare
State, Oxford, Oxford University Press, pp. 238–264.

Ebbinghaus, B. (1995), 'The Siamese Twins: Citizenship Rights, Cleavage Formation,
and Party-Union Relations in Western Europe', International Review of Social
History, 40, 51–89.

Ebbinghaus, Bernhard and Jelle Visser (2000), *The Societies of Europe: Trade Unions
in Western Europe Since 1945*, London: Palgrave.

Ferrera, Maurizio (1997), 'The Uncertain Future of the Italian Welfare State', in
Martin Bull and Martin Rhodes (eds), *Crisis and Transition in Italian Politics*,
London: Frank Cass, pp. 231–249.

France Pratique (2003), *Retraite de Base de la Sécurité Sociale*, http://www.pratique.
fr/vieprat/emploi/retraite/daf3603.htm, visited 12 March 2003.

Hering, Martin (2004), 'Turning Ideas into Policies: Implementing Modern Social
Democratic Thinking in Germany's Pension Policy'', in Giuliano Bonoli and
Martin Powell (eds), *Social Democratic Party Policy in Contemporary Europe*,
London: Routledge.

Hinrichs, Karl (2001), 'Elephants on the Move. Patterns of Public Pension Reform in
OECD Countries', in Stephan Leibfried (ed.), *Welfare State Futures*, Cambridge,
UK: Cambridge University Press, pp. 77–102.

Hinrichs, Karl (2003), *Between Continuity and Paradigm Shift: Pension Reforms in
Germany*, paper presented at the workshop 'Social Policy Responses to
Population Ageing in the Globalisation Era', University of Hokkaido, Sapporo
(Japan) 27 February – 1st March.

INPS (Istituto Nazionale di Previdenza Sociale) (2001), TuttoINPS, http://www.inps.
it/Doc/TuttoINPS/TuttoINPS.htm (visited 23/07/2001).

Kitschelt, Herbert (1994), *The Transformation of European Social Democracy*, Cambridge, UK: Cambridge University Press.

Langen, H.-G. (1998), 'Rentenreformgesetz 1999 – verbesserte Bewertung', *Die
Angestellten Versicherung*, **45**, March.

Lehmbruch, G. (1993), 'Consociational Democracy and Corporatism in Switzerland',
Publius: The Journal of Federalism, **23**, 43–60.

Leonradi, G. and M. Peruzzi (1995), 'Pensioni', *Italia Oggi*, **5** (197) (special issue).

Myles, John and Paul Pierson (2001), 'The Political Economy of Pension Reform', in Paul Pierson (ed.), *The New Politics of the Welfare State*, Oxford, UK: Oxford University Press, pp. 305–333.

Myles, John and Jill Quadagno (1997), 'Recent Trends in Public Pension Reform: A Comparative View', in Keith Banting and Robert Boadway (eds), *Reform of Retirement Income Policy. International and Canadian Perspectives*, Kingston, Ontario: Queen's University, School of Policy Studies, pp. 247–272.

Natali, David (2002), *La Ridefinizione del Welfare State Contemporaneo: La Riforma delle Pensioni in Francia e in Italia*, IUE Florence, PhD Thesis.

Neidhart, Leonhard (1970), *Plebiszit und pluralitäre Demokratie. Eine Analyse der Funktionen des schweizerischen Gesetzesreferendum*, Bern: Frank.

Nöcker, Ralf (2001), *The Recent Pension Reforms in Germany: Individual Pension Accounts as a Replacement for State Pensions*, mimeo, London: Centre for Pensions and Social Insurance, Birkbeck College, University of London/City University.

Pierson, Paul (1994), *Dismantling the Welfare State. Reagan, Thatcher and the Politics of Retrenchment*, Cambridge: Cambridge University Press.

Pierson, Paul and Kent Weaver (1993), 'Imposing Losses in Pension Policy', in Kent Weaver and Bert A. Rockmann (eds), *Do Institution Matter? Government Capabilities in the United States and Abroad*, Washington, DC: The Brookings Institution, pp. 110–50.

Regini, M. and I. Regalia (1997), 'Employers, Unions and the State: The Resurgence of Concertation in Italy?', *West European Politics*, **20** (1), 210–230.

Riksförsäkringsverket (National Social Insurance Board) (2001), *Den nya allmänna pensionen,* http://www.pensions.nu (visited 23/07/2001).

Rosanvallon, Pierre (1995), *La Nouvelle Question Sociale. Repenser l'Etat-Providence*, Paris : Seuil.

Schludi, Martin (2002), *The Politics of Pensions in European Social Insurance Countries*, Cologne: Max-Planck-Institut für Gesellschaftsforschung, Discussion Paper 01/11.

Schmähl, W. (1993), 'The 1992 Reform of Public Pensions in Germany: Main Elements and Some Effects', *Journal of European Social Policy*, **3** (1), 39–52.

Schmidt, Manfred G. (1996), 'Germany: The Grand Coalition State', in Josep M. Colomer (ed.), *Political Institutions in Europe*, London: Routledge, pp. 62–98.

Tsebelis, G. (1995), 'Decision Making in Political Systems: Veto Players in Presidentialism, Parliamentarism, Multicameralism and Multipartyism', *British Journal of Political Science,* **25**, 289–325.

Tsebelis, George (2002), *Veto Players. How Political Institutions Work*, Princeton, NJ: Princeton University Press.

9. Ideas and the Politics of Labour Market Reform

Robert Henry Cox

INTRODUCTION

The politics of reforming European labour markets is fundamentally a battle of ideas. Pressures from globalization are forcing actors in all European countries to confront a new reality and this means the political assumptions and behaviours that informed past policy developments need to be re-thought and new approaches need to be developed. Ideas are crucial to this process. The countries that have made the greatest advances in reforming and reinvigorating their labour markets have done so by developing new ideas to justify the reforms, and persuading enough actors that those reforms would help to address the concerns of competitiveness as well as social justice. As a result, these new ideas inform new notions of the welfare state and its labour market regulations. In countries such as the Netherlands and Denmark, an internal debate among national actors circulated new ideas about work and welfare and in turn fostered a new consensus to pursue reform.

But the battle of ideas is not being engaged everywhere. A second pattern can be seen in countries where labour market reform has been accompanied by only a modest, if any discussion of new ideas to justify the reforms. The reforms to be found in these countries follow a pattern known as 'policy drift' (Hacker 2004). In some countries policy drift can result in dramatic change, but most frequently policy drift is the result of reforms that are in-cremental and incomplete, taking place in ways that are not immediately apparent and involving changes whose effects only become evident after a number of years. In either case, what makes these countries good examples of policy drift is the failure of new ideas to provide a new direction for labour market policies. Sometimes this is because reforms are little more than ad-ministrative adjustments attended to by a rather small circle of actors, rather than legislative changes that involve a more public discussion (Pierson 1996). In such countries, public opinion proves unaware of the changes. In Sweden, for example, there continues to be a widespread sense that the 'Swedish Model' remains intact, even while policy drift in labour market reforms represents a departure from the Swedish Model.

Most frequently, however, policy drift takes place in countries where new ideas fail to dislodge strongly entrenched supporters of the status quo. In Germany, for example, reforms have been attempted and have been accompanied by bold ideas about how labour markets need to change to meet the needs of the global economy. This description also fits Italy, where, as in Germany, there has been no serious challenge to the 'post-war settlement' responsible for the creation of labour market regimes in the 1950s and 1960s. Other countries that fit this pattern are France and Belgium, though they are not discussed in this chapter. In these countries, political parties cling to their post-war ideological foundations and new ideas wither. Policy drift happens in these countries because a few small remnants of the bold reforms do manage to take hold. The result is persistent and high unemployment (especially among the youth), low job creation, and deteriorating labour market performance. Once seen as superior examples of labour market governance, these countries now stand as the problem cases within Europe. Most remarkable among them is *Modell Deutschland*, whose labour market regime once was praised for its combination of industrial peace, high productivity and competitiveness, and ability to train a highly skilled workforce. These countries demonstrate that resistance to new ideas allows institutional 'path dependencies' to stifle the adaptation of labour markets to the new global realities.

My objective in this chapter is to outline how the politics of labour market reform is defined by the introduction of, or resistance to new ideas. The chapter begins with a discussion of the role of ideas and how they challenge the orthodoxy of the labour market regimes and especially of the actors that have dominated policy discussion in this area. Then, I discuss how these new ideas often are introduced and try to identify why they lead to successful labour market reform in some cases and not in others. Finally, I briefly examine the countries that represent these two patterns of labour market reform, highlighting where new ideas succeeded and failed, and exploring why.

WHY IDEAS MATTER

Most explanations for labour market regulations focus on the way they balance the interests of stakeholders who have influence in the policy process. Specifically, labour and business have certain interests that are potentially at odds with one another. Labour seeks better working conditions, job and income security, and improvements in compensation. Business leaders are interested in containing costs and maintaining flexibility in their decisions over how large a work force to have and how to assign job duties. In most European countries, the 'post-war settlement' (Kesselman 1987) that governed labour market policies balanced the interests of business and labour. Labour won job security, stable incomes and control over many workplace decisions. Business won wage restraint, less disruption in the form of fewer strikes, and enjoyed a profitable environment. All this was supervised and enforced by national governments.

In an age of globalization, these interests have not fundamentally changed. But, globalization has diminished the ability of labour, business, or even national governments to control their environments. This means that continued pursuit of their interests forces the 'social partners' (management and labour) into more uncertain positions as they seek to minimize the threats posed by globalization. Sometimes this leads them into more antagonistic relationships, as each blames the other for its growing uncertainty. Labour blames managers for making their jobs more insecure, and managers blame labour for keeping labour costs high in a global environment more sensitive to price competition. If we assume that the interests of all parties are stable, then the preference of each is to return to the *status quo ante*. Globalization, as well as Europeanization, however, makes this impossible.

The only direction out of the dilemma is for interests to change, thereby setting up an opportunity for a new consensus around a new set of labour market policies. This is where ideas enter as important vehicles for change. As a theoretical issue, the most common assumption is that the interests of actors are stable. This does not means the interests of an individual actor never change; certainly they do, but only as the situation changes and the individual is confronted with a new circumstance and new information. Rather, the assumption is that any person in a similar situation would have the same interests. Applied to the analysis of European labour markets, this leads many to assume that the social partners prefer policies that preserve the status quo. For the social partners, and especially labour, the post-war settlement is a comfortable status quo, whereas globalization only presents risks. Even some actors in the business community, faced with a choice between an imperfect status quo and a risky and potentially worse future, often prefer what they know to what they do not. At the very least, the business community is divided between the large multinational firms that favour liberalization of every-thing, including labour markets, and the small- and medium-sized enterprises, which are suspicious of some aspects of liberalization.

Scholars who study the role of ideas in policy making, however, have observed that ideas often have the power to transform interests and thereby to realign policy preferences, and that this happens independent of a change in circumstance. As Colin Hay (2004) has observed, interests are not fixed and stable, but are 'constructed' by people as they interpret their material circumstances. This means that two people in the same situation would not necessarily perceive their interests in the same way. How people interpret their environment is always influenced by what they hear others saying. In other words, the discourse that surrounds a policy decision will have a large influence on how people perceive their own interests (Schmidt 2002). Ideas are the currency in any policy discourse. Policy actors struggle to make their ideas the dominant ones, and to have the dominant ideas interpreted in ways convenient to them. Material interests are important to those who promote ideas, but the ideas are broader, also encapsulating people's notions of social justice, or what is a legitimate course of action for public policy.

In addition to helping to transform individual interests, ideas are the coin of political debate. Political actors seek to persuade others that their particular perspective on a problem, and the policy action it suggests, is the most reasonable. In this discursive process, ideas are important rhetorical devices that help to unseat opposition to a proposed course of action. The new ideas allow people to think of new ways to arrange their interpretations of the world so that their interests are still preserved (Béland 2005).

When new ideas gain currency, they open political space for new actors in the policy process. Often these new actors are the original advocates of new ideas, and use the ideas to insert themselves into the policy discussions. The arrival of these new actors and their ideas usually further accelerates the transformation of interests within the debate. But, the receptivity of the political system to new actors is not the same in all countries. Political institutions are known for being more or less open to the input of new actors. Some political systems allow for multiple veto points (Immergut and Jochem 2006) where new actors can exert pressure for change. Other political systems are notorious for being closed and immune to new pressures, thereby preserving the privileged access enjoyed by well-entrenched interests. The countries in Europe where labour market changes are most profound are also the countries where new actors have established themselves in the discussion. By contrast, the countries with the least change are those where the social partners of the post-war settlement have effectively repelled any challenge to their policy role.

For example, a central idea in labour market policy is the 'breadwinner' concept, at least for countries of continental Europe. This idea links together the values of income and family security by suggesting that men should earn enough to support their entire household while women perform the domestic chores of the household. The result of this idea is a preference for policies that provide job tenure and high salaries for men while encouraging the exit of women from the work force. Upon its introduction by Christian Democrats in the 1950s, the breadwinner concept quickly was embraced as a positive development in many countries by workers who saw the reforms as a way to have a luxury previously enjoyed only by the middle class. Giving working class men enough income and security to allow their wives to stay home (like middle-class women) was desired by workers who thought more leisure was in the interest of their families. Electoral competition quickly forced social democrats in these countries to embrace the breadwinner concept or risk losing votes to Christian Democratic parties (Cox 1993).

As an idea, the breadwinner concept is no more in the interest of workers than is the idea of working-class solidarity, or of payment based on individual merit. In each case, workers can construct their interests based on their perception of what is available to them and their own values. In countries where workers readily see themselves as part of a class, they believe collective action is an important way to pursue their common interests. But, in countries where workers tend to view their society in liberal terms, i.e. as comprised of individuals rather than classes, solidarity has a weaker effect on the way workers perceive their interests. Workers tend to see their own interests as more intimately connected to their own effort, and might understand themselves to be in competition rather than solidarity with their fellow workers.

Labour market policies in countries where the breadwinner idea prevailed have looked different from countries where workers are seen as individuals or members of a class, rather than as heads of households. For example in countries with stronger degrees of class solidarity, working-class parties have successfully pursued labour market regulations that promote equality in wages, benefits and labour regulations. The results are more wage compression and greater universality in social benefits (Wallerstein 1999). These policies promote solidarity by underscoring the link between collective action and collective benefits. In countries where more individualistic ideas define the worker, wider wage differences are accepted, female participation in the workforce is higher because households expect that their well-being demands that they have more than one person active in the work force, and child care opportunities are more abundant (Esping-Andersen 1990).

For the past 15 years, labour market reforms have challenged these ideas, and the reforms have been based on new ideas. For example, 'flexicurity' is an idea from the Netherlands, which was widely discussed in Europe in the 1990s. 'Flexicurity' was promoted as a way to link the value of job security to the notion of part-time employment. Unlike under the previous labour market regime, within which security was best attained by providing full-time employment to male breadwinners, flexicurity is a term used to describe reforms that allow part-time workers to also enjoy the same social security benefits normally associated with full-time work. Implementation of the idea facilitated a greater participation of women in the Dutch workforce, and changed the breadwinner to a 'one-and-a-half jobs' model (Visser and Hemerijck 1997). The idea behind the one-and-a-half jobs model was that both partners in a household could work part-time, allowing them to share household duties and still enjoy some leisure time. To make this attractive, however, the Dutch government had to adopt reforms that moved away from the breadwinner model. Following the Dutch example, Danes imported the idea of flexicurity and also used it to give a positive image to their own labor market reforms (*The Economist* 2006).

'Activation' has been another important idea prodding countries to reverse some of the key features of the breadwinner model, especially to reform benefit assistance (Clasen 2002). At its introduction, activation was the idea that existing systems of transfer payments were too passive because they simply provided money to people who left the workforce, rather than inducing them to return to work. According to the activation critique, not only were such high levels of benefits expensive, but they also led to a depreciation of skills and high levels of social isolation among people who stayed on benefits for a long period of time. Instead, activation proponents argued, benefit systems needed to move people back into the work force. The idea of activation served to reframe the situation in a way that allowed stakeholders to be more receptive to policy reform. Active labour market policies do not have to be a sign of an uncaring society that commodifies labour. Rather, they allow people to re-enter the work force and to maintain the social attachments they acquired through their jobs.

Ideas, therefore, help people to conceive of their interests, suggest what types of public policies will best help them realize their interests, and are the discursive vehicles for people to communicate their understandings and build support for their positions. Labour market reform occurs under any situation, but truly dramatic policy reform requires new ideas and a reorientation of people's preferences to support new policies. Today in Europe, the war of ideas pits the adherents to the breadwinner model against the advocates of flexicurity and activation.

IDEAS AND POLITICAL PARTIES

Political parties are the most important merchants of policy ideas. Most of Europe's large political parties can still be identified with a particular ideology. But today, the pressures of globalization are forcing political parties to fundamentally reconsider their ideological foundations. This confrontation has been most severe for social democratic parties, who see the post-war settlement as a social democratic victory, representing the triumph of the working class for social justice. In the words of Gøsta Esping-Andersen (1990), social welfare and labour market regulations led to the 'decommodification' of labour, freeing the working class from the choice between work and lifestyle.

Today, the social democratic parties that have a positive impact on labour market reforms are those that have re-examined their ideological foundation, often only to rediscover a positive vision of work at the heart of their ideology. To put it in simple terms, social democrats take pride in having put into practice Karl Marx's dictum 'to each according to his need', but they overlooked the first part of the dictum, 'from each according to his ability'. Today, the most innovative social democratic parties are augmenting their well-developed theories of distribution with equally well-considered theories of production. The new idea in social democratic circles is to enact 'social investment' policies that place a premium on training, upgrading of skills and re-integrating labour market 'outsiders' who have been discriminated against by existing regulations of the labour market. For example, in Great Britain, Tony Blair's transformation of the Labour Party from a traditional social democratic to a 'new left' political party has basically followed this route, as have social democrats in the Netherlands and Denmark (O'Brien 2000).

The ironic paradox in this shift is that social democratic reformers employ instruments that are indistinguishable from those advocated by their opponents on the right side of the political spectrum. Upgrading skills requires not only that people enrol in retraining programs, but that these programs also lead to jobs within a specified period of time. Such notions have been the hallmark of neo-liberal labour market reforms. When US President Bill Clinton advocated a five-year limit for benefits, European social democrats derided this as a punitive reform only imaginable in America. Now, such time limits are increasingly common in Europe and receive the endorsement of social democratic parties. Also, social democrats are advocating tighter conditions for the award of benefits (Taylor-Gooby 2004).

To highlight the theoretical statement in this chapter, the material condition of the social democratic constituency has not changed. Rather, new ideas have allowed social democrats to reconcile labour market reforms with their ideologies. Social democrats make a special effort to distinguish their form of labour market activation from what is proposed by their neo-liberal opponents. The basic distinction, as articulated by many social democratic parties, is that they are trying to use the power of the state to allow people to return to and thrive within the labour market. Mobilizing the capacity of the state, rather than allowing market forces to make adjustments is a hallmark of social democracy, and social investment policies are the idea that links the ideology to the realities of globalization. The irony is that the mechanisms advocated by social democrats are often those that also have the support of parties to the right on the political spectrum.

Though the ideological challenge has been strongest for social democratic parties, parties on the right have also been affected by the new realities. The challenge on the right, at least among the neo-liberal parties, is to accept that unregulated markets, especially labour markets, do not operate ideally. Rather, markets need some sort of regulation to prevent them from realizing suboptimal outcomes. For example, the deregulation of labour markets is often seen to remove a major obstacle to female participation in the labour force. But, the actual participation of women in the work force is dependent upon the availability of child care options for those who chose to work. Curiously, the Scandinavian countries enjoy the highest participation of women in the work force, largely because the state underwrites a myriad of child care options. Indeed, publicly-subsidized child care itself is a major source of female employment. Countries with more liberal labour market regulation, on the other hand, find that women are best able to enter the work force if they can do so at a high income, or if they have a spouse who also works. Lone mothers, especially those who have marginal labour skills, often find that the child care options available in the market place make it difficult, if not impossible for them to balance work and family duties (Lewis 2006). Consequently, liberal parties are learning to accept some ideas from the left that require more state intervention in the labour market, such as subsidized child care or retraining programs.

Parties on the right which have a more *dirigiste* tradition also are facing challenges to adapt. Christian democratic parties and the French Rally for the Republic have long supported heavily regulated labour markets. Indeed, they were the architects of the present forms of labour market regulation, taking credit for such ideas as the breadwinner concept (Kersbergen 1995). For them the challenge is to move away from the idea of corporatist economic management. The cosy relationship between the state and the social partners has proven to be the single largest obstacle to labour market reform in countries where christian democrats or *dirigiste* parties were responsible for creating the present labour market regimes. Corporatism allows labour unions to protect existing jobs, with the adverse result that employers are reluctant to take on new workers. Widely known as the 'insider-outsider problem' (Lindbeck and Snower 2001), this cosy relationship is responsible for high levels of youth unemployment and a degradation of skills in the workforce. As well, the entry of women into the workforce challenges these parties to consider that women could have multiple roles in society and not just be mothers and home makers. *Dirigiste* parties have proven to the most reluctant to adjust their ideological foundations and embrace the new ideas.

All parties of the right have proven supportive of activation programs, but their ideologies impose some limits to how much activation they believe is desirable. Neo-liberal parties are hesitant about expecting public officials to be proactive in finding jobs for beneficiaries, preferring instead that individuals assume the responsibility to find their own jobs. For *dirigiste* parties, the cosy system of corporatism allowed for a quick removal of unproductive workers from their jobs. Real levels of unemployment were hidden by extensive utilization of disability and early retirement programs to remove less productive workers. These programs required little state activity beyond the disbursement of benefits, especially in countries where enforcement of disability requirements was lax. These parties are now learning to accept that programs of labour market activation demand that employment services be more engaged in finding jobs and that social service case workers exercise more discretion to move people back into the work force.

Thus for all political parties, the current trends in labour market reform have demanded adjustment of their ideological principles, as well as an effort to conceive of an arrangement different from their inherited policy legacies. As we shall see, some have embraced the idea of activation because they have come to see it as an idea that addresses the current reality in a legitimate way.

PATTERN ONE: THE NEW CONSENSUS ON LABOUR MARKET POLICY

The countries that have booked the most dramatic changes in labour market policies have done so because new ideas about what the labour market should achieve have been widely discussed, these new ideas have been embraced, and they have created a legitimate basis for the new reforms. For many years, Denmark and the Netherlands were considered the best examples of successful labour market reform, and here is where the most innovative policy activity has taken place. The specific details of labour market changes in Denmark are carefully spelled out by Irene Dingeldey's contribution to this volume (see Chapter 4), so I will not recount them here. Instead, I would like to highlight the ideas that gave justification to these remarkable reforms and devote more attention to the Dutch case.

In the Netherlands, the reform of labour markets began in the 1980s and reflected a slow adjustment to a problem created by the most generous breadwinner model in Europe (Cox 1993). A very generous system of benefits developed by the middle of the 1970s. By the late 1970s, an economic downturn set in and this same system became a form of hidden unemployment. To avoid layoffs, many workers were encouraged to visit their doctors and apply for disability assistance. The result was that by the middle of the 1980s, the Netherlands had the highest percentage of disabled workers in all of Europe. This high level of inactivity was especially pronounced among older and low-skilled workers. At the same time, more young women began to pursue careers and were frustrated to encounter formal regulations and informal discrimination that discouraged them from taking jobs. When the European Commission began a campaign to reduce gender discrimination in the workplace, the Netherlands was singled out for its extremely low level of female participation in the work force (Commissie van de Europese Gemeenschappen, 1992).

Organizations representing women pushed for reforms that would allow all workers, including women with part-time jobs, to enrol in the social insurance system. Their criticisms focused on the regulatory obstacles that discouraged women from taking jobs if they also had young children to care for. This was the origin of the idea of the 'one-and-a-half-job' model, mentioned earlier in this chapter. Many men who were changing their own ideas of how to balance work with family found the prospects of part-time work attractive and the idea was embraced by a wider sector of the population.

The one-and-a-half-job model was an idea quickly embraced by the three major political parties. Christian democrats and liberals, who dominated coalition governments during the first half of the 1990s, both saw this as a way to encourage higher levels of labour market participation and thereby relieve pressure from the unemployment and disability programs. When social democrats joined the government in the latter half of the decade, they saw this as one means to promote their broader agenda of gender equality.

A more dramatic change in ideas prompted a reconceptualization of active labour market policies. The basic idea, known as activation (*aktivering*) both in Denmark and in the Netherlands, was that the entire system of cash transfers created too many disincentives to work. The critique was somewhat controversial, but the reforms received fairly broad support. Governments in both countries sought to reduce the take-up rates in benefit programs by reducing the amount of the payments, reducing the duration of benefits, and otherwise providing incentives for people to move back into paid employment. These changes were encapsulated in a phrase coined by the Rotterdam Social Service Office, which argued that the new program represented a shift 'from the safety-net to the trampoline', (Gemeentelijke Sociale Dienst Rotterdam, 1985). As in Denmark, the major mechanism for this was a budget-based decentralization of authority to municipal governments and to works councils to better supervise the implementation of their programs.

To justify strict enforcement of active labour market policies, officials in both Denmark and the Netherlands articulated a notion of reciprocity between rights and responsibilities.

The basic idea was that a worker who had a right to unemployment and other benefits also had a responsibility to be actively seeking work, and to take any available job. In the Netherlands, activation policies were supported by a legislative change that required people receiving unemployment benefits to seek jobs of comparable worth. This was a large departure from the old system, which allowed a person to continue to receive benefits if he could not return to the job for which he had been trained. In Denmark, controversy over the strictness of the activation measures led the Social Democrats, who controlled the government, to temper the activation responsibilities with more worker rights. These took in the form of a job-rotation program that allowed workers to take leave for family care, retraining, or for sabbatical. Except for the family care provisions the program was disliked by employers, and was sharply curtailed shortly after its adoption (Martin 2005).

It is important to note that activation programs received strong support not only from the political right, but also from the left in both countries. In 1996, commenting on his vision of active labour market policies, the Dutch Minister for Social Affairs, Ad Melkert, was quoted as saying 'I have always believed that those who don't work, shouldn't eat'. A less provocative comment was offered by the leader of the Labour Party, who suggested that in order to do more for those in need, benefits had to be targeted more directly on those who truly need them (Versteegh 1996: 4).

Flexicurity was another idea that had a strong impact on policy reform. The term originated in Dutch academic circles but was quickly embraced by policy reformers in the Netherlands and Denmark. In both countries, the appeal was twofold: on the one hand, it provided a positive frame for viewing the historical form of labour market regulation in the two countries. Both countries historically had combined relatively low job protection with generous benefits (Benner and Bundgaard 2000). Social democrats embraced the idea as a positive way to maintain employment and high benefits in an environment of increasing global competition. Flexicurity was also attractive because it framed reforms of the labour market in a way that facilitated consensus between labour and business interests.

In short, the pattern in both Denmark and the Netherlands was one of creative problem solving, thinking up new ideas to reconceptualize the balance between work and welfare, and the balance between job and home. The creative ideas helped to reorient the positions of political actors. Social democrats as well as the political right supported many forms of activation, as well as the cutbacks in cash transfers. The language of rights also resonated across the political spectrum. These ideas encourage active labour market policy, combining flexibility in the labour market with an assurance that those who take part-time jobs will still enjoy social security benefits. Ideas such as 'flexicurity,' 'activation' and the 'one-and-one-half-jobs model' encourage people to think of labour market provisions in a new way, one that reflects the contemporary reality of working women and a work force that requires periodic upgrading of skills. As such, these ideas mark a departure from the post-war settlement on labour market policy and build a foundation for a more globally competitive labour market. It should be noted that these ideas were not so much new ideas that led reform as much as they were important new ways to frame reforms that already were taking place.

PATTERN TWO: POLICY DRIFT IN LABOUR MARKET POLICY

The battle of ideas has not been successful everywhere in Europe. Sadly, the more pervasive pattern is one we can call policy drift; a set of small, incremental reforms that are enacted by policy leaders who fail to engage a large scale overhaul of their labour market regimes, or whose bold ideas for reform are struck down by advocates of the status quo.

Sweden provides a good example of a country where a number of labour market reforms were enacted in the 1990s, but without a broader engagement of new ideas to justify the changes. During the 'golden age' of the welfare state, a system of centralized wage bargaining maintained equality in wages and benefits. Strict job tenure rules limited the capacity of employers to reduce their work force. Generous job training programs allowed the skills in the work force to respond to pressures for structural adjustments in the economy, and the Swedish welfare state became a significant employer providing retraining and child care programs to the unemployed and working mothers, respectively. These were not activation programs in the contemporary sense. There was little effort to place people in jobs at the end of their retraining period, and it was not unusual for people to cycle through a number of retraining programs. The official level of unemployment in Sweden would be about 4 per cent higher if those enrolled in retraining schemes were actually counted as unemployed.

Since the 2000 Lisbon summit of the European Union declared them a desired direction for future reforms, active labour market measures have had growing significance in Sweden. There have been efforts to enforce the work requirements that have always been on the books in the unemployment scheme. The strictness of the work requirements does serve to 'recommodify' labour and establish a more punitive environment for the long-term unemployed (Larsen 2002). But, as in the Netherlands and Denmark, this is more of a supportive than punitive form of activation. While there has been much debate on the desirability of labour market activation in Sweden, some of the more significant labour market reforms have taken place without a great deal of public discussion.

Decentralization of wage bargaining, and deregulation of the labour market are two reforms that are having a substantial impact on the character of the Swedish labour market, but have received far too little public attention for the potential size of their impact. Decentralization of wage bargaining has been an issue in a number of countries, but especially in Sweden (Iversen 1996). Centralized wage bargaining was once praised for producing wage restraint and wage solidarity (Huber and Stephens, 2002). This is because the bargaining power of the strongest unions benefit the entire work force. But, with decentralization, those sectors of the work force that have a stronger bargaining power are able to negotiate their own agreements. Because their greater usefulness to the firm affords skilled unions stronger bargaining positions than unskilled unions, they are able to negotiate better packages of compensation through sectoral rather than centralized bargaining.

In many countries, decentralizing in the bargaining system brings a growing spread in wages. In Sweden, this pressure has been moderated by the strong social norms in bargaining that enforce compliance with wage solidarity, however, there is growing pressure to provide other forms of compensation outside of wages, for example, by developing more flexible labour contracts (Iversen 1996; Pontusson and Swenson 1996). Such individualized forms of non-wage compensation seriously undermine the Swedish Model. Not only are they contrary to the ideals of labour solidarity, but flexible labour contracts are difficult to track and monitor. Thus, as a consequence of decentralization of wage bargaining, new forms of compensation and job flexibility have entered the Swedish labour force.

This presents a dilemma for those who assess the continuing viability of the Swedish model, and especially the Social Democrats, the political party most closely associated with the Swedish Model. If one takes a standard view of the model and simply looks at traditional outputs of centralized bargaining, such as wage inequality, one is likely to find confirmation that the model is intact. But if one takes a broader view of the model and searches for evidence of growing disparities in non-wage compensation, one might find evidence that the model is being undermined. What makes this a good example of policy drift is the fact that these changes are taking place at the same time the public discourse declares that the Swedish model is still intact.

For the Social Democrats, their legacy as the architects of the Swedish Model explains their difficulty in admitting that the system is changing. The model has become part of their identity. As the most fully developed welfare system in the world, any direction in which it would reform would be a reversal of the party's prized achievement. This has led the Social Democrats to adopt rather awkward positions, arguing that the model is intact while accepting the decentralization of labour markets, cutting back on collective benefits, and targeting assistance. This is unfortunate, because as the Dutch and Danish cases show, the parties that are able to find positive ideas to describe the new reality will benefit more than those that do not. The election of September 2006 transferred power from the Social Democrats to centre-right coalition, and arguably one of the major issues in the election campaign was the persistent high unemployment in the Swedish Model.

Italy is another case where labour market reforms have been few and have occurred without a comprehensive strategy. In the 1980s, the idea of deregulation entered the policy discourse in Italy and inspired a number of labour market reforms. A law passed in 1984 allowed for more flexibility in the labour market by permitting work sharing agreements, work and training contracts for young workers (aged 15–29) and part-time work. Like in Denmark, these reforms had differential success. The most successful was the training program for young workers because it provided financial incentives to employers who hired young workers. Work-sharing and flexible labour provisions were not well utilized (Ferrera and Gualmini 2004: 89–91). In the 1990s, a 'new deal' for the labour market promoted the decentralization and privatization of employment services, new policies for local development, and a stronger promotion of flexible labour contracts. The main inspiration behind these changes was external to the country. For example, the liberalization of employment services and temporary employment contracts followed two European Court of Justice rulings against the country for failing to comply with EU directives (Ferrera and Gualmini 2004: 100). Italy, therefore, is a good case of policy drift. The reforms have been modest, have had very little affect on the country's high level of unemployment, especially among the youth, and to this day Italy has one of the most heavily regulated labour markets in Europe. The few reforms the country has enacted were forced on the country from outside, particularly from the European Commission.

Among Italian political parties, old ideological lines have not changed much and help to explain the policy drift. Initially, it was the moderate left who enacted the new provisions on temporary work. But, when Silvio Berlusconi's right-wing government came to power, it lowered the wages paid to the temporary workers below that of permanent workers. This change was designed to encourage employers to actually make use of the provision. Controversy over this decision was an issue in the 2006 election campaign. The left, which won the election, has promised to reform the law to prevent it from eroding job security of permanent workers. Thus, in Italy there has been change, but not much, and serious departures from the post-war consensus are not successful.

Germany presents another case of labour market drift. For the past 20 years, many proposals have been floated to reform the German labour market, yet none has had a substantial impact. To some extent the challenges faced by Germany are unique, owing to the huge impact of the reunification of East and West Germany after the end of the Cold War. Workers in the former East Germany had poor skills and suffered from a dearth of employers willing to locate in the eastern provinces. Integrating this group of workers into the new unified economy occupied attention during the 1990s.

Labour market problems persisted in Germany, however, and in 1998 a serious effort was made to bring the social partners together to devise new policies. Dubbed the *Bündnis für Arbeit*, this initiative was launched with considerable ambition but quickly bogged down as the social partners set themselves in opposition to almost every issue placed on the agenda. By the time the initiative was abandoned in 2002, its only accomplishments were a few minor improvements in job-placement services (Blancke and Schmid 2003).

Instead, in 2002, Gerhard Schroeder's government undertook a bold initiative to break the labour unions' stranglehold on labour market reforms. He established the Hartz Commission, named for it chairman, Peter Hartz, and which included major industry leaders, but almost no representation from labour or small business. The Hartz Commission issued a number of bold recommendations that Chancellor Schroeder promised to implement after the election of 2002. Indeed, he followed through on most of this, as reforms were passed that tightened the rules for unemployment assistance, and to make it possible for people to take part-time and temporary jobs. More controversial provisions were passed in 2003 that shortened the period for receiving unemployment assistance to 12 months, and which integrated public assistance with unemployment assistance (Streeck and Trampusch 2005; see also Chapter 4 by Irene Dingledey in this volume). Policy drift is seen in the slight movement to remove the social partners from their historical role as administrators of labour market programs, and to curtail many benefits. But these changes are being enacted without a larger vision that provides a legitimate foundation for their broader acceptance.

At each step in the process, efforts to reform the German labor market have lacked a sufficiently engaging set of ideas to make the reforms compelling. At various points in the debate, ideas were borrowed from other countries that were not seriously promoted in Germany, or ideas that originated within Germany tended to galvanize opposition more than they paved a path for reform. For example, the debates that preceded the establishment of the *Bündnis für Arbeit* focused on the problems of competitiveness in the German economy. Known as the *Standortdebatte*, high wage costs and rigid labor market policies were seen to be the obstacle to maintaining Germany's strong position in the global economy. At least, this was the position of those who advocated reform. Labor unions and others opposed to reform, by contrast, argued that it was exactly the existing policies that had made Germany competitive in the first place. Unlike the debates in Denmark and the Netherlands, where new ideas like flexicurity created new coalitions in support of welfare reform, the Standortdebatte fueled the tensions between global industry on the one hand, and labor and small enterprise, on the other (Lamping and Rüb 2004). The ideas proved to polarize political actors rather than create a coalition in support of reform.

Nor were German reformers very effective when they imported ideas from neighbouring countries. Especially in the 1990s when Denmark and the Netherlands became the models for positive labor market reform, German officials spoke of active labor market reforms, flexicurity and equating rights with responsibilities. And, in 1999, Chancellor Schroeder borrowed Tony Blair's ideas for a 'new deal' for labor. However, those who imported ideas frequently lost the courage to propose bold change. Instead, they suggested that the reforms would strengthen, rather than alter the German 'Social Market Economy'. Germany simply lacked leadership for a new vision of the labor market and social reform that would build a broad coalition of support.

In short, the more common pattern of labor market reform in Europe is one of policy drift. Usually policy drift takes the form of small changes that are adopted without a larger discussion of their significance for the overall character of the country's labor market profile. Sometimes these changes are the small bits of bold reforms that were scuttled by fierce opposition, usually from organized labor. For these countries a special problem persists. The labor market regimes still are characterized by the ideas of the breadwinner concept and the post-war settlement that created corporatism. In an era of globalization, these countries are failing to articulate a new vision for the labor market that recognizes the global realities. Some policy reforms push towards a more globalized work force, but more could be accomplished if these reforms were more broadly accepted and if they were promoted with ideas that built support.

CONCLUSION

The objective of this chapter is to outline the politics of labor market reform in Europe. My argument is that labor market reform has been more successful in countries where reforms were accompanied by the articulation and promotion of new ideas about how these reforms will bring about positive change. It is no coincidence that the countries that have been the most successful at reforming their labor markets have also developed the most innovative ideas for understanding the new purpose of labor market regulation. And, these new ideas have received broad support and form the foundation for some far reaching reforms.

Political parties are important to this process. In the countries that have had successful labor market reforms, parties have revisited their ideological foundations and discovered ways that they can support the new ideas. Perhaps most important is for parties of the moderate left, i.e. social democrats, to embrace labor market reform. It is telling that in countries where the reforms were successful, social democratic parties have been the champions of the new ideas, and have used those ideas to make their appeal to voters more in tune with the realities of globalization.

The countries that have been less successful at reforming labor markets, by contrast, have failed to win the battle of ideas. In many cases, the ideas that underpin the existing labor market systems continue to resonate with the public and manage to create strong coalitions to oppose reform. Ideas like the Swedish Model, or the German Social Market Economy have a strong foundation in the public mind, are deeply identified with the current system of labor market regulation, and therefore make it easy to view all attempts to reform the system as serious threats to an aspect of national identity.

Again, political parties, especially the role of social democrats, have made a difference in these countries. Parties on the right have advocated, and even implemented labor market reforms in Sweden, Italy and Germany (as well as France). But when social democrats are unable or unwilling to be the champions of new ideas, or when they become vigorous defenders of the *ancien régime*, they prove to be powerful at mobilizing opposition to reform.

Yet, labor market regulations are being changed in every country. For the countries where this is done in the absence of new ideas, the reforms are a type of policy drift. The reforms move in the direction of making labor markets more effective in the global economy. Yet, they are not clearly understood by a public (and many political parties) who believe the old labor market regimes are still intact. For these countries, policy drift will continue to be a source of distress and consternation in the coming years. Policy drift is likely to continue, and it is likely to move further away from the ideas that are now under attack. An adjustment in the public understanding is inevitable. But, it will take place after policy drift has created a labor market regime that no one ever discussed or clearly understood. The result will be that the inevitable adjustment to new ideas will cause even more public discord.

REFERENCES

Béland, D. (2005), 'Ideas and Social Policy: An Institutionalist Perspective', *Social Policy and Administration*, **39**, 1–18.

Benner, Mats and Torben Bundgaard (2000), 'Sweden and Denmark: Defending the Welfare State', in Fritz Scharpf and Vivien Schmidt (eds), *Welfare and Work in the Open Economy*, Volume Two, Oxford: Oxford University Press, pp. 399–466.

Blancke, Susanne and Josef Schmid (2003), 'Bilanz der Bundesregierung Schröder im Bereich der Arbeitsmarktpolitik 1998–2002: Ansätze zu einer doppelten Wende', in Christoph Egle, Tobias Ostheim and Reimut Zohlnhöfer (eds), *Das Rot-Grüne Projekt: Eine Bilanz der Regierung Schröder 1998–2002*, Wiesbaden: Westdeutscher Verlag.

Clasen, J. (2002), 'Modern Social Democracy and European Welfare State Reform', *Social Policy and Society*, **1**, 67–76.

Commissie van de Europese Gemeenschappen (1992), 'De Positie van vrouwen op de arbeidsmarkt', *Vrouwen Van Europa*, nr. **36**, 53 p.

Cox, Robert Henry (1993), *The Development of the Dutch Welfare State: from Workers' Insurance to Universal Entitlement*, Pittsburgh, PA: University of Pittsburgh Press.

Esping-Andersen, Gøsta (1990), *The Three Worlds of Welfare Capitalism*, Princeton NJ: Princeton University Press.

Ferrera, Maurizio and Elisabetta Gualmini (2004), *Rescued by Europe? Social and Labour Market Reforms in Italy from Maastricht to Berlusconi*, Amsterdam: Amsterdam University Press.

Gemeentelijke Sociale Dienst Rotterdam (1985), *GSD, Vangnet of Trampoline*. Rotterdam: Gemeentelijke Sociale Dienst.

Hacker, J.S. and P. Strauss (2004), 'Privatizing Risk Without Privatizing the Welfare State: The Hidden Politics of Social Policy Retrenchment in the United States', *American Political Science Review*, **98**, 243–260.

Hay, C. (2004), 'Ideas, Interests and Institutions in the Comparative Political Economy of Great Transformations', *Review of International Political Economy*, **11**, 204–226.

Huber, E. and J.D. Stephens (2002), 'Globalization, Competitiveness, and the Social Democratic Model', *Social Policy and Society*, **1**, 47–57.

Immergut, E. and S. Jochem (2006), 'The Political Frame for Negotiated Capitalism: Electoral Reform and the Politics of Crisis in Japan and Sweden', *Governance*, **19**, 99–133.

Iversen, T. (1996), 'Power, Flexibility, and the Breakdown of Centralized Wage Bargaining: Denmark and Sweden in Comparative Perspective', *Comparative Politics*, **28**, 399–436.

Kesselman, Mark (1987), *European Politics in Transition*, Lexington, MA: D.C. Heath.

Lamping, W. and F.W. Rüb (2004), 'From the Conservative Welfare State to an 'Uncertain Something Else': German Pension Politics in Comparative Perspective', *Policy and Politics*, **32**, 169–191.

Larsen, C.A. (2002), 'Policy Paradigms and Cross-national Policy (Mis)Learning from the Danish Employment Miracle', *Journal of European Public Policy*, **9**, 715–735.

Lewis, J. (2006), 'Employment and Care: The Policy Problem, Gender Equality and the Issue of Choice', *Journal of Comparative Policy Analysis: Research and Practice*, **8**, 103–114.

Lindbeck, A. and D.J. Snower (2001), 'Insiders versus Outsiders', *The Journal of Economic Perspectives*, **15**, 165–189.

Martin, C.J. (2005), 'Corporatism from the Firm Perspective: Employers and Social Policy in Denmark and Britain', *British Journal of Political Science*, **35**, 127–148.

O'Brien, D. (2000), 'Reconstructing Social Democracy: New Labour and the Welfare State', *The British Journal of Politics and International Relations*, **2**, 403–413.

Pierson, P. (1996), 'The New Politics of the Welfare State', *World Politics*, **48**, 143–179.

Pontusson, J. and P. Swenson (1996), 'Labor Markets, Production Strategies, and Wage Bargaining Institutions: The Swedish Employer Offensive in Comparative Perspective', *Comparative Political Studies*, **29**, 223–250.

Schmidt, V.A. (2002), 'Does Discourse Matter in the Politics of Welfare State Adjustment?', *Comparative Political Studies*, **35**, 168–193.

Streeck, W. and C. Trampusch (2005), 'Economic Reform and the Political Economy of the German Welfare State', *German Politics*, **14**, 174–195.

Taylor-Gooby, P. (2004), 'New Social Risks in Post-industrial Society: Some Evidence on Responses to Active Labour Market Policies from Eurobarometer', *International Social Security Review*, **57**, 45–64.

The Economist (2006), 'Denmark's Labour Market: Flexicurity', September 7.

van Kersbergen, Kees (1995), *Social Capitalism: A Study of Christian Democracy and the Welfare State*, London and New York: Routledge.

Versteegh, K. (1996), 'De Overheid als Weldoener: Armoede in Nederland Volgens De Clerus en de Politiek', *NRC Handlesblad*, 11 May 1996, p. 4.

Visser, Jelle and Anton Hemerijck (1997), *A Dutch Miracle: Job Growth, Welfare Reform and Corporatism in the Netherlands*, Amsterdam: Amsterdam University Press.

Wallerstein, M. (1999), 'Wage-setting Institutions and Pay Inequality in Advanced Industrial Societies', *American Journal of Political Science*, **43**, 649–681.

10. Agenda Setting and Political Institutions in Education Policy: A Cross Country Comparison

Michael Baggesen Klitgaard

INTRODUCTION

Public education has received scant attention in welfare state research. One probable reason is that it often makes little sense to analyse educational reforms as social policy retrenchment, which is a typical definition of the dependent variable in contemporary welfare state research. Reforms in education policy and other welfare services are more commonly associated with changing forms of governance, in which welfare states adopt a new mix of state and market for the provision of collectively financed services (Christiansen, 1998). Due to the so-called 'crisis' in welfare state governance, reforms have received much attention in public administration research since the late 1970s and early 1980s. The factors that combined to create the welfare state crisis included excessive public spending, especially on welfare-related policies, a rigid public sector focused on input rather than performance, cost-awareness and societal demands (Premfors, 1998). Since the early 1980s, the hope has been that new modes of governance can improve cost efficiency and service quality as well as make the welfare state more output-oriented and responsive. The reforms that have been introduced typically include mechanisms designed to increase competition between public and private service providers, the extension of parental choice and the delegation of political authority to lower levels of government.

However, it is argued in this chapter that welfare states have generated varying responses to the common drive to reform education policy. There are two reasons for these differing responses. Firstly, it is assumed that the institutional legacy created by a country's education policy determines whether that policy is included on the governance reform agenda. This is likely to occur if existing education policy is dominated by uniform public institutions delivering a standardised education service within a system that also restricts parental choice. The inclusion of a delegitimated school policy on the reform agenda is a necessary but not sufficient condition for the initiation of reform. Secondly, the system of political decision-making has to be capable of translating policy proposals into legislation (Weaver and Rockman, 1993). Countries in which decision-making power is concentrated in central government are generally believed to have a stronger capacity for reform and are hence more likely to undertake far-reaching policy changes than countries in which power is shared among different branches and levels of government (Immergut 1992; Pierson 1995; Bonoli 2001).

These hypotheses are advanced in order to account for the diversity of the reforms affecting the governance of primary school systems in the US, Germany, Sweden and Denmark that were introduced between 1980 and 2000 and which are analysed in this chapter. The analysis concentrates on two types of change in primary school governance: 1) the introduction of parental choice of primary school; and 2) the decentralisation of political responsibility for the provision of primary education. These types of reform are normally associated with the new public management approach and have been discussed in connection with the education reforms undertaken in many OECD countries (OECD 1994, 2002; Arnott and Raab 2000). The empirical analysis focuses on the output, or lack of output, from the reform processes that were initiated and shows that the four countries investigated differed somewhat in their approach to reform. Nevertheless, there are signs of what could be termed path-dependent convergence. At the end of the period in question, all four countries had moved towards more decentralised forms of governance and were also beginning to offer parents a greater degree of choice. In other words, there was convergence towards a lower level of state intervention (see Chapter 1 in this volume). Nevertheless, there remained significant differences in the actual design of policies on parental choice and political regulation.

ANALYTICAL FRAMEWORK

In comparative analyses of public policy, it is commonly assumed that policy choices at t_2 depend on the situation at t_1 – an assumption closely associated with the concept of path dependency (Mahoney 2000; Pierson 2000). This assumption has been applied not least in recent studies of welfare state restructuring (c.f. Rothstein and Steinmo 2002), but it has also attracted fierce criticism, at least when it comes in a stylised version. It has been argued that this kind of explanation is too deterministic and merely predicts enduring stability (Thelen 1999: 385). Furthermore, this critique is related to the more general criticism of the new institutionalism within the social sciences, namely that it does little to resolve the problem of formulating coherent and plausible theories of change (Immergut 1998).

According to scholars such as Levi and Mahoney, however, it may not be so difficult to explain why policies, or institutions, are stable over time but also undergo change, since the mechanisms guaranteeing stability can be replaced at certain critical moments by the forces of change. To be sustainable over time, public policy institutions require, among other things, popular legitimacy, which depends on the ability of those institutions not only to provide citizens with the goods and services they want but also to be perceived as socially and economically fair (Levi 1997; Mahoney 2000: 525). If public policy institutions do not provide what the public wants, governments come under pressure to make changes. If, in other words, public policy institutions are not sufficiently responsive to taxpayers and are also increasingly inefficient in the delivery of public services, they run the risk of losing their legitimacy (Levi 1997, 1998). For example, in a period characterised by increased individualism and stronger demand for individualised public services (Inglehart 1990; Rothstein 1998), a uniform and centrally planned public school system that also restricts parental choice is at risk of losing legitimacy and public support. As a result, it may find its way on to the reform agenda. This in turn may trigger attempts to develop new approaches that would radically change governance structures (Baumgartner and Jones 1993). Hence, on the one hand, policy legacies may give rise to stability and path dependencies; on the other hand, if they lose their legitimacy, they may rise to the top of the political agenda and become targets for change (Baumgartner and Jones 1993, 2002).

Delegitimated governance structures and successful agenda setting are necessary but not sufficient conditions for the implementation of major reforms. Proposals for change must be fed into decision-making systems capable of transforming them into legislature. During the 1980s and 1990s, the role of formal institutions in structuring the policy-making process was increasingly recognised. It follows from this that those institutions may constrain or facilitate governments' ability to implement reform. There is general agreement that governments in unicameral parliamentary systems are more likely to undertake radical reforms, since power is concentrated within the cabinet, in contrast to governments in bicameral systems or those in which power is distributed among several branches (separation of powers). A government's capacity for action in a political system characterised by multi-tiered decision-making structures is assumed to be constrained by the numerous opportunities such systems provide for opposing interests to exercise their power of veto (Immergut 1992; Tsebelis 1995; Bonoli 2000).

Furthermore, in certain policy areas, the capacity to push through changes depends on the degree to which formal authority is shared between different levels of government authorities. In federal systems, such as those in the US and Germany, central authorities coexist with authorities in the units constituting the federation, which may have constitutionally guaranteed autonomy in certain policy areas. Central governments in unitary states such as Sweden and Denmark are normally able to decide what has to be done and then implement their preferred policy choices (Pierson 1995: 451). Federal systems, in comparison, are usually more constrained, since governmental authorities at all levels seek to control policy, which is why policy changes in such systems are often obstructed by joint decision-making traps and disputes between competing centres of political authority (Scharpf 1988; Pierson 1995).

The theoretical argument put forward in this chapter is that the extent of governance reforms in primary education policy depends on a combination of agenda setting and the capacity of the political decision-making system for reform (see Figure 10.1). If education policy rises to the top of the agenda and becomes a dominant political issue in a political system in which the capacity for reform is relatively low due to the dispersion of political power, then a low or moderate level of reform activity is to be expected. This means that certain reforms may be enacted within the existing system. If education policy is not even recognized as a major issue in a system with little capacity for reform, then the level of reform activity can be expected to be even lower. On the other hand, a combination of a delegitimated education policy that makes its way slowly to the top of the political agenda in a system that also has a strong capacity for reform can be expected to result in a rather higher level of reform activity. Finally, if education policy continues to be regarded as legitimate, the level of reform activity can be expected to be low or moderate, even if the political system has a relatively high capacity for reform.

		Reform capacity	
		Weak	*Strong*
School policy delegitimated and placed on the reform agenda	*Yes*	1: Low or moderate reform activity	3: High reform activity
	No	2: Low reform activity	4: Low or moderate reform activity

Figure 10.1   Conditions for school reform – an analytical model

The following section of the chapter sets out to examine whether these hypotheses can be substantiated with empirical evidence by analysing governance reforms in the public education systems of the US, Germany,

Sweden and Denmark between 1980 and 2000. As the empirical analysis will show, these countries have different combinations of characteristics that place them in different cells in Figure 10.1.

US: EDUCATION POLICY ON THE AGENDA, BUT GOVERNMENT ACTION CONSTRAINED

In the early 1980s, the US school system was dominated by non-selective public schools delivering free and compulsory education.[1] However, it was not a uniform system as American public schools are governed by the education policies of their respective states, which are constitutionally responsible for public education (Chubb 2001: 27). In the early 1980s, however, the federal government provided little financial support to private schools, and most of that was indirect (tax relief, etc.). Nevertheless, private schools, many of them run by the Catholic Church, accounted for approximately 10 per cent of school enrolments (OECD 2002).

The debate on education policy intensified and became one of the key issues of the early 1980s. At this time, decision-makers at federal level began to look at ways of extending parental choice, firstly by introducing school vouchers. In a voucher system, the government provides funding directly to parents in the form of vouchers that can be exchanged for a place in a public or private school of their choosing (Chubb and Moe 1990: 217). However, one particular event brought education to the top of the political agenda in 1983. In that year, a national commission declared the United States 'a nation at risk' because of the poor quality of its education system (Pappagiannis et al. 1992: 12). Since then, education reforms have commanded the nation's attention and occupied its political leaders (Moe 2001: XV). In other words, the lack of parental choice and the perceived poor quality of America's schools gave rise to strong agenda setting in this policy area. However, because of the federal government's weak capacity for reform – not least in the field of education policy – our theoretical arguments would suggest that this would result in only moderate reforms.

The main issues in the debates on how to resolve the crisis in America's schools were vouchers and parental choice. The federal government was active in putting the choice and voucher issues on the political agenda and tried in 1983, 1985 and 1986 to get the Democrat-controlled Congress to approve educational voucher plans (Moe 2001: 25, 36–7). However, even though the proposed programmes were modest in scope, they were all defeated (Henig 1994: 72). At the beginning of the 1990s, the first President Bush, who had declared his intention of becoming the 'education President' (Henig 1994: 90), presented to Congress a bill that would have provided

$1000 vouchers to children from low-income families; this bill too failed to get through Congress. The voucher issue continued to be a central issue in all presidential election campaigns throughout the 1990s and in 1998 Congress, now dominated by the Republicans, passed a bill authorising vouchers for the children of low-income families in Washington, DC. However, the bill was vetoed by President Clinton (Moe 2001: 36–7).

Despite these deadlocks at national level, however, there were a number of developments at a more local level. In 1990, the first public voucher programmes were introduced in Milwaukee for children from low-income families (Mintrom 2000: 24; NCSPE 2003). A similar programme was established in Cleveland in 1996. The first state-wide voucher programme was introduced in Florida in 1999, but it was restricted to students from failing public schools. Although policy innovations in some states are often taken up by others, that fact that education policy is a preserve of the individual states means it is uncertain whether this will happen with school vouchers. State constitutions vary widely and while some can be interpreted as allowing such a policy innovation, others are either very restrictive or at the best uncertain in this regard (Kemerer 2002). Local referendums on vouchers have consistently been defeated by sizeable margins, with political opposition easily mobilised (Belfield and Levin 2002).

Overall, little progress has so far been made with vouchers and parental choice due to the fragmented political system. On the other hand, reforms introducing greater decentralisation into the public school system but without exposing it to competition have progressed further. The US has a long tradition of decentralisation and local control of education policy. More than a century ago school governance was separated from general local governance and non-partisan elections for school boards were introduced (Chubb 2001: 24). Charter school reforms and the implementation of school-based management (SBM) in the 1990s took decentralisation a step further.

Charter schools are public institutions, supported by public funds, but they enjoy greater freedom from state regulations than traditional public schools. They are typically free to hire and fire personnel, design their curricula and promote specific values (NCSPE 2003). The first state to adopt charter school legislation was Minnesota in 1991. Since then, the charter school programme has become one of the fastest growing educational reforms in the US and has won support from various proponents and faced much less resistance than vouchers, since they constitute less of a threat to public institutions (Moe 2001: 40; Stoddard and Cocoran 2006). SBM reforms were implemented in at least three different forms throughout the 1980s and 1990s. In one approach, school principals were given greater powers and held accountable for results – sometimes with parent and teachers acting in an advisory function. In a second model, power was devolved down the hierarchy by establishing a group of teachers elected by their colleagues as the school's policy-making board. In a third form of SBM, power was devolved to parents and community members under community control (Wholstetter and Sebring 2000: 165).

The move towards decentralisation has proceeded much more quickly than attempts to extend parental choice. One probable reason is that decentralisation is wholly consistent with the characteristics of American school governance; SBM and charter schools, for example, constitute less of a threat than vouchers to the established system. The teaching unions, which strongly opposed vouchers and the extension of parental choice and used their links with the Democratic Party to block such reforms, have been more willing to accept further decentralisation, since these reforms often give teachers greater influence over school policy decision-making and pose no financial threat to the public system.

GERMANY: TWO DECADES OF NON-REFORMS

The German school system that evolved after World War II parallels in some instances the American school system, since education is primarily a matter for the *Länder*, which are responsible for most of the funding, maintaining schools, teacher training, educational standards and the curricula (Theodoulou 2002). In other respects, the German public school system is very different from the non-selective US system. After four years in primary school, German pupils transfer to a tripartite secondary school system in which lower (*Hauptschulen*), intermediate (*Realschulen)* and upper (*Gymnasien* or *Fachoberschulen*) secondary schools cater for students of varying ability and ambition. There have been attempts to make the system non-selective, but the comprehensive school movement has generally failed to overcome resistance from secondary schoolteachers and conservative politicians (Manning 1998; Ambler and Neathery 1999: 448).

Private schooling is relatively limited in Germany: approximately 6 per cent of pupils attend private (but primarily tax-funded) schools, most of which are denominational (Manning 1998: 87). The federal constitution enshrines the right to establish and run private schools with equal rights to public schools. Following a Federal Administrative Court ruling in 1966, private schools fulfilling the statutory requirements for authorisation have also had a legal right to financial support from the state (Weiss and Mattern 1991: 55). However, the vast majority of private schools also depend on fees, which vary according to the type and character of the school (Weiss and Mattern 1991: 57). The public funding of German private schools is similar in some respects to a voucher system, in that it extends parental choice. According to our general theoretical proposition, a fairly decentralised school system that provides a good level of choice is at little risk of being delegitimated and adopted as a central issue on the governance reform agenda. Furthermore, the strongly federal character of German education policy means that the role of central government is constrained in this area. Taken together, these factors lead us to expect a relatively low level of reform activity in Germany.

In 1982, a coalition government consisting of the Christian Democrats and the small liberal party (FDP) came to power in Germany. The government's first programme bore some resemblance to the neo-liberal programmes being implemented at the time in the US and the UK. However, the public sector restructuring and governance reforms introduced in Germany were more modest in scale (Clark 2000). This is not to suggest that there were no changes in the organisation of the German welfare state. In general terms, however, the legalistic administrative system and bureaucratic state were not challenged to any great degree by the market prescriptions. The most significant changes occurred with the reunification of East and West Germany in the early 1990s, when the East German system was adapted to the existing West German model of public administration (Clark 2000: 34).

If political attempts to marketise the public sector were generally weak and limited in Germany in this period (Clark 2000), they were even weaker in relation to the school system and the structures of educational governance. There was no serious political debate about replacing the existing bureaucratically and politically controlled schools with quasi-market arrangements or making schools compete for pupils and financial resources. One reason why vouchers and parental choice debate never made it on to the political agenda in Germany in this period is that the existing structures already provided parents with good opportunities to send their children to private schools (Weiss 1993; Manning 1998: 92; Wilde 2002). However, there were some intense debates about the quality of German schools – first in the early 1990s and especially in the wake of the publication of a PISA report in 2001. However, these debates have not yet resulted in any significant reforms.

Nevertheless, parental choice in Germany's tripartite secondary school system was an object for debate and political consideration in two ways. Firstly, debates on parental choice were linked to the question of selecting pupils for one of the three types of secondary school (Plachetta 1988: 49). The school-leaving certificates awarded by the different types of school play a crucial role in the allocation of subsequent education and training opportunities and it was recognised as a problem that an ever increasing share of parents wanted their children to obtain the upper secondary school certificate (*Abitur*) (Weiss 1993: 313). Secondly, debates on parental choice were also part of a more general political debate about public institutions. This led to increased parental demands not for market-based private schools but for church and other types of schools believed to uphold traditional values (Weiss and Mattern 1991: 51). Problems of delegitimisation were also countered with measures introducing greater decentralisation and parental participation, which resulted in the transfer of decision-making competences to lower levels of the political system. It has been reported that this period saw a general trend towards further decentralisation in the Federal Republic, with individual schools being granted greater autonomy. However, such decisions are a matter for the *Länder*; consequently there was no uniform national trend. Nevertheless, reforms intended to increase the involvement of teachers, parents and pupils in decision-making in individual schools were introduced in Hessen and Bremen, for example (Weiss 1993; Manning 1998).

The most significant reforms were introduced in the wake of German reunification at the beginning of the 1990s, the main aim being to adapt the former East German to the West German school system (Wilde 2002: 40). Thus the German school system, which for generations had been designed to preserve and reward status, was still more or less intact by the end of the period under review. This was due not only to inertia on the part of successive governments and a strong degree of federalism in education policy but also to the considerable influence wielded by churches and other religious institutions over education policy and decision-making (Manning 1998: 85). If the reforms introduced in East Germany following reunification are disregarded, the two decades between 1980 and the year 2000 saw little significant change; this recently caused *The Economist* to describe the German education system as being brilliant at what it was designed for: selection (*The Economist*, 11 February 2006: 8). Students continue to be channelled into different educational tracks at an early stage, which is one of the main obstacles to increasing Germany's relatively low level of social mobility (Pisa 2003: Chapter 4).

SWEDEN: STRONG AGENDA SETTING UNDER STRONG GOVERNMENTS

By the early 1980s, the Swedish welfare state had put in place a centralised and strongly regulated primary school system, based on the principle of providing all children with a standardised form of basic education. This public school system was the dominant form of primary education and constituted a virtual public monopoly, since only around 0.2 per cent of pupils attended private schools in the early 1980s. The political intentions behind the expansion of this school system were the same as those that had driven the post-war expansion of the Swedish welfare state. Equal opportunities for all within the education system was a central element in the Social Democratic Party's strategy for creating a society characterised by high degrees of social equality (Ambler and Neathery 1999: 442). The hypothesis advanced with regard to the Swedish case is that the governance structures of the Swedish school system in the early 1980s were likely to rise to the top of the political agenda. Furthermore, Sweden has a political system in which the central government enjoys a remarkably strong capacity for reform, which leads us to expect that Swedish education policy during the period in question would have been the object of some fairly radical reforms.

In the late 1970s, the Swedish welfare state was being increasingly criticised for its predilection for excessive bureaucracy and red tape. When the Social Democrats returned to power in 1982 after six years in opposition, they launched a comprehensive public-sector reform programme in order to facilitate governance reforms in the Swedish welfare state. The administrative framework and state-dominated regulation of public schools soon became the central issue on the reform agenda. And there were good reasons to focus on this policy area in particular. A major survey of Swedish people's perceptions of their ability to influence the public services they used, conducted in the second half of the 1980s, revealed a general feeling that it was difficult to exert influence within the public school system. The attitude toward schools, for example, was that Swedes found it difficult both to influence the teaching offered to their children and to choose a school that met their own preferences (Peterson, Westholm and Blomberg 1989: 262).

The proposals set out in party election manifestos found their way on to the policy agenda in 1988, triggering a process that fundamentally altered the governance structures of the Swedish school system. Between 1988 and 1991, the administration of Swedish schools was devolved to municipalities and freedom of choice between public as well as between public and private schools was introduced with a sort of universal public voucher. During this process, successive governments broke with the traditional corporatist and consensus-seeking style of politics; as a result, the teaching unions and other interest groups were frequently left out in the cold, unable any longer to block government proposals (Lindbom 1995: 71; Klitgaard 2004).

In 1988, responsibility for public primary schools was delegated to the municipalities, while the role of central government was reduced to the formulation of general policy objectives, the provision of funding and quality evaluation (Prop. 1988/89:4:9). As part of the decentralisation process, schools were also given opportunities to develop special academic or pedagogical profiles and to adapt their curriculum and teaching to local needs and demands (Prop. 1988/89:4: 53–6). In the autumn of 1989, municipalities were also given responsibility for school personnel (Prop. 1989/90:41: 12); in 1990 and 1991, a new funding system was introduced (Prop. 1990/91:18:

25). After the municipalities became the employers of teachers and head teachers, it was decided to allocate funding in the form of block grants earmarked for schools and other educational purposes but without their precise use being further specified. This gave municipalities greater freedom to use their resources and organise public schooling as they saw fit.

New forms of parental choice also evolved. Having been given an opportunity to develop their own particular profiles, schools were obliged to reciprocate by meeting parental preferences with regard to the choice of school for their children, at least as far as was practically and economically possible (Prop. 1988/89:4: 53–7). However, parental choice was not limited to the public sector. The introduction of school vouchers meant that private schools could now attract public funding on the same basis as public schools. The Social Democrats had an ambiguous view on the public funding of private schools during the 1980s. They feared that public schools would be drained of pupils and resources, which in turn would threaten the political cohesiveness of the universal welfare state (Klitgaard 2007). In the end, however, the Social Democratic government did introduce a voucher system based on means testing in which municipalities were obliged to allocate resources in accordance with need; parents and pupils were allowed to choose between public and publicly-financed private schools (1990/91:UbU17:23).

The Conservative-led coalition government that came to power in 1991 abandoned means testing and decided that private schools should have the right to receive an amount per pupil equivalent to 85 per cent of the average cost per pupil in public schools. When the Social Democrats returned to office in 1994, they reduced this to 75 per cent due to the economic crisis, but decided in 1996 that private schools should be given the same funding per pupil as public schools. Furthermore, private schools were not allowed to charge parents any additional fees (Klitgaard 2007). As a result of this major institutional overhaul of the Swedish education system, one of the most centrally regulated school systems in OECD member countries became, in the course of just a few years, a strongly decentralised school system offering parents and pupils a considerable degree of choice (Skolverket 2001; Blomqvist and Rothstein 2000; Svensson 2001; Klitgaard 2004: Chapter 7).

DENMARK: TWO DECADES OF PATH-DEPENDENT REFORMS

Denmark has a long tradition of allowing for choice in its education system, mainly through the establishment of largely publicly-funded private schools. Since the Free School Act of 1855, parents and organisations have been entitled to set up their own schools and private schools have been an integral part of the system ever since. Non-selective public schools still predominate, although private schools increased their share of pupils from just above 7 per cent in 1980 and 1981 to approximately 12 per cent in the 1990s. Danish private schools are highly dependent on public funding, which covers approximately 85 per cent of the costs, with user fees covering the remainder (Christiansen 1998; Green-Pedersen 2002). The public school system is regulated by national legislation but has traditionally been administered by municipalities. According to the hypotheses outlined above, this would make Danish education policy a less likely candidate for a leading position on the public-sector reform agenda. This expectation is by and large confirmed. Occasionally, however, education policy has attracted political attention and the centralised form of political decision-making has allowed decision-makers to introduce some moderate reforms relatively unhindered.

The Conservative–Liberal government that came to power in Denmark in 1982 launched a major programme of governance reforms in the Danish welfare state. Throughout the 1980s, successive centrist governments of varying composition committed themselves to the so-called 'Modernisation Plan' of 1983. The plan was based on a series of proposed reforms, including the devolution of budgets, governance by the market, free choice, new modes of funding for public services, increased responsiveness to consumers and deregulation (Christiansen 1998: 273). Clearly, the new Danish government shared many of the concerns and policies of the conservative US and UK governments of the time; however, rigorous market solutions to welfare state governance held little attraction for the Danes. And in contrast to contemporary developments in Sweden, for example, governance reforms in Denmark were never really tied up with welfare state issues but seen rather in the context of economic restructuring. At the beginning of the 1980s, Denmark's economy stood on the 'brink of the abyss' and along with unemployment macro-economic issues ranked at the top of the political agenda (Green-Pedersen and Klitgaard, forthcoming).

As Danish education policy was already decentralised to a considerable extent and could hardly have been more liberal with regard to school choice, it was difficult for this policy area to become a key issue on the reform agenda. During the 1980s, the Danish education debate was largely subsumed into a more general political debate about cost containment in the public sector. In the late 1980s, however, the minister of education managed to direct political attention toward proposals for more comprehensive institutional changes in the governance and administration of Danish schools. In 1988, he launched a plan for 'perestroika in Danish schools'. Political intervention in schools and education policy should be relaxed, it was argued, and detailed regulation from above replaced by management by objectives (Haarder 1988). Moreover, parents should have a choice not only between public and private schools but also within the public sector and more political authority should be delegated to municipalities, schools and parents (Lindbom 1995: 109; Andersen 2000).

In 1989 a bill was enacted, stipulating that each school should establish a mandatory governing council, consisting of elected representatives of parents, pupils and employees. This measure strengthened parental influence over the activities of individual schools, since they were allocated a majority of the seats on the councils. Since the governing councils were obliged in law to set out the principles governing all activities in their schools, this initiative delegated responsibility for local schools to users to an astonishingly high degree. However, the authority of head teachers was also increased with the abolition of the bodies representing school employees. In addition, the stipulation that all proposals for discussion by the school council had to come from the head teacher's office meant that school heads were in a good position to act as gatekeepers (Folketingstidende, register, 1988/89: 167).

A year after the establishment of school councils, the minister of education presented another bill introducing further deregulation, which got through the parliamentary process with just slight modifications. Under this new legislation, much of the education ministry's regulatory power was transferred to municipalities and school councils. The law also introduced the principle of choice within the public school system. Municipalities could, if they wished, allow for school choice within their local school district, although pupils were still to be guaranteed a place in the school nearest to their home. Furthermore, if their children were accepted by a school in a district other than the one in which they resided, parents were given the right to opt for that school (Folketingstidende, tillæg A: 5189–5202). However, this reform was shown to be devoid of any real substance, since local authorities laid down strict regulations governing parental choice (Christensen and Pallesen 2001: 186). The process of decentralisation was continued when a Social Democratic-led coalition came to power in 1993 and enacted a new education bill in 1994. However, as in the 1980s, education policy in the 1990s was never a key issue on a political agenda dominated by the economy, particularly unemployment.

PATH-DEPENDENT CONVERGENCE IN EDUCATION POLICY

The analytical framework adopted in this chapter assumes that the scope and character of reforms in education policy are a function of agenda setting and central governments' capacity for reform. It has been argued that education policy is likely to be delegitimated and included on the reform agenda if a school system provides a standardised service and/or does not allow for parental choice. Such governance structures are likely to develop legitimacy problems as they do not meet users' preferences for individualised social services, autonomy and freedom of choice. However, they are likely to be radically changed only if the central authorities have the power to push through reforms. The US, Germany, Sweden and Denmark are characterised by different combinations of agenda setting and capacity for institutional reform, which is why the reform processes in the different countries varied in scope and character. Despite this, trends towards convergence in the development of education policy could also be observed (Seeliger 1993). This means that school governance in the various countries has become more similar since the early 1980s, even if notable differences still exist.

School governance structures became a central issue on the reform agenda in the US and Sweden in the early 1980s. However, only Sweden had the necessary combination of strong agenda setting and an institutional capacity for radical reform, which is why there were considerable differences in the scope and nature of the reforms that could be implemented in the two countries. Sweden managed to devolve political regulation to the municipalities and also introduced a voucher system in order to extend parental choice. In the course of this reform process, successive Swedish governments of varied composition exploited the decision-making power enjoyed by central government in that country, although they also had to build coalitions with opposition parties in parliament (Klitgaard 2007). However, interest groups, primarily the teachers' unions, were left in the cold without any opportunities to block the reforms.

During the 1980s, Republican administrations in the US tried on several occasions to introduce various forms of parental choice and school vouchers, but were blocked by the Democrat-controlled Congress. Not the least of the reasons for the Democrats' opposition was the party's strong affiliation with the teachers' unions. The unions were more successful than their Swedish counterparts in blocking the reforms because divided government structures give organised interest groups more opportunities to influence political decisions. Moreover, due to the decentralisation characteristic of the American school system and education policy, the education voucher movement also encountered a series of obstacles that in the end led to its failure – at least at the national level of government. Charter schools and school-based management made much stronger progress, since they did not threaten to drain the public system of pupils and financial resources to quite the same extent as vouchers and parental choice (Mintrom 2000; Moe 2001). These reforms were more acceptable to the teachers' unions.

By comparison, agenda setting with regard to education policy was less strong in Denmark and Germany. The Danish school system has always been a matter for the municipalities, although the central state is responsible for legislation concerning curricula and standards. The Danish school system has also provided a considerable degree of parental choice, which is why Danish education policy was regarded as a less likely candidate for delegitimation and inclusion as a key issue on the reform agenda. However, Danish education policy was the subject of considerable political debate during the period under investigation and reforms aimed at further decentralisation and allowing parents to choose between public schools as well as between public and private schools were implemented. However, education featured only fitfully on the political agenda. Nevertheless, whenever it did attract a degree of attention from politicians, Denmark's centralised form of decision-making allowed the policymakers to implement their preferred policies relatively efficiently.

German education policy also remained remarkably stable during the period under investigation. That period has been described as two decades of non-reform, meaning that Germany stayed loyal to its selective tripartite school system. As in Denmark, the German school system allowed parents to send their children to private schools that were largely publicly funded. In Germany too, however, there were calls for greater autonomy and parental influence, although such issues were not major concerns for central government. Some *Länder* and city authorities did introduce reforms in this area on an experimental basis (Weiss 1993; Manning 1998). The most significant reform initiatives in Germany during this period were launched in the wake of reunification in order to bring the school system of the former East Germany into line with that of West Germany. Although the *Land* of Brandenburg introduced a non-selective comprehensive school system, by and large it was the traditional West German system that replaced the old East German system. Thus the German system continues to channel pupils into different types of schools depending on ability, to reward status and to maintain the social order.

Even though the reform processes were very diverse, a certain degree of convergence with regard to certain aspects of primary school policy can also be observed, although this has not led to the abandonment of specific national institutional characteristics. Policies on parental choice and decentralisation continue to be implemented differently. Sweden, Germany and Denmark have sought to extend parental choice by subsidising private schools with public money, while the US continues (at least as a national policy) to refrain from this. Private schools in Denmark and Germany charge parents an additional fee, while this is illegal for private schools in Sweden. In Denmark and the US, there is a formally constituted body through which parents can influence what goes on in individual schools; such a body exists only in certain areas in Germany and is completely unknown in Sweden. Thus in the midst of all the variations there is also some degree of convergence, which is why it may be reasonable to talk of a kind of path-dependent convergence.

Social scientists have been reluctant to acknowledge convergence as a relevant concept in the last 20–25 years. However, education policy is characterised by certain dynamics that make it especially susceptible to convergence. In all affluent democracies, it is a conventional wisdom that the highest achievable educational standards are essential if a country is to remain competitive in the knowledge-based economy. Not only are most countries therefore willing to spend a significant percentage of GDP on education, but they are also focusing strongly on comparative assessments of educational performance, as conducted by the OECD, for example, with its PISA programme. Germany's below-average ranking in the 2001 PISA report, for example, was a real shock for the country and did trigger some reforms, albeit within the existing system. Similar reactions to PISA have been reported in Denmark and the US (Andersen 2006; Education Week 2004). At these critical moments, when it becomes clear that other countries are performing better in certain areas of education, the under-performing countries have a strong incentive to learn from other countries with a view to emulating what are, presumably, better ways of organising schools and education. Thus in the knowledge-based society, in which student performance in other countries is becoming more transparent due to programmes such as PISA, there is every likelihood that policies will be more widely diffused, that countries will learn from each other and that there will be a greater degree of convergence in education policy as a result.

NOTE

1. Editor's note: since there may still be a few people unaware of the difference between American and British usage in this area, it is worth pointing out that, in the US, public schools are what in the UK are known as state schools, i.e. schools funded by the taxpayer. In the UK, public schools are, confusingly, independent fee-paying secondary schools.

REFERENCES

Ambler, J.S. and J. Neathery (1999), 'Education Policy and Equality: Some Evidence from Europe', *Social Science Quarterly*, **80** (3), 437–56.

Andersen, V.N. (2005), 'Kontinuitet og forandring. Gennemsigtighed og åbenhed i uddannelse', *Politica*, **38** (1), 40–56.

Arnott, Margott A. and Charles D. Raab (eds) (2000), *The Governance of Schooling. Comparative Studies of Devolved Management*, London: Routledge & Falmer.

Baumgartner, Frank R. and Bryan D. Jones (eds) (1993), *Agenda and Instability in American Politics*, Chicago: University of Chicago Press.

Belfield, Clive R. and Henry M. Levin (2002), *Does the Supreme Court Ruling on Vouchers in Cleveland Really Matter for Education Reform?*, National Center for the Study of Privatization in Education: Columbia University, see http://www.ncspe.org/.

Betænkning 1990/91, UbU17.

Blomqvist, Paula and Bo Rothstein (2000), *Velfärdsstatens nya ansikte*, Stockholm: Agora.

Bonoli, Giuliano (2001), 'Political Institutions, Veto Points, and the Process of Welfare State Adaptation', in Paul Pierson (ed.), *The New Politics of the Welfare State*, Oxford, UK: Oxford University Press, pp. 238–264.

Christensen, J. Grønnegård and T. Pallesen (2001), 'Institutions, Distributional Concerns, and Public Sector Reform', *European Journal of Political Research*, **39** (2), 179–202.

Christiansen, P.M. (1998), 'A Prescription Rejected: Market Solutions to Problems of Public Sector Governance', *Governance,* **11** (3), 273–95.

Chubb, John E. (2001), 'The System', in T. M. Moe (ed.), pp. 15–42.

Chubb, John E. and Terry Moe (1990), *Politics, Markets & America's Schools*, Washington, DC: Brookings Institute.

Clark, D. (2000), 'Public Service Reform: A Comparative West European Perspective', *West European Politics*, **23** (3), 25–44.

Education Week, December 7 (2004), US Students Fare Poorly in International Math Comparison.

Folketingstidende (1988/89), *Register.*

Folketingstidende (1989/90), *Tillæg A.*

Green-Pedersen, C. (2002), 'New Public Management Reforms of the Danish and Swedish Welfare States: The Role of Different Social Democratic Responses', *Governance*, **15** (2), 271–94.

Green-Pedersen, Christoffer and Michael B. Klitgaard (forthcoming), 'Between Economic Constraints and Political Entrenchment. Welfare State Developments in Denmark, 1982–2005', in Klaus Schubert, Simon Hegelich and Ursula Bazant (eds), *European Welfare Systems*, Wiesbaden: VS Verlag für Sozialwissenschaften.

Henig, Jeffrey R. (1994), *Rethinking School Choice*, Princeton, NJ: Princeton University Press.

Immergut, Ellen (1992), 'The Rules of the Game: The Logic of Health Policy-making in France, Switzerland and Sweden', in Sven Steinmo, Kathleen Thelen and Frank Longstreth (eds), *Structuring Politics. Historical Institutionalism in Comparative Analysis*, Cambridge: Cambridge Studies in Comparative Politics.

Inglehart, Ronald (1990), *Culture Shift in Advanced Industrial Society*, Princeton, NJ: Princeton University Press.

Kemerer, Frank R. (2002), *The U.S. Supreme Court's Decision in the Cleveland Voucher Case: Where to From Here?*, National Center for the Study of Privatization in Education: Columbia University, see http://www.ncspe.org/.

Klitgaard, Michael B. (2004), *At beskytte et politisk våben. Når Socialdemokratiet dekollektiviserer den universelle velfærdsstat*, PhD Dissertation, Department of Economics, Politics & Public Administration, University of Aalborg.

Klitgaard, M.B. (2007), 'Why Are They Doing It? Social Democracy and Market Oriented Welfare State Reforms', *West European Politics*, **30** (1), 172–194.

Levi, Margaret (1997), *Consent, Dissent & Patriotism*, Cambridge, UK: Cambridge University Press.

Levi, Margaret (1998), 'A State of Trust', in Valerie Braithwaite and Margaret Levi (eds), *Trust and Governance*, New York: Russel Sage Foundation.

Lindbom, Anders (1995), *Medborgerskapet i Velfärdsstaten*, Stockholm: Almqvist & Wicksell International.

Mahoney, J. (2000), 'Path Dependence in Historical Sociology', *Theory & Society*, **29**, 507–48.

Manning, Sabine (1998), 'Restructuring Education in Germany', in Holger Daun and Luciana Benincasa (eds), *Restructuring Education in Europe. Four Country Studies,* Stockholm: Institutionen för Internationell Pedagogik.

Mintrom, Michael (2000), *Policy Entrepreneurs and School Choice*, Washington, DC: Georgetown University Press.

Moe, Terry M. (ed.) (2001a), *A Primer on America's Schools*, Stanford: Hoover Press.

Moe, Terry M. (2001b), *Schools, Vouchers and the American Public*, Washington, DC: The Brookings Institution.

NCSPE (2003), *Frequently Asked Questions*, National Center for the Study of Privatization in Education: Columbia University, see http://www.ncspe.org/.

OECD (1994), *School: A Matter of Choice*, Paris: OECD.

OECD (2002), *What Works in Innovation in Education. School: A Choice of Direction*, Paris: OECD/CERI.

OECD (2003), *Learning for Tomorrow's World – First Results from PISA 2003*, Paris: OECD.

Pappagiannis, George J., Peter A. Easton and J. Thomas Owens (1992), *The School Restructuring Movement in The USA: An Analysis of Major Issues and Policy Implications*, Paris: International Institute for Educational Planning.

Peterson, Paul (2001), 'Choice in American Education', in T. Moe (ed).

Peterson, Olof, Anders Westholm and Göran Blomberg (1989), *Medborgernas Makt*, Stockholm: Carlssons.

Pierson, P. (1995), 'Fragmented Welfare States: Federal Institutions and the Development of Social Policy', *Governance*, **8** (4), 449–78.

Pierson, P. (2000), 'Increasing Returns, Path-dependence, and the Study of Politics', *American Political Science Review*, **94** (2), 251–67.

Pierson, P. and M. Smith (1993), 'Bourgeios Revolutions? The Policy Consequences of Resurgent Conservatism', *Comparative Political Studies*, **25** (4), 487–520.

Plachetta, B. (1988), 'Disputes over School Policy in the Federal Republic of Germany', *IPW Berichte*, **17** (7), 48–51.

Premfors, R. (1998), 'Reshaping the Democratic State: Swedish Experience in Comparative Perspective', *Public Administration*, **76**, 142–59.

Proposition 1988/89:4, *Skolans utveckling och styrning*.

Proposition 1989/90:41, *Ansvaret för skolan*.

Proposition 1990/91:18, *Om vissa skollagsfrågor m.m.*

Rothstein, Bo (1998), *Just Institutions Matter*, Cambridge, UK: Cambridge University Press.

Rothstein, Bo and Sven Steinmo (eds) (2002), *Restructuring the Welfare State. Political Institutions and Policy Change*, New York: Palgrave Macmillan.

Scharpf, F. W. (1988), 'The Joint-decision Trap: Lessons from German Federalism and European Integration', *Public Administration*, **66**, 239–78.

Seeliger, R. (1996), 'Conceptualizing and Researching Policy Convergence', *Policy Studies Journal*, **24** (2), 287–306.

Stoddard, Christina and Sean P. Corcoran (2006), *The Political Economy of School Choice: Support for Charter Schools Across States and School Districts*, National Center for the Study of Privatization in Education: Columbia University, see http://www.ncspe.org/.

Theodoulou, Stella Z. (2002), *Policy and Politics in Six Nations. A Comparative Perspective on Policy Making*, New Jersey: Pearson Education.

The Economist, 11 February 2006.

Tsebelis, G. (1995), 'Decision Making in Political Systems: Veto Players in Presidentialism, Parliamentarism, Multicameralism and Multipartism', *British Journal of Political Science*, **25**, 289–325.

Weaver, R. Kent and Rockman, Bert A. (eds) (1993), *Do Institutions Matter? Government Capabilities in the United States and Abroad*, Washington, DC: The Brookings Institution.

Weiss, M. (1993), 'New Guiding Principles in Education Policy: The Case of Germany', *Journal of Education Policy*, **8** (4), 307–20.

Weiss, Manfred and Mattern, Caroline (1991), 'The Situation and Development of the Private School System in Germany', in Hasso von Recum and Manfred Weiss (eds), *Social Change and Educational Planning in West Germany*, Frankfurt am Main: German Institute for International Educational Research.

Whitty, G. and T. Edwards (1998), 'School Choice Policies in England and the United States: An Exploration of their Origins and Significance', *Comparative Education*, **34** (2), 211–27.

Wilde, S. (2002), 'Secondary Education in Germany 1990–2000: "One Decade of Non-reform in Unified German Education"?', *Oxford Review of Education*, **28** (1), 39–51.

11. Conclusion: The Governance of Welfare State Reform

Heinz Rothgang and Irene Dingeldey

In the previous chapters, we investigated, from an international comparative perspective, the change in governance structures in four policy areas, with reference both to actual policies and the associated political processes. Naturally, the investigations led to the identification of a number of specific characteristics. However, no overall picture can emerge until these individual elements are brought together. It is the aim of the present chapter to provide just such a synoptic overview. To this end, the key findings of the studies gathered together in this volume will first be briefly summarised. Then, drawing on this material, we will examine the basic questions broached in the introduction: has there been a change in governance structures and, if so, what form does it take? In attempting to answer these questions, we will seek to ascertain, firstly, whether common trends can be identified that extend beyond individual countries and policy areas, secondly whether individual dynamics have their roots in particular policy areas, specific national characteristics or types of welfare system and, finally, how far politics and policies can be disentangled.

SUMMARY OF FINDINGS

In the first chapter in the book, Heinz Rothgang investigates the change in governance structures in healthcare systems over the last 40 years. The starting point of the investigation is the observation that, in OECD countries by the 1960s and 1970s, three types of healthcare system had emerged, characterised respectively as national health service, social insurance system and private insurance system. The UK, Germany and the USA are singled out as representative of each of these three types for the purpose of a three-country comparison. The typology of healthcare system is based on funding (level and structure), provision of services and the governance of regulation.

Although this last element is the sole object of analysis in the chapter, it is, nevertheless, capable of clearly revealing system differences.

With regard to governance structures, a distinction is made between the actors' level and the interaction level. The regulating actors considered are state actors, societal actors engaged in self-governance and market participants. If this level is cross-tabulated with the interaction level, at which hierarchy, collective negotiations and competition are identified as the relevant modes of interaction, a nine-field matrix is produced. The ideal types of the governance structures are located on the main diagonal and can be characterised as state hierarchical regulation (NHS systems), societal self-regulation through collective negotiations (social insurance) and private competitive regulation (private insurance system). At the beginning of the observation period, the governance structure in the three countries under investigation closely resembled the ideal types; over the last 40 years, however, there have been considerable changes. Since the beginning of the 1990s, competitive structures have been introduced into the British NHS that have permanently changed the mode of governance. The same applies to the German system. Here, the introduction of competition between insurance funds has led to a whole series of further reform measures intended to increase the functionality of the competition. In neither country, however, has competition necessarily led to any weakening of state hierarchical governance. On the contrary, it has to be stated that in Germany the still dominant self-regulatory structures have come under pressure from two quarters: on the one hand, from increased competition and, on the other, from increased state hierarchical regulation. A dual trend can also be observed in the USA. On the one hand, state hierarchical regulation has increased solely because the state insurance schemes have increased in importance in quantitative terms. On the other hand, the governance vacuum has led to the emergence of hierarchical governance structures, albeit in the private healthcare market. With the managed care revolution of the 1980s and 1990s, a functional equivalent for non-existent state governance developed to some extent in the private health insurance market.

Overall, healthcare systems have seen a shift away from pure forms of governance towards more hybrid forms. In each case, modes of governance that did not previously exist in the pure type of governance have been incorporated, giving rise to a trend towards convergence and a 'blurring of system types'.

The hybridisation of previously pure types is a subject that Thorsten Hippe also addresses in his chapter on the change in policies on old-age insurance. As with the assumed trend in healthcare towards more market-driven and competitive systems, so there has been a trend in old-age insurance towards privatisation and a shift from pay-as-you-go to funded insurance systems. As Hippe rightly notes, it is not sufficient simply to consider the level of coverage. Account must also be taken of the way in which private insurance systems are regulated. To this end, Hippe distinguishes between three governance strategies (social democratic, social-liberal and neo-liberal) on the basis of the way in which they are able to react to the four forms of market failure that he identifies (myopia, volatility risk, choice risk and administrative charges). The ensuing developments in three groups of countries are then investigated. These three groups are the English-speaking early funder countries, the European early funder countries and the European late funder countries. One representative of each group – the USA, the Netherlands and Sweden respectively – is examined in detail, while a total of 11 further countries provide supplementary evidence for the relevant group.

Specific developments can be observed for each group of countries. Thus the European late funder countries have significantly reduced the level of collective responsibility for resolving the problems caused by market failure, while in the English-speaking countries something of a counter-trend can be observed. Among the European early funders, there have been at most only slight reductions in collective responsibility. Overall, therefore, the variance between the various regulatory regimes has not disappeared but has probably reduced. If the level of collective intervention and the variance are considered jointly, then the configuration described in the introduction as 'convergence towards a reduced level of intervention' emerges. Hippe's results point to a 'cross-national, albeit not ubiquitous trend towards intermediate degrees of collective responsibility for status maintenance' (Chapter 3). Thus he finds evidence in favour of the hybridisation hypothesis, which postulates a converging trend towards mixed or hybrid forms of governance.

Changes in the goals of welfare state policies, which are encapsulated in largely normative concepts such as the workfare or the enabling state and the social investment or the activating welfare state, provide the starting points for Irene Dingeldey's investigation in Chapter 4 of the change in governance in the implementation of activating labour market policies in Denmark, the UK and Germany since the beginning of the 1990s. Her analysis focuses on the changes that have taken place in the welfare state's regulation, firstly, of the tension between the commodification and decommodification of individual labour market participation and, secondly, of the division of labour in the provision of labour market services between the welfare state and private (collective) actors.

Dingeldey's analysis shows that, on the one hand, entitlements to decommodification have been restricted in all countries by reducing the duration and/or level of transfer payments, increasing the conditionality of benefits and extending the obligation to work. On the other hand, the goal of promoting employability 'for all' has also required an expansion of labour market policy and social services in the shape of improved placement services and an increase in vocational training programmes (except in Germany) and childcare provision. The analysis further demonstrates that, in all three countries, regulatory responsibility as well as responsibility for guaranteeing the delivery of and access to services in the sphere of labour market policy remains largely with central state actors. Nevertheless, there has been a shift of responsibility towards private actors and an increase in competition or co-governance in the provision of labour market policy services. It is only in the financing of welfare benefits that contrary trends can be observed. Thus in Denmark, financing by the social partners has been introduced, while in the UK and Germany there has been an increase in funding out of taxation following an expansion of needs-based transfers. Ultimately, therefore, the changes in governance outlined in Dingeldey's analysis confirm the thesis that the welfare state is being reshaped.

It is true that this implies a blurring of regimes, since individual welfare regimes can no longer be characterised by their own individual governance principles. Nevertheless, differences in initial conditions and reform strategies mean that differences persist between the various regimes that have emerged on the basis of the new governance mixes.

In Chapter 5, Kerstin Martens and Anja P. Jakobi examine the growing influence of the OECD as an international actor in national education policies, thereby highlighting a shift in the territorial dimension of governance (cf. Figure 1.1 in the Introduction). At the same time, however, Martens and Jakobi point to a change in forms of governance within the OECD itself. By virtue of its institutionalist approaches, the OECD is characterised as a policy entrepreneur in the field of education policy; it uses three instruments of governance in order to influence national policies, namely agenda setting, policy formulation and policy coordination.

The change in the OECD's role and in the instruments it uses is investigated through a comparison between the 1970s and the 1990s based on two examples: the spread of 'lifelong learning' and the benchmarking of education indicators. In both cases, Marten and Jakobi show that the OECD has considerably expanded the range of its influence. In the 1970s, this influence was largely confined to agenda setting; since the 1990s, however, it has been extended to encompass policy formulation and coordination as well. In concrete terms, this means not only that general problems are broached (agenda setting) but also that 'best practice' is identified by benchmarking or the use of internationally comparable statistics and proposed solutions put forward accordingly.

Thus the OECD's exertion of influence through agenda setting, policy formulation and policy coordination is based on so-called 'soft' modes of governance – modes that are listed in Figure 1.1 under the headings of 'moral persuasion' and 'discourse'. This form of governance is now paradigmatic, however, and is also used by other international organisations, for example the EU with its open method of coordination, in order to influence national policies.

It is clear from the chapters on the change in governance in health policy, pension policy and, in some cases, labour market policy that convergence processes can be observed. This raises the question of how far these findings can be generalised and whether convergence is also evident at the outcome level. It is this search for the 'big picture' that is the focus of Starke and Obinger's chapter. Whereas the previous chapters investigated convergence processes in governance, in Chapter 6 Starke and Obinger first adopt a quantitative approach in order to ascertain whether these convergence processes are reflected in the levels, structure and financing of welfare benefits. They then adopt a qualitative approach in order to examine convergence in policies.

The chapter begins with a discussion of notions of convergence, divergence and persistence, and various forms and degrees of convergence are outlined. A quantitative empirical analysis of the social expenditure ratio in 21 OECD countries shows that such expenditure is not declining and that there is, therefore, no 'race to the bottom'. On the contrary, the share of social expenditure in GDP is rising in 19 of the 21 countries. The share of social expenditure in total public expenditure is also rising. At the same time, social expenditure ratios are converging. Thus the coefficient of variation as a measure of cross-national dispersion declined by a third between 1980 and 2001, from 0.31 to 0.21 (σ-convergence). The other measures of dispersion considered (range and standard deviation) confirm this. This convergence is driven by catch-up processes in countries in which, at the beginning of the observation period in 1980, levels of public expenditure were low, in other words by a process of β-convergence. Thus as Table 1.1 shows, the evolution of social expenditure overall is characterised by 'convergence with an increased level of intervention'.

Convergence can also be observed in various, though not all structural parameters. Thus expenditure on transfers in cash (which are characteristic of the Continental European welfare states and some of the English-speaking countries) and expenditure on transfers in kind (which are characteristic of the Scandinavian welfare states) have converged significantly. Convergence can also be observed in welfare state funding. All the indicators considered (total taxation as a share of GDP, social security contributions as a share of GDP and social security contributions as a share of total taxation) display σ-convergence and β-convergence. As far as replacement rates are concerned, which serve as indicators of individual protection levels, convergence is observed only in the case of unemployment insurance but not in standard pensions or in cash benefits in the event of illness. Finally, no convergence can be observed with regard to the extent of decommodification.

The concluding qualitative analysis of changes in the fields of pensions, labour market policy, health care and family policy confirm the finding of the quantitative analysis: there is little evidence of convergence towards a uniform welfare state model, but welfare states are certainly borrowing heavily from each other. Thus according to Starke und Obinger, the process they describe can best be characterised as a 'blurring of regimes' or as 'trespassing'. In general terms, the various welfare state regimes have not disappeared, but they have become significantly less clearly differentiated from each other and a trend towards 'upwards convergence' is clearly discernible.

Thomas Gerlinger's Chapter 7 marks the beginning of the second part of the book, which is concerned with the politics of welfare state reforms. However, the chapters in this part make it clear that politics cannot be discussed without serious attention being paid to policies as well. Gerlinger examines how regulatory activity in the Swiss, Dutch and German healthcare systems has changed since the beginning of the 1990s. In particular, he discusses the extent to which the changes tend in the same direction. In that sense, this chapter also addresses the theme of convergence. Gerlinger comes to the overall conclusion that in the last two decades the three healthcare systems have been through 'a process of change which has taken them in essentially the same direction', but that they have reached different points along this path and, despite the shared characteristics of the process, have to date retained the core of their institutional regimes.

Having described the initial situation in the three countries 'on the eve of the structural reforms', that is about the end of the 1980s, and the main features of the structural reforms in chronological sequence from the beginning of the 1990s onwards, Gerlinger supports his argument that the changes have tended in the same direction by citing five examples. Firstly, a general obligation to take out insurance has been introduced in all three countries. No such obligation existed previously. While the Netherlands and Switzerland now insure their entire populations within an integrated system, Germany has retained the division between public and private health insurance, although the two systems are drawing closer together. According to Gerlinger, the likelihood of Germany also having an integrated system in future depends on which parties form the next government. Secondly, in all three countries costs have been privatised by co-payments and co-insurances. At the same time, funding out of taxation is playing an increasingly important role in health insurance. In some cases (Switzerland, for example), this development is a direct consequence of the reforms but in Germany, on the other hand, it is a measure intended to support the reforms. Thirdly, in all the countries under investigation, the state has played an active role as the architect of the new order. This finding, based on an assessment of the politics of healthcare reform, contradicts the argument that these healthcare systems are inherently incapable of pushing through reforms, an argument that was commonly made at the beginning of the 1990s. The reasons given for this inability were the dominance of strong interest groups, the frequent need to form coalition governments and, in Germany and Switzerland, federalism. In fact, it emerges that all three governments were prepared to drive the reform process forward and to take on the powerful doctors' organisations because they feared that, if they continued to resort to the kind of cost reduction measures that were common in 1980s, then the consequent increase in the financial burden on insurees would give rise to legitimation problems. As a result, fourthly, the healthcare systems in all three countries have a higher level of regulatory density following the reforms. This is in part a direct consequence of reforms intended to strengthen competition, which have necessitated wide-ranging re-regulation by the state. This reclaiming by the state of its ability to act cannot, however, be characterised as a return to the primacy of politics. Finally, Gerlinger finds that regulatory competences have been centralised in all three countries and that there is a new trend towards standardisation of the general framework within which healthcare systems function and the elimination of existing regional differences. As a result, there has been a shift in governance at the territorial level.

The starting point for Guiliano Bonoli's Chapter 8 is that pension reforms are particularly difficult for politicians to push through against defenders of the status quo. Thus Bonoli argues that reforms entailing cuts in pension entitlements cannot succeed unless they take the form of a 'modernising compromise', to which important societal actors, and particularly trade unions, are persuaded to acquiesce by means of quid pro quos. This give and take can manifest itself in a wide diversity of forms. The probability of such a modernising compromise emerging depends, according to Bonoli, on four factors. It is higher, firstly, in countries in which non-standard workers are not covered by existing pension arrangements, since a reduction in the general level of entitlements can be combined with an improvement in the situation of this category of workers. Secondly, it also increases with the number of veto points, since the need necessary to involve any possible veto players also increases. Thirdly, the probability of a modernising compromise rises when the trade unions represent not only (older) workers in standard employment relationships but also a larger share of younger and female employees, as well as workers in precarious employment relationships. On the one hand, Bonoli argues, this increases the unions' ability to gain acceptance for reforms, while on the other hand it makes it easier to push through reforms by improving the situation of non-standard workers. Fourthly, and finally, the probability of a modernising compromise is higher when there are close links between the trade unions and a social-democratic party.

Bonoli then tests these arguments by examining five case studies, namely the pension reforms in Sweden, France, Switzerland, Italy and Germany. It emerges that three of the four factors that facilitate modernising compromises are present in Sweden and Switzerland, whereas in Italy and Germany only one is present. And in fact Bonoli notes that both Sweden and Switzerland have introduced reforms that can be described as modernising compromises, while the German reforms give little indication of any such compromise and those in France and Italy cannot be described as modernising compromises at all. Because of the disparity between the number of variables and the number of cases, Bonoli cannot of course verify the influence of each of the listed factors. However, the starting hypotheses are, overall, confirmed by the case studies.

Thus Bonoli's contribution shows that there has also been a change in governance in the political dimension. It is true that the success of reform attempts continues to depend on whether an exchange of interests between the usual suspects can be achieved and whether the trade unions in particular can be involved. However, this 'log rolling' is no longer necessarily institutionalised within the framework of corporatist governance or within a tripartite structure, as the highest form of corporatist governance. True, the outcome depends on the political parallelogram of forces and thus reflects traditional pluralistic notions. However, factors such as the composition of trade union membership and the situation of non-standard workers, i.e. factors in the political sphere, are playing an increasingly important role in determining the enforceability of certain policies. Bonoli himself actually highlights this in the title of his chapter, in which he suggests that class conflict (albeit in a different form) is influencing policy outcomes.

In Chapter 9, Robert Cox points to the importance of new ideas and their mediation by political actors as an explanation for differences in the capacity for reform and differing degrees of success in reforming labour market policy. The Netherlands and Denmark are regarded as successful in this regard, since they have managed to break up the post-war welfare state settlement and restructured their labour markets in response to the demands of a globalised economy. New ideas such as labour market activation programmes and flexicurity, as well a shift away from the male breadwinner model, have been combined with the traditional values of each national welfare state regime. They have played a key role in framing the reform process, not least by providing a basis for re-establishing the consensus between the various political actors.

In contrast to these two examples, the labour market policy reforms in Sweden, Italy and Germany are characterised merely as a form of policy drift, that is as marginal adjustments that have received only limited attention from the general public and led ultimately only to minor and largely inconsistent changes in the various national post-war models of labour regulation. In the case of Sweden, Cox points to the Social Democrats' inability to distance themselves from the Swedish model and adapt new ideas on labour market regulation as the cause. The changes that have been introduced in Italy are assessed in a similar way. In the case of Germany, on the other hand, the strong attachment to the post-war model of the social market economy and the largely antagonistic discourse around reform are adduced as causes. The main obstacle to the emergence of a new consensus on reform was, in Cox's view, the 'lack of leadership for a new vision of the labour market and social reform' in the Social Democratic Party. Thus according to his argument, the successful mediation by political actors of new and wide-ranging ideas for reform is of crucial importance in the implementation of welfare state reforms that call into question the post-war consensus in order to adapt national welfare state regimes to the new socio-economic challenges. This means that, over and above the institutional and power-political preconditions that have to be fulfilled, the discursive mediation of new ideas can be regarded as a fundamental element of the governance of welfare reform.

In Chapter 10, Michael Baggesen Klitgaard examines the reform of primary school systems in the USA, Germany, Sweden and Denmark between 1980 and 2000. At the heart of his analysis are, on the one hand, the introduction of parental choice of primary school and, on the other, the decentralisation of political responsibility for the provision of primary education. These reforms are generally associated with the change in governance resulting from the new public management and the reform of public authorities.

Although all four countries had, by the end of the observation period, put in place decentralised forms of governance and had given parents increasing freedom to send their children to the primary school of their choice, significant differences still persist. Thus Sweden, Germany and Denmark guarantee parental choice by subsidising private schools out of public funds, while this does not happen in the USA. In Germany and Denmark, parents pay fees to private schools, while this is forbidden in Sweden. Furthermore, parental influence over the activities of individual schools is formalised in Denmark and the USA, while it is a feature in only some of the German *Länder* and is completely absent in Sweden.

Klitgaard adopts an extended institutional approach in order to explain both the change in governance and the variance between countries. In his view, the scope of the governance reforms in primary education policy depends on agenda setting and the capacity for reform of the various political systems, which is influenced by the national institutional environment. Consequently, the change in governance is greatest when demands for reform appear on the policy agenda because the existing system has lost its legitimacy and the government in question has sufficient power to implement them.

Ultimately, this ideal combination of circumstances applies only to Sweden, where a strong central government willing to build cross-party coalitions was able to implement demands for reform that led to a change in governance based on radical decentralisation and a voucher system introduced in order to increase parental choice. In contrast, the debate on the introduction of vouchers in the 1980s in the USA came up against Democratic opposition in Congress and ultimately came to nothing. In Germany and Denmark, the reform of primary education did not occupy a very important position on the political agenda. Nevertheless, demands for increased decentralisation and increased freedom of choice between state and private schools were successfully pushed through in Denmark's centralised decision-making system. In Germany, sporadic demands for increased parental influence have been made, but only in a few of the *Länder* have the authorities taken heed of such demands. Consequently, it is in Germany that the greatest continuity is to be observed, particularly since the highly selective tripartite education system remains largely in place and, following reunification, was transferred to most of the East German *Länder*.

WHAT CAN WE LEARN FROM THESE CASE STUDIES?

What generalised conclusions can be drawn from these separate findings? The first question that must be asked is certainly whether any change at all can be detected in welfare states and, if it can be, where it might be found. One possible answer, which is very prevalent in the literature, lies in the assumption that the dominant trend is one of continuous retrenchment and a 'race to the bottom'. This argument is refuted in Starke and Obinger's Chapter 6. There is no indication, either in individual benefit entitlements (as measured by replacement rates) or in aggregate welfare expenditure (as measured by the social expenditure ratios), that the welfare state is being dismantled. In fact, welfare state activities have increased, and countries once regarded as 'laggards' in this respect have caught up considerably in the last two or three decades. Overall, this has led to increased harmonisation of social expenditure ratios (convergence trends). Thus there is no evidence here of a dramatic changes of the kind implied in the notion of a 'race to the bottom'. However, consideration of social expenditure and of individual benefit levels can only ever give us part of the picture. It is also necessary to take account of governance structures, and specifically those in the spheres of politics and policy. Once that is done, the studies collected in the present volume provide evidence of a clearly perceptible change.

Let us begin by comparing the chapters concerned with actual *policies*. Such a comparison reveals some noteworthy congruences as well as some specific characteristics, depending on the policy sphere in question. The most striking finding is the consistent pattern of convergence trends that can be observed in healthcare systems, old age insurance policy and, to some extent, in labour market policy, as well as across the various spheres of the welfare state as a whole. The various chapters show that, in all policy areas, the differences that previously existed between systems are becoming less distinct; this phenomenon is variously described as a 'blurring of systems' and a trend towards mixed types (Rothgang, Chapter 2), 'hybridisation' (Hippe, Chapter 3) and 'trespassing' (Starke and Obinger, Chapter 6). It is in healthcare systems that the incorporation of hitherto alien elements into existing governance structures is most pronounced. In pensions policy as well, however, it appears that the predominant governance structures are being augmented by elements that have their origins in another regime. In labour market policy, a trend towards convergence is observed, which results from the adoption of a new policy paradigm; at the same time, however, the significance of the differences that still persist has to emphasised (Dingeldey, Chapter 4). Recommodification constitutes a sort of mega-trend, but one that the various regimes assimilate through different routes.

In contrast to these largely uniform trends in the governance of policy implementation, which cut across the various policy areas, a significantly more differentiated and less uniform picture emerges with regard to the change in the governance of the corresponding reform processes (politics), which is characterised by the increasing integration of societal actors or changed patterns of interaction.

A key factor, primarily in labour market policy but also in educational policy, seems to be the emergence of 'new' ideas and political objectives, which are developed and disseminated through transnational discourses. Another relevant factor appears to be whether and how interest groups or even federal veto players are involved. According to Bonoli (Chapter 8), pension reforms are more likely to be successfully implemented within a framework of co-governance in which what he describes as a 'modernising compromise' can be reached. In health and pension policy, however, the pressure exerted by urgent problems and the consequent increase in governments' readiness to take on opponents of reform, on the one hand and, on the other, the instruments of power at their disposal are identified as being of crucial importance to the implementation of reform projects. In addition, the territorial dimension seems to be of particular importance in this policy sphere; it manifests itself both in the transnationalisation of the agenda-setting function, as Martens and Jakobi describe in Chapter 5, and in the strong or increasing decentralisation of competences, as is apparent according to Klitgaard (Chapter 10) in the reforms in Sweden and Denmark and, to some extent, Germany as well.

Another factor worthy of note is that the capacity for reform and/or the implementation of welfare state reforms in the individual policy spheres can be explained both by similar forms of governance in decision-making in the various countries (Gerlinger, Bonoli Chapters 7 and 8) and by different national models (Cox, Klitgaart Chapter 9 and 10). Thus Gerlinger's chapter examines efforts to overcome obstacles to reform in healthcare systems and the state's reclaiming of its ability to act as key factors in explaining the changes that have taken place in the last decade and a half. Bonoli shows that a modernising compromise can be seen as the common denominator in many reforms in pension policy, although the enforceability of such pension policies depends on other, country-specific combinations of factors. Cox and Klitgaart, in contrast, give greater emphasis to country-specific differences. Thus Cox emphasises the important role played by ideas in labour market reform. These ideas are debated in all countries and similar labels, such as activation and flexicurity, are attached to them; however, very different configurations of actors and institutional contexts mean that that they are interpreted and implemented in very different ways. Cox's findings are echoed by Klitgaart, who considers the combination of pressure for reform and institutional opportunities as crucial in determining the capacity for reform in any given country or policy sphere. It follows from this that fewer common trends than country-specific trajectories are to be observed in education policy. For this reason, no single trend in the governance of the political process can be identified either across the various policy spheres or in the various countries: policy sphere and national characteristics do matter.

Against this background, no connection can be established between the (uniform) trend in the change in the governance of policies or the associated increased convergence in the evolution of the welfare state (regarded as dependent variables) and the governance of politics (as independent variables). With regard to policies, governance structures are moving closer together and they are doing so to a greater or lesser extent in all the policy areas examined in the present volume. However, the trend does not point to more or less state involvement or to a uniform shift to one form of governance or another. What is emerging, rather, is a process of hybridisation and 'regime blurring', which is giving rise in turn to converging trends but not to the complete disappearance of the existing differences. The policy formulation process, i.e. politics, on the other hand, continues to be dominated by factors specific to each policy sphere, which determine the success or failure of reform efforts, and by country-specific differences in the form these factors take. At most, certain tendencies pointing in the same direction can be observed, but certainly not convergence. There has also been a clearly identifiable increase in the importance of 'soft governance' or of discourses, not just at national level but also as a consequence of the increasing involvement of international organisations that do not possess 'hard' decision-making competences (Martens and Jacobi, Chapter 5).

The findings on the governance of welfare state reform that are summarised above suggest that the questions posed in the introduction require differentiated responses. Although there have been no dramatic reductions in individual benefit levels, there has nevertheless been a change in the governance of welfare state reform that manifests itself in a withdrawal of the state from service provision and a simultaneous extension of the state's responsibility for guaranteeing the delivery of and access to services. The correspondingly uniform trends in reform have contributed to the break-up or blurring of the hitherto unique or system-specific forms of governance in the various individual welfare state regimes. On the other hand, over and above the generally increasing importance of soft governance, the explanations for the corresponding reform dynamics (politics) are to be found primarily in different national institutional environments and actor-specific conditions, as well as in political success factors that are specific to individual policy areas.

Index